OPERATIC LIVES

Also by Alberto Savinio

SPEAKING TO CLIO

Alberto Savinio

OPERATIC LIVES

Translated by John Shepley

The Marlboro Press
Marlboro, Vermont

Originally published in Italian as
NARRATE, UOMINI, LA VOSTRA STORIA
Copyright ©1942 Casa Editrice Valentino Bompiani, 1942.

The publication of the present volume has been made possible
by a grant from the National Endowment for the Arts.

Manufactured in the United States of America

Library of Congress Catalog Card Number 88-60730

Cloth: ISBN 0-910395-42-X
Paper: ISBN 0-910395-43-8

THE MARLBORO PRESS

T M P

MARLBORO, VERMONT

The lives of Michel de Nostradamus, Eleutherios Venizelos, Felice Cavallotti, Paracelsus, Arnold Böcklin, Jules Verne, Vincenzo Gemito, Collodi, Antonio Stradivari, Guillaume Apollinaire, Giuseppe Verdi, Lorenzo Mabili, the *torero* Cayetano Bienvenida, and Isadora Duncan. Thirteen men and a woman immersed in the gelatin of history, some more deeply and others less. We have treated these characters as opera librettos, and our task has consisted mainly in setting them to music. Depending on the case, this has resulted sometimes in operas, sometimes in operettas.

Contents

Felice Cavallotti   1

Arnold Böcklin   18

The Wily Cretan   34

Two Venizelian Moments   44

Gemito's Second Life   53

Guillaume Apollinaire   74

Antonio Stradivari   81

Jules Verne   95

Lorenzo Mabili   109

Verdi, Man of Oak   123

Life and Death of Cayetano Bienvenida   131

Collodi   138

Nostradamus   154

Isadora Duncan   195

Bombastus's First Love   262

Felice Cavallotti

Bleached by a dawn that already wore the mantle of Italy, the spires of the cathedral rose into the sky of Milan like bunches of asparagus. Around the fires of a small bivouac at the beginning of the Corsia dei Servi, early-rising Milanese were imbibing *el caffè del geneucc*, their "knee coffee," which you drink standing up and between sips resting the cup on your knee. The *spazzitt* dragged their brooms over the pavement, and the *lattée* went from door to door delivering milk. All of a sudden, from the second floor of a modest house in Piazza San Giovanni in Conca, resounded the first cry of someone who would eventually hurl many more.

It was 6 December 1842.

Francesco Baffo Cavallotti, when he got his first look at the newborn infant, who in color and appearance resembled a cotechino sausage, realized that the honor of a family descended from illustrious ancestors in the Veneto, whose names were inscribed in the Golden Book of the Serenissima and who had owned houses and gondolas in the Venetian Arsenal, was saved. This having been acknowledged, Baffo Cavallotti swore to teach the child German, since Baffo, the son of one of Napoleon's captains, a student of Silvio Pellico, a pupil at the military college of San Luca, a cadet in the Austrian Bellegarde regiment, a clerk at the Land Office, and a scholar in the severe disciplines of philology, was highly versed in the language and literature of the Germans. Lying in the middle of the conjugal bed, emptied like a bagpipe that

1

has ceased its playing, Vittoria Gaudi Baffo Cavallotti dimly felt that her nocturnal labor had given the world a poet. Her lips, like dry leaves, smiled at the white snowflakes falling in a fringe outside the window.

Clio had reserved a special welcome for the future bard. He was scarcely knee high to a grasshopper when, to strike the imagination of the predestined child, Milan rose up against the foreigner, and for five memorable days drove the Austrian sharpshooters out the Porta Vittoria. When Cavallotti re-evoked that memory, his watery dreamer's eye saw once again *"a tall, splendid, aristocratic figure of a blond woman, preparing bandages and rosettes, encouraging the combatants, and affixing rosettes to their civilian clothes."*[1]

Already the Muse has her eye on the boy. Felice, at the age of ten, declaims Berchet and Mameli, making the knees of "right-thinking" people who come to visit the Baffo Cavallotti home quake in fear. At twelve, Felice stuffs the school desks with patriotic songs. At sixteen, a student at the Porta Nuova *liceo*, he foments a demonstration against the teachers, who to commemorate Franz Josef's visit to Milan have had a plaque set in the wall at the top of the school staircase. In the meantime he learns from the *Guerin Meschino** to defend the weak and oppressed. At seventeen, he publishes a political pamphlet, and since meanwhile his poet's heart has blossomed with love, he goes up to Ghevio where

shrouded by a veil of clouds

he finds

the blond goddess clothed in sky.

But here it is 1859. Cavallotti would like to wield a rifle, but when he tries to enlist in the Piedmontese army, the answer is: *trop cit* ("too young").

---

1. The italicized words are Cavallotti's.
* A satirical political newspaper of the time. (Tr.)

2

Who can forget the storm at sea on 9 June 1860, between Liguria and Cagliari? The *George Washington*, flying the United States flag, bobbed on the water with its whole cargo of youths, some their eyes ablaze with heroic imaginings, others with codfish eyes and on their cheeks the greenish pallor that comes from upset stomachs. When a torrent appeared on the horizon, both the ardent and the seasick rolled like barrels in the hold; then when the danger was past, they went back up on deck and formed a group around one who in the midst of the storm, his hair flying in the wind and with semaphoric gestures, spoke of freedom and democracy, and of the rights of man.

Once Cape Spartivento had been doubled, the storm subsided, and the stars twinkled over the calm sea. Cavallotti fell asleep with the sky as his ceiling, his mouth teeming with words that had not yet emerged as sound. And when next morning the sun shone on the sea and puffs of white smoke announced the vicinity of a volcano, the orator arose, no longer a simple tribune but a bard, and sang:

> *O, salvoes of Etna—glorious land,*
> *You broke the yoke—brandished the sword!*
> *Brothers are we—of the great Garibaldi,*
> *We ran to the voice—that thundered war!*

On his return from Sicily, Cavallotti stops in Naples, and goes to the Castel dell'Ovo, to a splendid villa whose terraces and rose gardens project over the sea. Mandolins trill around the fat mulatto with sausage lips and woolly hair, who from the pile of Oriental carpets on which he reclines proffers a pudgy hand.

"Cavallotti?"

"Maestro!"

"I love young poets. Would you like to write for my newspaper?"

The eyes of the youthful bard shine in the shadows.

Alexandre Dumas was *fou* for Garibaldi. He had followed the Thousand by sailing along the coasts of Sicily, Calabria, and Campania in his small schooner, the command of which

3

was entrusted to that boyish figure dressed as an admiral*
whom Cesare Abba in his memoirs calls "the little lazy-
bones." And so Cavallotti began writing fiery articles for the
Indipendente, the sheet with which the author of *The Three
Musketeers,* in his enthusiastic and harebrained way, thought
he was helping Garibaldi's cause.

But writing articles for the *Indipendente* barely taps the
energies of the volcanic youth. Moreover, Garibaldi, worried
about the heat to which Dumas's enthusiasm has risen, urges
a change of air on the novelist. In Milan, while great plans
mature for the *Gazzettino Rosa,* Cavallotti lends his pen to the
Fuggilozio.

Meanwhile the first civil songs blossom from his antimo-
narchist heart, and the Association of the Victims of Kings
proclaims him an "anti-Caesarean poet."

Ines Galbusera, who lives in a mezzanine flat in Via San
Pietro all'Orto, is awakened one morning by a great clash of
steel in the street. Fearing that the Austrians have come back,
she goes to the window, and at the entrance to the *Gazzettino
Rosa* sees a youth with adolescent moustaches who, sword in
hand, aroused as a lion, lunges at the assembled officers of
the Hussars of Piacenza regiment. Like a splendid tourna-
ment, and while the population scattered flowers and kisses
from the balconies and windows, that unequal contest,
generated by young Cavallotti's pen in the columns of the
Gazzettino Rosa, moved through the streets, squares, court-
yards, and gardens of Milan, until finally, the circuit completed, the inexhaustible fencer was seized by the guards and
carried bodily off to prison.

The contradictory results of a single event have not been
sufficiently considered: the bersaglieri, who in September
1870 entered Rome by the Porta Pia, in Milan released
Cavallotti from prison.

Freed by the amnesty, Cavallotti returns to his poet's
study. The minute the door is closed, it reopens and in
comes a beautiful woman in a dressing gown: the Muse. Not

---

* Dumas's mistress Emilie Cordier. (Tr.)

the one with whom Cavallotti has customarily dealt, but another one. Cavallotti will again be a poet, but in a different manner. He seizes his pen, and *I Pezzenti* emerges from it in a flash. The word *finis* is scarcely written at the end of the manuscript when there comes a knock at the door. Not the Muse this time, since Muses enter without knocking. "Come in!"

It is two friends, one of them Cameroni, the "Pessimist" of the *Gazzettino Rosa*. The Pessimist takes a step forward, exclaims "Your Honor!" and embraces the new member of Parliament. Cavallotti has been elected by the people and republicans of Corteleona. Italy of princes and black cassocks, beware! He whom your sons will carry aloft in the clear light of free thought and electoral reform has arrived.

A grave matter of conscience dampened the joy of the young republican as he journeyed in triumph from Milan to Rome. How is he to take the oath when he doesn't believe in God? Under the weight of the dilemma, Cavallotti gradually bows his head in sleep.

In Rome thirty centuries of history await Cavallotti at the station. He greets them and takes a carriage to the editorial offices of *La Capitale*. The night in the train has brought counsel to this "purist."

In his letter to *La Capitale*, Cavallotti explains that the oath is "a simple ticket to enter the Assembly of the people's representatives." The electricity builds up, the storm bursts. Next morning, to the president of the Chamber who calls upon him to take the oath, Cavallotti hurls his unforgettable statement: "I swear, but I demand the floor." Applause on the Far Left, where bristling beards and long rebel moustaches are amassed, "uh! uh!" on the right and in the center where gentlemanly beards are aligned in orderly fashion. Cavallotti is denied the floor. The applause and cries of "uh! uh!" swell in volume. "Have respect, you guilty consciences, for consciences that are at ease!" Cavallotti shouts at the gentlemanly beards. The marble sentence hangs suspended in the middle of the chamber like an aerial monument.

That day, in the cafés in Piazza Colonna, the heat of discussion made the ice cream melt.

Cavallotti lives in great poverty. What does a poet do when living in great poverty? He writes a play in hendecasyllables, then lies on his back and waits for gold to rain down into his mouth. This is what Cavallotti did, and that was why in 1879, under the Cairoli-Depretis government, he wrote *La Sposa di Mènecle,* a play set in Greece, preceded by an essay on the "penalties for adultery in Athens."

Under this same government, and for the reasons already stated, Cavallotti was offered the chair in Greek literature at the University of Palermo. Not an opportunity to be missed. And yet Cavallotti refused. He was a formidable Hellenist. Many, however, know classical languages only in the privacy of their studies.

One further shadow. In the new elections, Cavallotti is defeated. No matter. The special elections of '83 were to be a triumph for the champion of free thought. The candidate of the republic carries six constituencies. Piacenza gives him six thousand votes, her entire self. What will Depretis think? Cavallotti dips his pen in the ink of irony and telegraphs his enemy: "Sincere condolences for all the efforts expended for such meager results. We'll talk in Rome about poor liberty." Now that's sarcasm for you!

Spring in Milan brings the wonder of unexpected apparitions. That morning it threw open the window and spread itself all over the eighteen-year-old poet's writing desk. A virgin sheet of paper awaits the contact of the pen, which trembles between Felice Cavallotti's fingers. The poet, in a state of advanced inspiration, is about to set forth the motto of the new era. The back of his neck gleams with boils. Victor Hugo, with the eye of a Saint Bernard with distemper, peers at him from the wall. "No more the will of sovereigns, but the free aspirations of peoples." Ideas race through Cavallotti's head like millipedes. The paper is devirginated: "Freedom! Unity! Brotherhood!" The bard looks over his shoulder, a suspicion cuts across him like a draft of air: where has he heard those words before? Victor Hugo, stuck on the wall, either doesn't know or isn't telling. No matter. Cavallotti will later produce the "Marseillaise of the Italians."

The program of *Libera e Una* is born, organ of the people's new life, as a chorus of thousands and thousands of voices, speculating on reality and the future, moves in tumult through the city:

> *Scourge! scourge! splendid paean,*
> *Strip the illustrious of their Punic faith,*
> *The friar Loyola of his black soutane,*
> *Slaves of baseness, kings of pride!*

Perfect in all else, *Libera e Una* has this sole defect: it was never to see the light of day.

Not long afterwards, Cavallotti will show us how to put out a whole newspaper single-handed. This feat is *Lo Scacciapensieri*, an illustrated weekly of sixteen large two-column pages, with elegant woodcuts, and offering Massimo d'Azeglio's *Disfida di Barletta* as a premium. The "elegant woodcuts" were borrowed from French newspapers. With Felice Cavallotti as editor, Cavallotti as journalist becomes "Falco Attevicelli" and sometimes "Homunculus." A portrait of Léopold I of Belgium gives Falco Attevicelli the opportunity to inaugurate a "Biographies" column. For the "Novels and Stories" column he writes *La donna e la pipa*. A print of the Zoological Garden in Vienna gives him the excuse to initiate the "Picturesque Journeys" column, and for "Useful Knowledge" he avails himself of the Caselli Pantelegraph and the automatic time clock. Salvatore Farina, who soon comes to his assistance, signs himself "Aristofane Larva" so as not to infringe on Attevicelli.

Anyone listening today to *Mefistofele* finds it hard to understand how this opera did not catch on immediately. In those days art was a battle. In the one for the "music of the future," the purest feelings melted like stracchino cheese and friends became enemies. It took two of the most outstanding signatures in the *Gazzettino Rosa*, "Anomalo" and "Avvocato

Trombone," to reconcile Cavallotti and Rovani. The Scala shone like a gold sequin. Boito stood upright on the podium, while the orchestra below him bent over the oars. "A thousand young men of this stamp," Cavallotti shouted from a box, "and our artistic rebirth is assured!" When he had finished speaking, the opera collapsed under the boos.

A terrible day, 18 March 1876. Disastrous news floors the athlete of the opposition: the upheaval in Parliament has brought the Left to power. What will Cavallotti do now that things are in his favor? The blow is a serious one but he doesn't lose heart. In those very days the children of Leo VII of the House of Lusignan, once king of Cyprus, descendant of the emperors of Byzantium, and displaced sovereign of Russia, arrive in Milan. What does Cavallotti do, this republican who devours a prince for salad at every meal? He launches a public subscription "For the children of a king," and saves these poor wretches who were languishing in the transepts of the Ospedale Maggiore.

Cavallotti likes people named Leo. For Monsignor Rotelli, his friend from Perugia, Leo XIII had written an elegy in pentameters and hexameters. What does Cavallotti do, this freethinker who devours a priest in a ragout sauce at every meal? He turns His Holiness's Latin elegy into italically rhymed hendecasyllables, thereby earning the plaudits of the black eminences. Delicious contradictions of a poet's soul!

Ricciotto Canudo, Cavallotti's spiritual heir, was asked one day if besides being a novelist he was also a poet. *"Surtout poète!"* Canudo replied.

Cavallotti too was *surtout poète,* ready at all times to turn any subject into bouncing rhyme. He belonged to that species of men made of slightly spoiled ricotta cheese, overwrought and with wine on their breath, always the life of the party, the *deus ex machina* of social affairs, the Orpheus of outdoor picnics, their lips spouting rhymes and little bubbles of saliva. While the others rummage in baskets, bring out the sausages, and uncork the wine, they, in shirtsleeves, waistcoatholes under the armpits, watch chain on the paunch with the number 13 on the fob, cuffs slipping, sleeves held up by bands of red elastic, shaggy-haired, cordial and talkative, pinch the children's cheeks, whisper off-color stories to the adults behind hands spread fanwise, warble madrigals to the ladies, hawk and clear their throats, and embrace all of humanity with their puny penguin arms. So much for Cavallotti the madrigal singer. For Cavallotti the bard, art is an apostolate.

> *Poetry is not*
> *The humble shop of shadows and sketches:*
> *It is an austere and gentle philosophy,*
> *It is the faith and priesthood of every faith.*

And well they know it, those unfortunates who thirty years ago had to commit Felice Cavallotti's drumming poems to memory.

And now, O gymnasium student of those old days, close your eyes and watch your poet's creations file past: *Sic vos non vobis*, deeply philosophical in its light garments; *Povero Piero*, social and psychological drama that tackles the subject of marriage as a right and duty; *Nicarete o la festa degli Alòi*, which gives off a classical aroma; *Le rose bianche*, which epitomizes the concept of girls who on the one hand cling to their ideals and on the other are on the lookout for husbands.

When Cavallotti was first elected, the Right, confident that the new deputy lacked any oratorical skills, consoled itself by saying that the Chamber would have one more of many "silent deputies." And instead . . . Cavallotti would agree with Demetrius Phalereus in saying that eloquence "is in assemblies what iron is in battles."

Cavallotti had an implacable enemy in the president's bell. When the enemy rang:

> *from the depths of the heart*
> *A troubled "je ne sais quoi" rises*
> *And the right hand makes a certain gesture*
> *As though touching the strings of a lyre.*

At the Monumental Cemetery in Milan, Cavallotti thus greeted a soldier, like himself of the ideal: "Farewell, poor dreamer! You lived displaced on this earth and you never realized it."

He was said to be so eloquent that he could even demolish an opponent with a burst of laughter.

Montecitorio, the seat of the Chamber of Deputies, sticks its chest out into the piazza. Bust forward, arms thrust back, for 292 years now this stone gymnast has gone on doing the same exercise for the development of the thorax. In addition to the main entrance, one can enter Montecitorio by the many smaller side doors on Via dell'Impresa and Via della Missione. Ever original, Cavallotti did not enter Montecitorio like the other deputies, but approached instead from Via in Aquiro, made a run for it, turned at the obelisk of Psammetichus, and sprinted through the main door of Parliament. Where did the poet run, the man nourished by exacting studies?

Even at Montecitorio, the library was the place that most lovingly summoned Cavallotti. There the bard and deputy spent hours and hours immersed in books, his nose glued to the page. The writing rooms, where he came in on the run, colliding with the unlucky politicians in his path, were also familiar with Cavallotti's diligence. He wrote. And when that quivering pen started writing, the hands of the big clock, the white eye of Polyphemus on Montecitorio's forehead, went on revolving, passed over the dinner hour and left it behind, but this man in the throes of inspiration was unable to tear himself away from his papers. Cavallotti wrote *La Figlia di Jefte* at white heat in the writing rooms of Parliament, on the stationery with the blue letterhead of the Chamber of Deputies.

In the Chamber, Cavallotti sat in the third row of the last section. The "watchdog" of electoral reform had many enemies in that hall, but one in particular: Francesco Crispi. One might think the entire width of the hall would have been insufficient to separate the two adversaries, and yet Cavallotti sat only one seat away from the "Africanist," and was always ready to cross oratorical swords with him over the head of poor Abele Damiani who sat between them. Cavallotti was a virtuoso of the parliamentary system, highly versed in the secrets, mysteries, arrangements, tricks, short cuts, behind-the-scenes maneuvering, deals, and twists and turns of parliamentary procedure, and even the most reckless had to think twice before trying to trip him up in this area.

Many years have passed, many changes taken place, many emendations been made at Montecitorio. But if some night one were to let himself be locked in this chamber, and hold his breath, and keep his ears cocked inside this wooden amphitheater, where even in the profound stillness of the night the figures painted by Giulio Aristide Sartorio dance in the wind like laundry hanging on a clothesline, he would hear once again, faint and far away, the voice of the deputy and bard who in order to make of Italy something between the Athens of Pericles, the Sparta of Leonidas, and the Paris of the Commune, killed "transformism" and sponsored the "mechanical meter of the grist-tax law."

Did Cavallotti love?

The guardians of public security, blue in the jaw and black with suspicion under their waxed cloth kepis, who patrolled the cobblestones of the alleyways in the Rome of the early parliaments, used to have a ballad vision of the "honorable deputy" going by with triumphant mustache and tilted homburg, a shapely brunette rustling with flounces hanging on his arm, wasp-waisted, with the hips of a draft horse and enormous bosom, and with a seagull spreading its wings on a hairdo high massed in imitation of the steaming heaps at the feet of ruminants in barns.

For the poet and tribune, woman was life, dedication, poetry.

Then, in a furnished room on Via della Scrofa, in the presence of the one-legged bedside table, the bed that enshrines a glimpse of rustic nature in a medallion with black

11

scrolls, the wallpaper with its little pink flowers and sticking to it the tiny corpses of mosquitoes, the ballad rhythm that in the street had filled the guardians of public security with nostalgia beat in triumph, punctuated by kisses that crackled like chestnuts in the fire. The dewy, quivering moustache descends to the encounter with an ardent mouth. On the divan the flounces, still warm from flesh, mimic the wave that foams against the cliff. On the back of the chair, its laces on the floor, lies the corset that sheathed her body, its upper edge retaining sweat like a stain of nicotine. From the top of the solitary clothesrack, the heron turns its glass eye on that tangle of free love.

> *Amid kisses and languid caresses and songs*
> *May the days fly rapidly, rapidly by.*

Plumbing was still in its primitive stages, but all the same the custom of having a rural hideaway was a widespread one among poets. Cavallotti loved Woman, but he also loved the mountains and the introspection of a solitary retreat.

> *Perched at the flowering brink*
> *Atop the verdant hill*
> *That happy with saplings yields*
> *To the kiss of blue-green Verbanus,*
> *Refuge in my most troubled hours,*
> *A laughing abode of dreams,*
> *My dear little Dagnente,*
> *Here one day my bones will rest.*

The bell tower in Arona strikes noon: Cavallotti disembarks from the paddlewheel steamer, and with a vigorous step starts climbing the road for Dagnente. Nature sings its paean, as iridescent horseflies bite the back of the poet's exposed neck. As he comes into view of San Carlone, his friends appear, headed by Giovanni Buffi. The friends stop, look smilingly at each other, and say: "But is it really Cavallotti coming, so casual and informal, he who knows all the great men of Italy? Look! Look!" The same scene is repeated for twenty years. The greetings over, Lina, the little dog to whom

Cavallotti has given the name of Crispi's third wife, frisks about among the legs of the friends.

Cavallotti's little house is of two stories, its shutters green, its eaves a splendid bright red. The dining room is crowded with souvenirs and family portraits. On the first floor two small bedrooms, for friends who come to visit the poet in his retreat. On the second, there is a bedroom for Bocelli, his friend and secretary, one for his daughter, Maria Cavallotti Villa, and finally Cavallotti's room, which also serves as his study. The enchantment of Lake Maggiore is framed by the window. Cavallotti contemplates it from the desk. He works seated on a small pouf, so that, for all his nearsightedness, he can hold his head over his papers without resting his chest on the writing desk or bending his shoulders too much. Seen from behind, it looks like the head of an old child doing his homework.

In the evening a little tippling at Buffi's, then upstairs to bed, in the iron cot, under the portrait of Pinchetti.

Who is Pinchetti? Pinchetti

> *Was a bard; Giulio was his name.*
> *Fifteen lustra weighed on him in the evening;*
> *Though on the wrinkled untamed brow*
> *The wrath of his austere soul quivered;*
> *He walked cursing; he scourged; he derided:*
> *"All is corruption!" he said . . . and killed himself.*

In the morning a shower.

Cavallotti had acquired the habit of a daily shower as a result of a serious cerebral illness, due to excessive mental effort during the composition of a literary work. In Rome, he went every morning from Piazza Rondanini, where he lived close to the Pantheon, to have his shower in a hydrotherapeutic establishment on Via dei Crociferi. But where do you find hydrotherapeutic establishments in Dagnente?

No such establishment, of course, but a fine, ice-cold spring, in a wooded spot off the beaten track. There, naked as truth, the soldier of democracy and athlete of free thought subjected his brain, prone to cerebral raptures, to the freezing water.

A few steps from the spring, channeled by a trough supported on four wooden forks, a considerable volume of water falls from a height of five meters. Next to the little cascade, Cavallotti had erected four poles with a sheet stretched around them, inside of which he undressed. But later, since every so often the wind tore away the sheet, he replaced this fragile shelter with a small wooden hut, suggesting one of those sad and solitary country outhouses.

On 31 January 1898, a leaden sky hung over the wretched houses of Dagnente. Ragged clouds clung to the sides of the mountains and pleaded to be allowed to stay. A few hours before leaving for Milan and Rome, the poet decided to climb up to the little cemetery with the faithful Bocelli. A presentiment? Cavallotti gave a forced smile, but in that deceptive light a vague thought of death flickered through his mind.

In Rome, in Piazza Rondanini, in the house of Signora D'Anna, who loves him like a brother, Cavallotti has lived for fourteen years in the same modest bedroom, with its iron cot, one side table, three chairs, desk, and two small bookshelves. Even the food is meager. Cavallotti pays for his board and lodging. Two daily meals: Signora Teresa charges one lira for lunch, two for dinner. When the deputy eats out, he is not charged for the meal. But sometimes—a poet's absentmindedness?—notice is not given in time, and next day Cavallotti writes in his little notebook: "February 2, dinner (for the cat) L. 2.00."

In Signora Teresa's pension, lunch was at noon and dinner at seven. Cavallotti ate at the same table with the other lodgers, with Cesare Orsi, Signora Teresa, and the servants of the pension. After dinner he went by the Chamber for the last post, then to Aragno's to read the newspapers and drink punch. Though not a big eater, he was an intrepid drinker. When his manager Montecchi turned up empty-handed, the poet used to say, "I am a Muslim, a fatalist." On days of political battle, when he didn't even go home for lunch, they dragged him out of Montecitorio like a limp rag. He did not go to bed until he had first marked down the day's expenses in his notebook, from coffee to newspaper and postage stamp. Until the end of 1897 he collected stamps assiduously.

It was to Signora D'Anna's house that Cavallotti was transported on the evening of 6 March 1898. They had placed his wide-brimmed hat on his stomach, and tied a handkerchief around his face to keep his jaw from falling.

Noon had struck in the sirocco-laden sky. Bizzoni and Tassi had emerged from Montecitorio, where they had met with Macola's seconds. Rendezvous for three o'clock, at Villa Cellere, outside the Porta Maggiore. Felice had to be informed. Their faces grim, the two seconds hurried toward Piazza Rondanini. Just think, this mess had been brought about by someone whose name sounds like a meow: Miaglia! As they went along Via delle Colonnette, a black cat crossed the street. They went up the stairs at Signora D'Anna's: Cavallotti had gone out. They came back down and ran into him in Piazzetta della Maddalena. He did not want to read the challenge. "It's all right!" he said. "You've handled it all well. Go on upstairs. I'll be back in five minutes."

Around the familiar stains of wine, coffee, and orange juice, there was an affliction of sad faces. Hands lay limply on the tablecloth like slices of ham. Instead of eating their hands, the diners look from one to another. Deputy Garavetti looked at Deputy Aggio, Deputy Aggio looked at Deputy Engel, and Deputy Engel looked at Doctor Montenovesi who was going to attend Cavallotti. Each held his breath.

Felice came in, and to Signora Teresa he looked like the sun. In any other circumstances Signora Teresa would have bemoaned the delay that had burned the rice, but that day . . . Cavallotti barely picked at his food, he went down to change clothes. On the dark stairs he ran into Doctor Ascensi who was coming to put his carriage at his disposal. The concierge's little girl was crying at the bottom of the stairs. Rinaldi returned with the fencing glove. Cavallotti

15

went back up to try it on. "I can't hold the saber with this thing!" he said scornfully, and threw that huge white hand across the table, which they had forgotten to clear. It looked like the hand of a sufferer from nephritis. Signora Teresa was sobbing over the orange peels. When Cavallotti had departed with Ascensi, the others, so as not to attract attention, followed in twos and threes. Rome was deserted. In the restorative siesta, its functionaries were gathering their strength for new efforts. Leaving the city, they skirted the Verano cemetery.

By that strange law that transforms one person's troubles into someone else's entertainment, the lady who owned the villa chosen as the field of battle had made preparations as though for a garden party. What if there had been no blood? Due to the proximity of ancient aqueducts, ruins are numerous in that part of the Prenestina, and in the bare yellowish countryside, under the leaden sky, they stand erect like illustrious beggars.

The countess was getting impatient. What was keeping those people? From the coupé, which is essentially an up-ended coffin furnished with wheels, the adversaries descended, black as crows.

On the open space behind the villa's chapel, the duelists faced each other. When Bizzoni saw how preposterous his Felice looked standing up against that tall robust man with the enormous spread of his legs, his heart shriveled and sank.

Fusinato had already called a halt after two assaults. At the third, after a couple of passes, Fusinato again cried "Halt!"

Cavallotti turned. "What's the matter?"

A stream of blood gushed over his shirt. He said nothing more. They eased him into a tavern chair, and carried him into the little oratory of the villa. The point of the saber had gone into his mouth, which in his breathlessness he had held open like a running mastiff. They tried artificial respiration. They turned the body upside down as though to shake the coins out of his pockets. All in vain! His teeth were clamped shut. With the jimmying motions of a burglar, Montenovesi tried to insert a knife and force them open.

"The barrier of the teeth," he would have said. Poor Cavallotti.

In a ruined castle near Fondi, heart of the Ciociaria region, lives a family of giant males, their sisters as tall and cylindrical as towers, the mother ancient and grooved with wrinkles like an oak tree. Not long ago, amid thunder and lightning, a sinister nocturnal ceremony was celebrated in this castle, and from the windows, doors, and chimneys dreadful curses spread out into the night. The family, meeting as a tribunal, tried the former editor of the *Gazzetta di Venezia* and sentenced him to death.

Sentence having been pronounced, the voice of a woman, the mother of those gigantic country gentlemen, called out three times: "Macola! Macola! Macola!"

And Macola, who had already been dead anyway for several years, was executed in spirit.

1906. Milan is celebrating. The crash of brass, the boom-boom and clang of the bass drum with cymbals abate at the station, and grow in front of an old gray façade, behind which the Codice Atlantico chews on dreams as hard as stones. A curtain hides the "surprise," which forms a hump in the middle of the square. The most illustrious cooks in Milan, a gastronomical city *par excellence*, have had a hand in this "surprise." The eggs in all the henhouses of Lombardy have been bought up, and when the unveiling takes place, the result of all those beaten egg whites shines forth.

Why does this nude Leonidas with a helmet on his head stand before the door of the Ambrosian Library? Associations and sodalities march past to the sound of clarinets, the battalions of that civilian army that Cavallotti had dreamed of in opposition to the military army.

That day passed too, and night descended on the little glasses lighting the windows. And when the last candle in the last glass was also extinguished, what remained? Leonidas remained, in a short chiton and surrounded by clouds, wherein the moon is partially hidden, partially revealed.

17

Arnold Böcklin

I

We start reading the tercets of the *Divine Comedy*, and gradually we feel our boat get underway, propelled by the wind, dipping its oars in the invisible sea and now and then dipping them again. The voyage has begun. Only a few pilots, very few, are capable of bringing us safely to our destination: their names are Dante, their names are Homer, their names are Beethoven. Others leave you halfway, still others do nothing but show you the route on the map.

What is this mysterious voyage? What is this goal, this continent or island, for which man yearns from the depths of his being and where it is so difficult to arrive?

We do not know. By convention and for convenience we call it the "poetic world," but this is an obscure designation that generates more misunderstandings than knowledge of that world.

Another of these reliable pilots who assure the whole voyage is Arnold Böcklin. But his reputation has been blackened, the man highly discredited, and in the absence of travelers who have any faith in him, you see him alone on the pier, frowning and staring at the dark and distant horizon, his gaze that of an ancient marine centaur, to which the heavy bags under his eyes add severity.

I said the *"Divine Comedy."* Some just say the *"Comedy,"* but this is not simplicity: it is an affected and irreverent form, like ostentatiously calling a famous person by his first name.

It was one day in 1924 at the Odescalchi Theater, which was then being built in Rome. In comes a little journalist and shouts, "Ciao, Luigi!" I turn to look: "Luigi" was Luigi Pirandello. Not to mention the stupidity and pretentiousness of these abbreviated forms, such as saying "the Ninth" for "Beethoven's Ninth Symphony," or in another context saying "I've taken a bed" when what you mean is you've reserved a single-berth compartment on the night train from Rome to Milan. Brevity is something to be praised so long as it also acts on the intelligence, which relentlessly abbreviates.

Michelangelo and *michelangiolismo*, Wagner and *wagnerismo*, Nietzsche and *nicceismo*.

The spelling *"nicceismo"* was consecrated by Panzini in his novel *La Madonna di Mammà*. This shows the great disparity that runs between the artist and his legacy.

Curious! The greater the artist, the more the "creator" type he is, the more of the order of "genius," the more he, his work, and his essence are subject to being vulgarized, compromised, and made ridiculous.

So is there a greater possibility of corruption, more death, in the man who in himself sums up a universe than in the artist of limited talent? It may be only a question of fat: a dead whale on the ice cap, its huge body exposed to the Arctic sun, and birds and polar bears crowding onto that enormous, "rich," and stinking blubber that lies open in monstrous lips. The fat man is the genius in the animal world, and Gargantua is the Beethoven of that world.

Böcklinism has been confined to the *Island of the Dead*, the *Self-portrait with Death,* and the *Hermit Violinist*, to which one might add a half dozen paintings of nereids and tritons. I am not the one who made this list: it was made by Monsieur Louis Gillet, author of three essays on Böcklin published in the *Revue de l'art ancien et moderne*, in its January-June 1908 series. Louis Gillet says that Böcklin was an execrable painter "lacking in touch," and when he decides to treat him with a little more respect, he compares him to Gustave Moreau and Puvis de Chavannes, but places him below them.

Monsieur Gillet is French, and one day Böcklin said, "I don't paint for the French." When Böcklin uttered this proud and scornful declaration, it rang true. There was grave opposition between "profound and dreaming" Germans and "manneristic and superficial" Frenchmen. Out of saturation and reaction against the profundity of the fatherland, the most capricious, restless, and hysterical (but also most far-sighted) Germans aspired, or pretended to aspire, to *esprit* as though to a contrary ideal: witness Schopenhauer and his library of four thousand French volumes out of a total of five thousand; witness Nietzsche who chooses *Carmen* as an antidote to Wagnerism and yearns to drink champagne on the very soil of Paris.

But today the positions have changed. The progressive march of the French toward depth, mystery, and dream, coincides with the contrary march of the Germans toward the surface, the non-mystery, the reality of the foreground. It is the adolescent, or else the old man, who turns his gaze to distant and sunless worlds, but at noon the shadows are short. Abandoned by their countrymen, the great Romantics today are welcomed in France like brothers, and the poetic shades and melancholy phantasms of Achim von Arnim find refuge in the former center of *clair esprit*. As always, artists have been "ahead of their time." Think of all the shocks and surprises that would have been avoided had anyone listened to them!

The center of Böcklinism was Munich, the capital of Bavaria. Böcklinism spread northward in triumph as long as it found houses inhabited by men and the life of reasoning animals. To the west it died in Alsace and in Italy it stopped at Milan, not because the South rejected it (in the Balkan peninsula it reached Athens and beyond) but because in Europe the currents of Romanticism follow the itinerary of the storks. In their periodic flights from Europe to Africa and vice versa, the storks cross France on one side and the Balkan peninsula on the other, but either they do not fly over Italy at all or else they do so in very limited numbers.

Böcklinism has been principally represented by the *Toteninsel*—the *Island of the Dead*. Death is much more fascinating than life. After the *Island of the Dead* Böcklin painted the *Island of the Living*, but the effect is decidedly inferior. Could this be one more demonstration that art must show man what he is unable to see for himself? Lithographic reproductions of the *Toteninsel*, the epitome of Romantic painting, printed in sepia or dark blue ink, in wooden Art Nouveau frames, embellished on both sides with three gold wires ending in three ruby drops, were hung over the black piano, next to the snub-nosed mask of Beethoven. The fraternal grouping of these three objects constituted a sure initiation into the world of the arts, a passport for the world of poetry.

There are as many places in Europe that inspired the *Island of the Dead* as there are beds in which Napoleon slept. A strange thing, all those beds for someone who boasted of needing so little sleep! Among the "sources" for the *Toteninsel* are the English Cemetery in Florence, the Pontikonisi in Corfu, and San Vigilio on Lake Garda. But they are apocryphal sources. Even Böcklin's wife was wrong when in her *Memoirs* she indicated the Castello of Ischia as the source for this all too famous painting.

Böcklin had come down into Italy from his native Basel, the way young German artists in those days came down into Italy: to be "reborn." In Rome he lived on Via Gregoriana, worked together with other German painters in a studio on the Passeggiata Ripetta, and fed like a faun on cheese, onions, and figs. This is the time of Böcklin the "draftsman" and "copier" of nature. He was a formidable walker. He meandered around the Roman countryside, setting his yellow eyes on the mountains, trees, and lakes. He liked the "Vale of Poussin," the Wood of Egeria, and Olevano, and he drew, drew, drew. But when he began to work seriously, to create "his" world, he no longer drew. Landscape, that form of

21

direct painting that the French call *sur le motif*, is a kind of picnic in the country, a depiction of taste. Some savor it with their lips: "I'd like to eat that white." There is much frivolity in nature and only by keeping his distance from it and being absorbed in himself can the profound artist, the creator, find the necessary seriousness.

Young Arnold's heart had already been opened to love, but she who had opened it, the Swiss Luisa Schmidt, died of meningitis.

One day Arnold was walking along Via Capo le Case, and at a window he saw Angela Pascucci. She was fourteen years old, her father and mother had died of cholera, and she lived with her aunt, Carlotta Balzer.

Arnold saw Angela, and for two years he went on seeing her at the window and loving her in silence. Whirlwind romance and abductions in the hussar manner are unsuitable for artists, who are considered stupid in love by the likes of hussars.

A "transformation" in Angela's appearance was needed before Arnold could decide to "declare" his love. Two years after the first look at the window, Böcklin met Angela Pascucci at a street fair. She was dressed in "Albanian costume," and only then did he find the courage to offer her a bunch of violets and ask her if she would consent to become his wife. But the matter can be explained this way: Arnold was not addressing the flowers and the question to Angela Pascucci but to the "Albanian girl," so that she in her turn might pass them along on to Angela Pascucci.

It was on Ponza that Böcklin found the inspiration for the *Island of the Dead*.

A lady with a great soul to be filled, a great melancholy in need of nourishment, commissioned from Böcklin "the most romantic picture ever painted." And no one can truly say that Böcklin failed to fulfill his patroness's wishes.

Böcklin liked to repeat the same picture several times. He left as many as five versions of the *Island of the Dead*. The cypresses become ever smaller, the rocks larger and larger.

Whatever bit of life was still present on the island of death is thus reduced, assuming it is legitimate to speak of life in connection with cypresses. Under the door to one of the tombs on the right, not far up on the overhanging rock, Böcklin, as was his custom, signed his name with only his initials: "A.B." Thus having built his island and reached the limits of that desolate sea, Böcklin reserved one of the burial niches for himself, to inhabit as a dead man or even a living one.

These signs of ownership, this way of "inhabiting" his own paintings, are a revealing feature of Böcklin's work, the key to his poetic situation. In the *Bark of Charon* Böcklin carves his initials on the side of the Stygian boat, not to indicate that Charon is himself but that the boat is his. This is how Böcklin's complete passage into the "poetic world" is demonstrated in the most legitimate and persuasive manner. Others, even such singular and lofty poets as Rimbaud, gaze long but from a distance at that world, in a despair sometimes filled with hatred, but the man himself is held fast by the shore and the dominant theme of his song is unhappiness. When you hear a poet suffer, remember that he suffers as a prisoner, and that he yearns for this impossible journey.

The tranquillity and well-being of the landowner who has paid his taxes shine in Böcklin's "circular" gaze (the poet who has only the "wish" for the poetic world gazes from only one side), in his way of looking all around and finding everywhere his earth, his sea, his sky.

In no other artist, since the world began, has man dwelt so fully within the poetic world.

Much has been said about Böcklin's "bad taste." As though Böcklin's condition were that of Cézanne, or in any case of painters who look at the "poetic world" from outside and far away, are bound by the rules and discipline of "good taste," and in their experiments with taste consume their will, energies, and dreams.

The precise degree of an artist's quality is measured by the quality of his admirers. The "type" of Cézanne lover is to be seen in the hero of S. S. Van Dine's detective stories. Philo

Operatic Lives

Vance, the character of whom I speak, transfers his dilettante soul from police investigation to tasteful painting and back again; he is incapable of creative acts, his intelligence is sharp but oriented in one direction alone, and confined to that "good taste" that specifically means balance and limitation. In any case, this limited and qualified intelligence allows Philo Vance and lovers of Cézanne to savor "tonal relationships," and to discover that underneath it all the music Toscanini most prefers is *La Bohème*.

Scientific philistinism has also seized on Böcklin's work. A member of the Berlin Academy of Sciences, Professor Du Bois-Reymond, of Huguenot descent, has written an erudite essay pointing out the anatomical unlikelihood of the creatures imagined by Böcklin, and has shown that his centaurs are equipped with a double chest cavity, four front limbs, four lungs, and two hearts. It is after due consideration that we mention Professor Du Bois-Reymond's Huguenot background: what we said about Louis Gillet goes for him as well. And we who have always dreamed of spare limbs!

Arnold's marriage to Angela was allowed to take place despite his Lutheranism and the strict Catholicism of her relatives. Angela's father had been a marshal in the papal guard. Arnold and Angela went on their honeymoon to Olevano, to places dear to his "draftsman's" pencil. When Victor Bérard, who devoted his whole life to the study of the *Odyssey*, married Adèle, he took her on the route of Odysseus's voyage. Böcklin, in the middle of his honeymoon, continued to draw furiously. For a short while the couple lived on Angela's small dowry, and when it was used up, Böcklin thought of the other "portion" left by Angela's father, and in a moment of discouragement thought of giving up painting and enlisting in the pope's Swiss guard.

It was Angela who dissuaded him from this desperate idea and encouraged him to persevere. She took her husband's paintings under her arm, the romantic *Landschaften*, the ruins amid cypresses, the fauns giving whistling lessons to the

24

blackbirds, and went around selling them in the cafés of Rome. At that time Cézannism did not yet exist, and Angela was able to get a little money for these paintings.

Angela was for Böcklin what Cosima was for Wagner, and Sophia Engastromenos was for Heinrich Schliemann. She taught herself to read and write, for although around 1840 the good sisters did indeed educate young girls, this did not mean that reading and writing actually formed part of education. And having learned to read and write in limited fashion on her own, Angela wrote copiously, embellishing her letters with conspicuous grammatical errors. She had considerable natural intelligence, but the innocence of her spirit underwent no changes. At the height of her mental maturity, the most that Angela Böcklin could manage when it came to reading was the prose of Edmondo De Amicis.*

Did Angela Pascucci understand her husband's work? We do not know. We do not wish to know. Besides, it is indelicate even to formulate such questions. What is certain, however, is that Angela "felt" Arnold had important things to do in this world and watched faithfully over his health and peace of mind.

The parallel, mentioned above, between Angela Böcklin and Cosima Wagner was only a formal one, because actually there was as much difference between Angela and Cosima as between Böcklin and Wagner—which is to say enormous.

There was no love lost between Böcklin and Wagner. They met three times and each meeting ended badly.

On the first occasion Böcklin arrived at the Wagners, and instead of finding the "maestro," he found Cosima, who took him by the hand, saying, "Come with me. I consider you worthy to witness the most beautiful sight in the world, but walk on tiptoe." And with infinite precautions she took him inside a room dim with shadow and led him to a vast divan covered in red satin, where among the cushions, wearing the dressing gown of a magician, his velvet beret over his ear,

---

* Author of *Cuore*, a children's classic. (Tr.)

Wagner was sleeping like a little Klingsor. Böcklin said nothing, but his face spoke volumes.

The second occasion was when Wagner invited Böcklin to hear some passages from *Götterdämmerung*, which Anton Rubinstein was playing on the piano in an adjoining room, but whether because of Böcklin's lack of attention, or the expression of boredom on his face, Wagner jumped up like a bantam rooster and shouted, "I see you have no understanding of music!" To which the painter replied, "More than you have of painting."

For Böcklin music was a distraction for a demiurge in repose. He liked Mozart, Cherubini, Paisiello. His favorite musical instrument was the flute, because "the sounds it gives are more solitary and profound." But to the flute itself he preferred the ineffable notes made by the pipes of his Pan among the reeds.

The third occasion was when Wagner asked Böcklin to come from Sorrento, as he was finishing *Parsifal* amid the roses of Ravello. He had thought of Böcklin as a possible stage designer for his theater in Bayreuth. It was a very hot day. Böcklin listened drowsily to the composer's plans and theories, then without making any reply, he asked for a glass of wine and took his leave.

The idea of combining three arts to make a single one stank to him of pastiche.

II

The damp winter night descends on Via Nomentana. The shadow of the trees deepens the shadow of the sky. I have difficulty finding the house.

A wild and overgrown garden opens behind an old gate. There was a time when the owners of these villas around Rome did not pay taxes, because the eucalyptus trees in their gardens purified the air.

This is an old house belonging to Professor Pallenberg, Arnold Böcklin's son-in-law. Red draperies hang from the walls, and the eyes of the portraits look at us from the shadows. What mysterious frontier have I crossed? I think of what is happening in the world, and am astonished to find in this house, protected by a family of eucalyptus trees, the charm, the deep love, the decorum of romantic life.

Among the attractions by which Italy summoned the poets and artists of the north—whatever happened to the pilgrim artist?—along with the sky and its now threatening, now peacefully drifting clouds; along with the Homeric quality of its sea; along with the still fresh traces of the gods, there was also the wine. Böcklin sacrificed often to Bacchus Lyaeus. The painter's love for the god "who loosens" was a youthful love; it went back to 1850, to the time when Böcklin, along with other painter friends, worked in the studio on the Passeggiata Ripetta, and wine, in the Rome patrolled by the red trousers of the Zouaves, cost twenty centesimi a liter. One's very recreations included wine, the excursions outside the gates, the halts at the Half-Mile Inn, at Porta Pia, the Marozzi Inn, the Artichoke Inn, the Baths of Caracalla, those excursions that combined relaxation with the contemplation of nature and fruitful disputes about art. In one of his self-portraits, Böcklin holds a glass filled with ruby-colored liquid in his right hand. Sometimes he remembered he was Swiss and took his wife to the Albrecht beer hall in Via Capo le Case.

Sunday is a day of rest. Sunday mornings, when other men in the cities and countryside were washing their feet, putting on their best clothes, and going to mass (in those days the custom of bathing was restricted to a few inhabitants of the extreme north of Europe), Böcklin would go into his studio and begin the painting he had in mind. He began his pictures on Sunday, because he considered it auspicious. The Church condemns work done on Sunday, but Böcklin's work was not the work of man. Like all serious painters, he prepared his canvases and paints himself. He liked his canvases very smooth. The painter conscious of his quality as a craftsman and his integrity as a worker begins his task with the preparation of his material. The urge to do well is greater in the painter who paints on a primed surface prepared by his own hands. I speak from experience: one paints differently, one paints better, one paints with greater self-confidence on a canvas that one has prepared oneself.

The way Böcklin began a painting also deserves to be known. He would apply a color to the prepared surface, almost always a gray. He would then stand in front of the gray canvas and with a sponge soaked in water broadly lay out the composition he had in his head. (The first sketch was done in his mind and deposited in his memory in the solitary hours immediately before falling asleep.) Then he would sit down and look at this premature ghost of his work. If the damp sketch satisfied him, he would go over it rapidly with paint and establish its lines; otherwise he allowed it gradually to fade away.

In drawing heads Rembrandt began with the eye; Böcklin started his picture at the horizon and came forward with crossed brushstrokes, in obedience to a mysterious centripetal force. He used to say that painting is a calculation made with volumes and colors. He tended to express himself violently. He wanted his painting to be stronger and stronger. He was happy if the cook, coming into the studio, was frightened at the sight of the new painting. He did not use a palette but a marble tabletop. He painted sitting down. The trite painter paints standing up, the one who, like Laszlo,* aims at effects. The serious painter paints sitting down, and is as careful and meticulous as a dentist. Böcklin experimented with the whole range of tempera paints, and was especially partial to egg tempera. Then he went on to the resins, and for him cherry gum, according to the recipe of a certain Theophilus, was a great discovery. Loving brilliant colors as he did, painting with cherry gum gave him great satisfaction, and like a good demiurge who likes to do everything for himself, he planted

---

* Philip Alexius Laszlo de Lombos (1869–1937). Hungarian painter and naturalized British citizen, best known for portraits. (Tr.)

cherry trees in the garden of his villa in San Domenico near Florence. He would slash the bark of the tree, let the gum trickle into a hanging container, carefully collect the precious secretion, and then with much knowledge, above all with much patience, prepare it for his painting. He liked Rubens but not Rembrandt. He also like Grünewald, and often traveled from Basel to Colmar to take another look at the putrefying Christ on the cathedral altar. He liked the Flemish, and spent long hours looking at their paintings. In San Domenico he had two villas and fields that were worked by tenants. He could not abide the elegant and handsome Feuerbach.* They had quarreled about money. Böcklin was cultured. He read Greek and Latin. He was very fond of Ariosto. At the age of sixty-five he had an attack of apoplexy. When he recovered, he went to Viareggio, then to Forte dei Marmi. At San Terenzo he had a sailor friend, who took him in a boat to visit the grottoes. He visited the islands of Ponza and Gorgona. His painting *The Pirates* was inspired by the Castello of Ischia. Ponza inspired the *Island of the Dead.* Böcklin died at the age of seventy-two. His wife survived him by fifteen years. She was strong and naive. She taught herself to write, and, pleased with the result, started writing furiously and left some "Memoirs." Böcklin was a friend of Burckhardt. But one day they quarreled. Böcklin had painted a *Pietà.* The head of Christ was turned to the right, Burckhardt persuaded him to turn it to the left. Böcklin listened to his friend, but the result was awful. Actually I would have expected the historian of our Renaissance to be more intelligent, or at least aware that one oughtn't to give advice to painters. Böcklin's character was solemn. He fell ill with typhus and on his recovery painted his self-portrait with Death playing the violin behind his back.

One evening, after supper, in the summer of 1898, the family was gathered on the terrace of the San Domenico villa.

---

* Anselm Feuerbach (1829–1880), historical and portrait painter. (Tr.)

Also present was a brother-in-law of Böcklin, who was re-evoking certain episodes of the 1870 war. Taciturn by nature, the painter listened and kept silent. All of a sudden a fire began blazing in the valley. Next morning, although it was not Sunday, Böcklin sketched with water the first of the four versions of *War*. The horse carrying Death on its back is inspired by the second horse of the group of knights in the *Triumph of Death*, in the Camposanto of Pisa.

One doesn't fly in order to shorten distances. Flying is a metaphysical wish of man, a dream, the memory of a most remote and monstrous life. What do you call a man in whom the memory of flying is still alive? One such man was Arnold Böcklin. Man is not naturally made for flying, just as neither is he made for swimming, and one day will not even be made for walking. Nevertheless he preserves an obscure memory of when he swam and flew, just as among future men a few will obscurely recall the time when men walked. Desire's perspective falsifies the direction, and projects into the future what instead lies in the past. Rather than desiring new achievements, we want to regain what we have lost. Illusion deceives us into thinking that we are advancing toward our desires, while actually our advance is a retreat. Our greatest aspiration, our deepest wish, is to return to the condition that preceded our birth, and since we are not allowed to re-enter the wombs of our mothers, we make do with a metaphor and re-enter the womb of the earth.

The memory of flight is sometimes rekindled in dreams, and there rediscovers its quality as a way of liberating ourselves from evil. We dream that some danger is pursuing us, we have no way to protect ourselves, and are about to succumb; but when our anxiety is most compelling, we suddenly reacquire our long-lost faculty and with an immense sense of liberation begin to fly once more.

Böcklin was an Icarian. He remembered when men flew and he wanted to return to that primitive condition. Between 1870 and 1880, in one of his most intense periods of work as a painter, he conceived, designed, and made gliders. He and two of his friends, zur Helle and von Pidoll, built the framework of the apparatus; his wife, daughters, and servants sewed the canvas to be stretched on the bamboo wings. Von Pidoll committed suicide in Rome. Zur Helle was a painter and had been one of Böcklin's pupils. Returning from a trip to Egypt, he brought his teacher the stuffed head of a crocodile, which inspired Böcklin's painting *Ruggiero and Angelica*. The paladin spreads his cloak to cover Angelica, his virgin kinswoman, naked and shrinking with shame, while the dragon's head, separated from its body, looks long and ironically up from the ground at this spectacle of love, honor, and chivalrous illusions. Böcklin drew inspiration from Ariosto for one of his finest paintings.

The glider experiment took place at Campocaldo, near San Domenico, just outside Florence, where Böcklin lived. Rumors about the "diabolical thing" had spread in the vicinity and the peasants, grim and threatening, stopped to watch from afar. Sometimes they threw stones in an attempt to destroy the instrument of Satan, and zur Helle and von Pidoll, both of them former officers, had to organize a defense. Intelligence is a long memory, but the peasant has a short memory and has forgotten that he too once flew, over an earth that was as yet uncultivated.

After his attempts to fly in Tuscany, and with people talking about his model gliders, Böcklin was summoned to Berlin by the German General Staff and asked to repeat his experiments. In Berlin Böcklin shared his Icarian studies with Otto Lilienthal, and in the apparatus conceived by the painter of the *Island of the Dead* the pioneer of glider flight first detached himself from the earth and made a flight of three hundred meters.

One day Lilienthal succeeded in placing a motor on the craft, but that day he crashed and was killed. Flying with a motor is not a natural thing. In order to take off on his flights, Lilienthal had had a hill made for his personal use. In the final analysis, what these "Icarians" remember is the time when man's life was one grand, continuous game.

Böcklin's mind was dominated by the idea of flight. When-

31

ever a sheet of paper fell into his hands, he placed it on his palm, shook it slightly to detach it, and watched it free itself in the air and drift slowly to the floor. One day he received in the mail a diploma from the University of Basel, naming him doctor *honoris causa*. Without bothering to read it, Böcklin took the beautiful sheet of paper and ever so slowly, with infinite delicacy, made it fly across the studio.

Böcklin was strong, robust, and exceptionally agile. At the age of sixty he could still turn somersaults. But he fainted at the sight of blood. He was unable to cut his own fingernails, and had his wife do it for him. He suffered whenever he saw someone leaning out a window. When his wife gave birth, Böcklin became so ill that he had to go to bed. In some Balkan countries, after the wife gives birth, the husband goes to bed and receives the good wishes of relatives and friends. Every symbol is the reflection of a reality.

Böcklin had fourteen children. In one of his many *Pietàs*, in which Christ lies on a marble sarcophagus and an archangel descends from heaven to receive him, the little angels grieving over the dead Redeemer are all children of the painter. Eight of them died, one was killed. A brother of Böcklin was also murdered. One of his sons died insane. Only one is still alive. He married a fortune-teller and lives in Munich, solitary and crippled by illness.

Two sons were painters: Karl, who was also an architect, and Arnold, who was named after his father and inherited from him his artistic talent.

Pallenberg gets up and takes me into the next room. It is the dining room, very large and decorated with tapestries and columns. The table is set, and by the little silver glasses and the napkins stuck in napkin rings I recognize the children's places.

Pallenberg takes a small painting down from the wall and brings it close to the lamp. It is the head of a little boy. A forceful painting, glazed, obviously painted with gum: one of the very few remaining ones by Arnold Böcklin the son. Spots have appeared on the canvas like fever blisters, impairing the child's sad sweet expression. Pallenberg attributes these spots to the proximity of the radiator. It is sad to think of this painter, burdened by a great name, dying young, and the victim of an adverse fate even in the beyond.

How to account for Böcklin's obsession with flying? In no other artist, since the world began, has man transported himself so fully into the poetic world created by himself.

In constructing his gliders, Böcklin perhaps dreamed of being able to transport himself physically into the world of his imagination.

The Wily Cretan

Fate had hounded the Venizelos family. Fate is still powerful on the island that witnessed the reign of Minos and Pasiphaë's perpetration of unheard-of monstrosities.

Three children had already been lost by the unhappy mother, before they had scarcely uttered their first cries, and the fourth, he who was to be known as "the wily Cretan," was about to be born. Moira had to be placated, but on Crete Moira has two faces: pagan and Christian. To placate the Christian Moira, the parish priest advised the mother, burdened with her pregnancy, to prostrate herself before the icon of the Virgin in the Panaghiota convent near the village of Murnies, on the outskirts of Khania, and make a vow to give birth to the child in a stable, in imitation of what She had done. For their part, the experts in ancient religions advised that the newborn infant be exposed in the countryside under a fig tree, in imitation of what had been done with the little Oedipus. Which of the two propitiatory acts to choose? So as not to play favorites, the Venizelos couple decided to perform both.

A few hours after the birth of Eleutherios, which means the "Liberator," friends knocked on the door of the Venizelos house.

"Who's that little fellow you're carrying in your arms?" asked Kiriakos Venizelos, gazing with a pleased eye on his baby boy still wrapped in his original slumber.

"He's an orphan who was exposed under a fig tree," the

friends replied, and one of them added, "We beg you to adopt him, O Kiriakos, you who are so kind and just."

And Kiriakos said: "The gods' will be done."

Thus Heaven was satisfied in its twofold pagan and Christian dignity, and the Liberator, unlike his little sibling predecessors, lived and thrived.

Eleutherios Venizelos was two years old when his father closed his small haberdasher's shop in the *Venetica stena*, or "Venetian quarter," of Khania, and with his wife and son moved to stony Sira. Once again the Cretans had risen against the Turkish yoke, and although duty required Kiriakos to join his oppressed brethren and fight together with them for freedom, a mysterious voice whispered to him to save himself and his wife, and above all to save the child born under such auspicious signs. The Venizelos family remained in Sira for six months. For Eleutherios this was the first of his many exiles.

On their return to Khania, a *didaskalos*, or teacher, initiated the future statesman into the rudiments of learning. Eleutherios did so brilliantly in his studies that some years later Kiriakos decided to send his son to Athens. There the student Eleutherios Venizelos not only gained a knowledge of law from that building with metopes and porticoes situated on University Street,* but became the recognized leader of Cretan irredentism. When in 1877 Eleutherios returned to Khania with the title of *dikegoros*, or "orator of justice," his name was already resounding clearly from one end of the island to the other.

Crete, which some have called the "polyglot island," never lived up to its name so fully as in 1888. In homage to the year of the three eights, the ancient land of Minos gave itself over to an orgy of blood. Greeks and Turks vied with each other in murder. The spirit of Vendetta took possession of the whole island. Religious differences inflamed the hatred between oppressors and oppressed.

Meanwhile Eleutherios Venizelos's career was proceeding

---

* Now Venizelos Street. (Tr.)

full tilt. Besides practicing law, he had launched into politics and been elected deputy to the Cretan assembly. The bloodbath grew. A colossal massacre was in sight. The more peaceful Cretans thought of their own safety. Once again, as with an enormous sneeze, Crete scattered a portion of its children to Melos, to Kythera, to the Piraeus. Venizelos himself, just as he had been about to make his debut in the assembly, again found himself in Athens, where he took advantage of his new exile to complete his education.

It was a mellow afternoon in autumn. His glasses trained on the page, Eleutherios Venizelos was perusing a passage in the *Peloponnesian War*, when his attention was distracted by the metallic bursts of a military band. He went to the window, and below on Stadium Street, packed with cheering crowds, he saw royal carriages going by carrying George I of Greece with his long mandarin moustaches and the Empress Augusta of Germany, Wilhelm II with his lightning-rod moustaches and Queen Olga of Greece, and the diadochos Constantine and Princess Sophia of Hohenzollern, all equally smiling and bestowing mechanical greetings to right and left.

The appearance of Wilhelm II, who had come to Athens to give his sister in marriage to the heir to the throne of Greece, struck the Cretan's mind like a dark thunderbolt. Eleutherios withdrew from the window, while the cortege proceeded amid cheers, but instead of going back to his reading of Thucydides, he concentrated his thoughts on the harm this monarch was about to inflict on the future of Greece. Hatred for the monarchy, latent in the breast of the twenty-five-year-old republican, suddenly burst forth.

The prestige of the young tribune grew and spread. Cretan unrest grew in equal measure. On 26 March 1895, the new vali, Alexander Karatheodori Pasha (Black Theodore), disembarked at Khania from the Austrian packet boat, and the arrival of this "Christian" governor general opened the cage to the most rosy hopes. In the name of the Cretan people, Venizelos sent Abdul Hamid his "grateful thanks." Next day two Muslims lay with their throats cut in the dust of Apokoroma, and soon thereafter four Christians paid with their blood for the lives of those two sons of Allah. Arson was added to bloodshed. Khania burned rapidly amid sinister rumblings. Discarding the toga for the sword, Venizelos recruited a corps of volunteers, established his headquarters at Akrotiri, three quarters of an hour from Khania, called a meeting of the Assembly, set up a provisional government, entered into negotiations with the admirals commanding the British, Russian, and French naval units anchored in Suda Bay, and declared his proposal to unite Crete with Greece to the representatives of the Powers.

While the negotiations between Venizelos and the representatives of the Powers were proceeding, the Sublime Porte declared war on Greece. Thus began, on 17 April 1897, that five-week war between Greeks and Turks, in which the diadochos Constantine, supreme commander of the Hellenic army, made the bold experiment of substituting gastronomy for strategy by appointing his mess director, General Sapunzakis, as chief of the General Staff.

The attempt to free Crete from the Ottoman yoke having failed, agitation on the island resumes with renewed fervor. The insurrectional assembly elects Dr. Sphakianakis as president (the ending "kis" is extremely common in Cretan surnames) and a month later Eleutherios Venizelos. The majority wants autonomy. Venizelos, as an advocate of annexation, is accused of being in the pay of Athens. On 25 August 1897, the assembly decrees the expulsion of Venizelos. The crowd besieges the fallen president in his home, bombards the windows with pails of garbage, and tries to set fire to the house. Venizelos, with some difficulty, succeeds in fleeing and takes refuge in Athens. The European chancelleries hand over the government of the island to Prince George, second son of the king of Greece. Venizelos returns to Crete and is elected deputy for Cydonia.

An important page in the life of Eleutherios Venizelos opens at this point. Prince George is not the sovereign, and yet to Venizelos's highly republican nose, the new governor smells like a monarch. Between the two that unrelenting struggle begins that some years later was to bring Venizelos to the height of tragicomedy.

In the middle of the inaccessible White Mountains, lies a godforsaken village called Therisso. There, in March 1905, men wrapped in black cloaks prowled about like bandits, their rifles on their shoulders. It was the headquarters of the ringleader Eleutherios Venizelos. "Join me," he said in his speeches, "for I represent Cretan freedom against the autocracy of Prince George." And in the manifesto of 11 March: "Today, 11 March 1905, the Cretan people, meeting in plenary assembly at Therisso in Cydonia, has proclaimed its union with the kingdom of Greece, in a single free and constitutional State."

The insurrection spread swiftly. Even the governor's advisers, Sphakianakis and Kriaris, went over to the rebels. To protect their ward, the great Powers proclaimed a state of siege. On 7 August a detachment composed of fifty Italian and fifty Russian marines arrived at the Venizelos camp. A rifleman ordered the rebels to lay down their arms. Half an hour later, and since the camp continued as silent as a tomb, the Russian marines opened fire. The Cretans came out in force, their pantaloons full of wind, and the Russians were forced to withdraw. From that moment, and for twenty-four hours, "General" Venizelos, in his alpaca jacket, starched cuffs, and spectacles was the victor over Europe.

Next day the Russians returned with four hundred men, and the Cretans took flight over the crags of the White Mountains.

Europe had beaten "General" Venizelos.

For many years, until 14 October 1912 to be exact, Venizelos belonged to the category of specialists. His specialty was preparing for the annexation of Crete by Greece. By posing as the liberator of Crete, he had succeeded in attracting a following of partisans. A military league for the independence of Crete had been formed in Athens, and it invited the "liberator" to the capital. King George had gone down to Phaleron by landau, an evzone on the seat, to breathe the sea air. They told him that Eleutherios Venizelos was on board that squat, chugging steamer heading for the Piraeus. King George, squinting his lids, watched the ship with his blue nearsighted eyes, and though his spirit was as meek as a girl's, said, "I hope Mr. Venizelos will soon be hanging from the yard of a warship." Greece at that time did not have an abundance of warships, but enough in any case to hang the "wily Cretan."

In 1910, having asked for an audience with the king, the man who had failed to be hanged declared, "If Your Majesty will accept my program and leave the choice of means to me, I will within five years present Your Majesty with a renewed and strengthened Greece, and one worthy of foreign respect." George I, who had trouble with his r's, replied, "Twy."

To keep his promise to this remote descendant of Hamlet, Venizelos set about the preparation of what was to be the masterpiece of his political career: the Balkan War of 1912. He contrived his diabolical plot in great secret with the help of the governments of Sofia, Belgrade, and Cetinje. On 8 October Montenegro, which the satirical journals of the time represented in the guise of a fox, declared war on the "Ottoman lion." On the 13th, Sofia, Belgrade, and Athens send a note to Constantinople, demanding the autonomy of the European vilayets. On the 14th, Athens, with an ultimatum, demands the lifting of the embargo on Greek merchant ships detained in Turkish waters. On the same day Venizelos proclaims the annexation of Crete by Greece, and with this proclamation concludes his career as a specialist. A few days later the overwhelming offensive of the confederates in Epirus, Macedonia, and Thrace begins. The "Ottoman lion" arrives back at the gates of Constantinople.

On 9 November old Abdul Hamid, no longer the Red Sultan and reduced to the state of no longer being able to offer "bad coffee" to his friends, is sitting on the terrace of the Villa Alatini, exploring the outskirts of Salonika with a small telescope. He sees horsemen swooping down from the heights of the Vardar in a cloud of dust. "Who are they?" the deposed Sultan asks his faithful Ali standing behind him.

And the faithful Ali: "They are the vanguard of the Greek army, O my padishah." "*Aman!*" sighs the old tyrant, reduced to impotence, passing his hand over his hooked nose and dyed beard. "Have they allowed the Balkans to unite? What fools! They're finished." The "fools" were the Young Turks.

Venizelos gave the finishing touches to his "masterpiece," perfected and polished it: first by refusing to participate in the armistice signed on 3 December between the Balkan states and Turkey, in this way preserving rule over the Aegean for Greece, then allying himself with the Serbs against the Bulgars and enriching Greece with Bulgar spoils, after having enriched it with Turkish spoils.

It was time to return to King George and say, "Sire, I have kept my promise, and in less time than foreseen. Now you have Epirus and southern Macedonia, Chalcidice except for Mount Athos (but who cares about a bunch of lousy, squabbling monks?), and almost all the islands of the Aegean: a total of 56,000 square kilometers." But in the meantime King George, passing in the vicinity of the White Tower of Salonika, his admiral's cap over his ear and a staff in his hand, had been stabbed by an individual who on being taken to the police station and interrogated had begun giggling and telling a story that made no sense.

Here ends the "heroic" part of Venizelos's life. From now on this life is nothing but one long intrigue.

With the outbreak of the European war, Venizelos and Constantine agree to place Greece in a position of benevolent neutrality. This agreement having been expressed, Venizelos wishes the king good night and goes home to bed. But at two in the morning, they come knocking at Venizelos's door. The German ambassador to Athens asks that the cruisers *Goeben* and *Breslau* be allowed to refuel in Greek ports. Venizelos gives the authorization and goes back to bed. Three days later Venizelos blames Foreign Minister Streit for granting permission and calls it a "criminal act."

On the 14th, unbeknown to the king and the other ministers, Venizelos asks the legations of the Entente if Greece, by coming to Serbia's aid and attacking Bulgaria, would be treated as an ally, and on 18 August 1914, in proposing in the council Greece's entry into the conflict on the side of the Entente, he adds, "And we'd better hurry up, because in three weeks the Entente will have crushed the Central Powers." Then, taking advantage of his colleagues' perplexity, he goes secretly to the ministers of England and France and offers them both, politely and unconditionally, the cooperation of the Greek army. Stunned by such generosity, the two diplomats look at the wily Cretan with dazed eyes, without answering either yes or no.

Venizelos continued this "peek-a-boo" policy, full of tantalizing hints and evasions, offering the meager Hellenic divisions sometimes to this one and sometimes to that one, until 22 September 1915. On that day, at two in the afternoon, the wily Cretan left Athens by the Patissia highway, in an automobile with lowered blinds, and set off for the royal castle of Tatoi, with its four small brick towers set among trees a short distance from the capital. The meeting between the king and the minister was a brief one. They discussed the possibility of a Bulgarian attack and studied the means of countering it, after which Venizelos left. At five in the afternoon the king received a strange letter from his minister, urging him once again to allow the Allies to land at Salonika. His suspicions aroused, Constantine sends Mercatis, his chamberlain, to Venizelos's home to demand an explanation. At that very moment Venizelos is returning from a visit to the British, French, and Russian legations, from whom he has requested a prompt landing at Salonika. Mercatis is stunned. "What's the matter?" replies Venizelos. "I didn't make this request in the name of Greece, but personally in my own name."

Next morning, Guillemin, minister of France, tells the king that Venizelos's proposal will not be acted on. Shortly before, however, the same Guillemin had informed Venizelos that his proposal had been transmitted to France and England, and favorably received. On 1 October, a British admiral disembarks at Salonika and requisitions quarters for the expeditionary force. Venizelos runs to the palace. "What scoundrels these English are!" he exclaims before the king. "Violating our territory! But I'll tell them a thing or two! Oh, won't I tell them a thing or two!" Indifferent to his minister's indignation, the king asks him to resign. Venizelos flees to Salonika, picks himself a villa with a garden along the sea, posts a sentry at the gate in bolero jacket and black pantaloons, and announces to the world that henceforth Greece has two sovereigns: Constantine I and Eleutherios Venizelos. The rest is known.

The rest is even more squalid. Venizelos cancels out the diplomatic victory at Versailles with a disaster in Asia Minor. What is Venizelos by now? A name. The name of a party. In 1928 the ridiculous seesawing begins: Venizelos against Tsaldaris. On the night of 6 June 1933, as Venizelos's automobile speeds toward the cool of Kefissia, murderous hands open fire on him, but fail to hit him: Tsaldaris against Venizelos.

Eleutherios retires to Crete. Venizelos had once dreamed of the union of this island with Greece: from this island Venizelos now contemplates the conquest of Greece. Thus was born that absurd revolutionary attempt that was buried under general reprobation. Defeated, Venizelos takes refuge in Italy and from Italy goes to Paris. He is finished. The government of his country condemns him to death. His property is confiscated. Then, after the restoration of the monarchy, even the old enemy of kings takes advantage of the amnesty granted by the sovereign. What will Venizelos do?

To find out the intentions of the "wily Cretan," a journalist presents himself at Venizelos's house. He is received by his son, who in memory of the haberdasher grandfather is named Kiriakos.

"My father," says Kiriakos, "is not concerned with politics."

"Pas possible!"

"He has never been concerned with politics. He is interested only in history. Just now he's working on a book about Thucydides, his favorite author. Would you like to see?"

Kiriakos opens the door of the study. The head is bent over

the desk, the face with the full beard rests on the book: the same Thucydides that Venizelos was reading on that mellow autumn afternoon in Athens, as the nuptial cortege of Constantine and Sophia went by on Stadium Street. The strange Phrygian cap he has worn for so many years has fallen on the carpet. It is the first time the old republican has bared his head before a majesty. But it is the majesty of Death.

Two Venizelian Moments

ATHENS 1906

His surname was Angelo, or *Anghelo* to be exact. He was a bad angel, the pernicious herald for that child I still was. Alongside my thankless fourteen years, his seventeen seemed the age of marvelous achievements, of supreme triumphs. Fancy waistcoats were the fashion: Anghelo's was oxblood, and its iridescent buttons shone like cats' eyes. Anghelo smoked a great deal and had frequent coughing fits. When the fit was over he would rap his chest with his knuckles and say: "I'm ruined." After this declaration he would flip open his silver cigarette case and light another "Barca." The best Greek cigarettes of the time bore the name of the Carthaginian who had caused glorious Rome so much trouble. Anghelo's cigarette case was an objet d'art. On the lid a beauty of the time, a sort of Belle Otero dressed as a tulip and raising a glass of champagne in her left hand, glittered in enamel. The case had a "secret" compartment in which Anghelo kept photos of his favorites. Anghelo was experienced in love, so much so that now women had come to bore him, and all he asked was to be left in peace. Short in stature, he used to boast of just one feat: he could empty half a bottle of cognac without passing out. They were bottles with a very long neck and shaped like the wooden Indian clubs used in gymnastic exercises. In the tricks, deceits, and violence practiced by Anghelo to wring money from his parents, the cunning of Odysseus was combined with the fury of Ajax. My father had died the year before. My mother, worried

44

about my fate, had warned me against bad companions. "That Anghelo is dragging you to perdition," she said, looking at me with mournful eyes. My conscience suggested to me I was behaving badly, my pleasures were ruined by scorching remorse, but where was I to get the strength to renounce this magnificent friendship? Anghelo possessed exquisite subtlety. He succeeded in abolishing the difference between us in age, to which others would have given God knows what importance. He treated me as an equal. He offered me cigarettes without first asking me if I "knew how to smoke." He once made me try some tobacco in which he told me hashish had been mixed: a crazy stunt! He was munificent. In the café he paid. He left the waiter princely tips. He never touched the change, as though afraid of burning himself. In Greece waiters are called "boy." Just see the effect of habit! It did not seem amazing that a seventeen-year-old with an imperious voice should call men who were often white-haired and bent over with age *paidi*. Following in the wake of this lord of life I presented myself in certain settings where, without my anghelic guide, I would never have dared to stick my nose: I penetrated the mysteries of the notorious Castalia.

These things happened in Greece. So it should not be surprising if a beer hall bore the name of the Phocian spring from which poets drew their inspiration and talent. It was more than a beer hall, it was a *café concert*, as they were called in those days, and there the *tarantella* of Don Pasquale Scognamiglio was performed with great success.

Anghelo was an *aficionado*, an *habitué*, of the Castalia. When he entered, a cigarette dangling from his lips and his thumbs hooked in his waistcoat, the music, whether dance or opera selection, immediately stopped and the mandolins struck up, as though it were the anthem for a sovereign, "Don Ciccí la caramella," this important customer's favorite song and illustrative of him, for I have forgotten to add that my companion kept a huge monocle of ordinary glass perpetually stuck in his left eye.

At that time tarantella companies occupied the place that

has since been taken over by chorus girls. There is not only
an identity in their artistic intentions, but also in the
discipline and austerity of their behavior. A dozen girls, both
blondes and brunettes, lovable bacilli who among the
jeunesse dorée of Athens had spread an epidemic of serious
crushes, but all of which were equally inoperative. Never
mind that from the stage of the Castalia these young
Neapolitan women scattered a profusion of smiles and
kicked their legs to the four winds. Once the show was over
and the footlights extinguished, these twelve budding roses,
enclosed in highnecked dusters and each with her dressing case in her hand, returned in formation, in single file,
under the watchful command of the Cavaliere Scognamiglio
and his wife to the Hotel Plato—*Xenodocheion tou Platonos*
(that is to say, the place, or rather the vessel, the receptacle
in which the divine Plato receives the transient foreigner).
On the sidewalk in front, tapping the pavement with
nervous heels, twirling their canes with three fingers, the
jeunesse dorée stared with lobster eyes at the closed shutters
of that house, which had taken its name from the father of
idealism.

It was an electoral autumn. Two parties were contending
for the government of Greece: the party of the "cord" and
that of the "olive." The "cord," composed of the national
colors, two twisted white and blue threads, was headed by
Delyannis, the "olive" by Theotokis the Phaeacian. Modern
Greek is a composite language and highly ideistic. The
meaning has not yet descended to the bottom of words, but
still remains on the surface. The same for proper names. It is
an amusing game to break up Greek words and see how they
are made internally. You thereby learn that Theotokis is "the
one begot by God" and Delyannis "Crazy John." When we
come to names more in the news today, we discover that
Condillis is "General Pencil" and Camenos "General
Burnt-out."

Delyannis was a rosy, florid, lovable old man. Gallant with
the ladies, affable with men, courteous and loyal with adver-

saries. But who were the adversaries of this moderator *par excellence*, this "nice papa"? In fine weather (the Athenian winter is so short!) Delyannis wore a gray frock coat, gray trousers, gray bowler. Three things on him shone: his white spats and the enormous gardenia in his buttonhole. His broad muttonchop whiskers made him look like a Franz Joseph in a civilian suit. As he passed through the streets of Athens with the polite trot of a teacher of etiquette, Delyannis scattered greetings to right and left with the gesture of a sower.

And yet this mild old man was stabbed, and right in front of the propylaea of Parliament, by someone who was neither an anarchist nor a political adversary—at that time, and especially in Greece, there were not even the shadows of communists. In reporting the assassination of the "faithful servant of the Fatherland," the newspapers used the verb form *klonizetai*, meaning "struck dead," and more precisely "transformed into a tree trunk." A highly appropriate meaning. I don't know why, but in the typical politician of the times to which the unfortunate Delyannis so intimately belonged, there was something arboreal, something oddly vegetal.

Athens that night was in the grip of political fever. The cord and the olive each had its own action squads, recruited primarily from the thriving guild of ambulant bootblacks. When cord and olive supporters clashed during elections, the impact was certainly forceful and rich in sounds, but no more bloody than those rock fights in which all of us have participated as boys. On that day, however, events had taken place that were less innocuous than usual. There was talk of broken heads, injured people, someone even mentioned "one dead." At ten the *astifilakes*, or guardians of the city, entered the Castalia to close the place. There was something sinister in the air. We were hardly out of there when I turned around suddenly at the sound of the iron shutter clanging down. A sharp cold wind blew, bending the gas flames and making the shadows dance. Many street lamps were out. Reddish clouds, as from the glare of a fire, passed low over the houses. We found ourselves, not following a group of people running toward Concord Square, but swept along by it. On the façade of the Hotel Independence loomed the shadow of a man gesticulating among the capital letters of the sign. Two torches burned on the second-floor terrace, the orator's pulpit. Silhouetted in the light from the window, his hands gripping the railing, he wagged his beard at intervals. In the gusts of wind passed gusts of violent and incomprehensible words. His glasses shone in the middle of his dark face.

The few people standing underneath with faces upturned to listen did not seem to belong to either the cord or the olive. They were almost all Cretans, recognizable by their black stamboulines and equally black pantaloons.

"Who's that?" Anghelo asked someone.

"Venizelos!" came the shrill reply.

"Venizelos?" repeated my companion. And after a pause: "Never heard of him."

PARIS 1911

A morning in distant childhood. We were hiking through one of the valleys that extend from the slopes of Pelion to the Gulf of Volos. The path led past a country school. Since then I have yet to find a more touching expression than this social concept: compulsory education. That hovel was living its scholastic life. A word divided into three beats, vigorously scanned, accented on the first syllable (the computation of syllables is classically done from right to left), declaimed more than pronounced, sung more than declaimed by the combined voices of many children, poured out from the windows, from the door, from the sheets of slate on which the walls were composed, from the tiles of the roof: "Cho-ri-gós . . . Cho-ri-gós . . ."

The rhythm of the childish chorus proceeded with the regularity of breathing. Over the sparkling voices of those little rustics, the adult voice of the *didaskalos* bore down with the force of the *keleusma*, the goading cry of the oarsman: "Cho-ri-gós . . . Cho-ri-gós . . . Cho-ri-gós . . ."

The life of the *scholeion* was completely expressed in those three syllables, just as the life of a construction yard is expressed in the voice and rhythm of its particular work activity. And the pupils' lungs were the machines of that little construction yard of knowledge in embryo.

I have no way of knowing why the didaskalos had chosen that word, which means "chorus conductor," in preference to others. The invisible pupils repeated it endlessly, with a kind of vital continuity, with the physical necessity of a beating heart, as though if that word were to cease to echo, didaskalos, school, and pupils would cease to exist. "Cho-ri-gós." A lesson in solfeggio, as in institutions for the cure of stuttering, and at the same time a strange duplication of the Dalcroze method, which among other things was certainly unknown in that wooded and mountainous part of Thessaly.

We went on our way. The countryside swarmed in the extended ferment of spring, the nearby sea mingled its voice with the more varied ones of the earth; but until we had left the valley, the vast chorus of nature was dominated by that hammered, deliberate, implacable one of rustic children learning to syllabify.

Many years later (1903–1911) and while I was on my way along the Champs Elysées in Paris in the direction of Valsamakis[1] house, for some reason or other it was just that school chorus that kept coming back insistently to my mind. True, it was spring, just as then in the Thessalian valley, and perhaps the return of nature in ferment, certain specific signs . . . It was not, however, the anarchic spring of an unculti-

---

1. The "kis" ending is characteristic of Cretan names. It also has a diminutive flavor—I don't say a diminutive value. The surname Valsamakis is simply the name Balsam, or rather the noun "balsam" with its resinous and aromatic connotations landing on the shores of Crete. The softening of the B into V should not mislead us: Beta is pronounced softly like "Veta."

vated countryside, but the orderly, highly groomed spring of the most civilized avenue in the world.

The horse chestnuts were in full bloom, and altogether it would not have been easy to find such thriving trees, but nevertheless that triumphant foliage preserved the discipline of dancers in crinoline, of hot-air balloons held in check. In the shade of these *messieurs* of the vegetable kingdom, children played with restraint, showing that even beginning with one's first steps in life one can be aware of what constitutes style.

Madame Amelia was waiting for me impatiently on the doorstep. Her triangular face became round under a hat as broad as an umbrella. O exquisite futility of nearsighted ladies! She handled her lorgnette with dexterity, yet didn't see me until I was right in front of her nose, and perhaps it was only by smell that that highbred woman recognized me. Fat, encased in a tight-fitting dress, grumbling and bustling, Madame Amelia was constantly busy, like all persons who have nothing to do. She was the chairwoman of the "Drop of Milk" for poor children of the Greek colony in Paris, the "Woolen Bodice" for the poor mothers of the poor children of the Greek colony in Paris, and the "Crust of Bread" for the poor husbands of the poor mothers of the poor children of the Greek colony in Paris. The vast pauperism, the majestic misery, the fate of all the needy Hellenes driven by the migratory wind from the shores of the Aegean to the banks of the Seine—Madame Amelia (or so she supposed in the simplicity of her charitable and childish mind) drew it all close like a bunch of radishes in her beringed, buttery hand.

To her philanthropic tasks, one should add all the tasks of representation whose burden had to be assumed by this ambassadress *honoris causa,* nor were they any less weighty. To give an example, that very day Madame Amelia had to receive in her home and with due honors a very high personage in Greek politics, who had been in Paris for the past few days. The Balkan League, which a year later mounted an assault on the Ottoman lion, was closing ranks. *Si vis bellum para pacem.*

Two Venizelian Moments

The automobile, its motor running, was waiting and swiftly transported us (I was crushed into a corner by that monumental lady, who with her inflexible whalebone was as rigid as a column) to the studio of the painter Gervex, who not only had the thick and shapeless brushstroke of the academic painter, but the faunlike beard, flabby hand, velvet jacket, and ineffable air as well.

The portrait loomed on the easel inside a massive, glittering frame, and was so stupid a likeness that between the one enclosed in the frame and the self-propelled column pacing the studio on invisible little feet, I was unable to tell which was the real Madame Amelia. Nevertheless, in accordance with an old habit of portrait sitters, Madame Valsamakis found that "that" nose was not hers, "that" mouth was not hers. And trusting, for some reason, in my intervention, she wanted me to persuade the artist to apply a few extra touches and catch that little something of charm and personality possessed by her features (*sic domina dixit*).

I didn't have to work hard to persuade him: it was an expensive portrait. The *cher maître* amiably helped madame to ascend the red velvet platform and make herself comfortable in the gilded armchair. And then in that studio, with its Bukhara carpets and Arab rifles, damascened blades and sacerdotal stoles, the admirable trick once used by Michelangelo in response to the gonfaliere Soderini's complaint about David's nose was repeated: the painter pretended to paint but didn't, and when madame was invited to judge the retouched result, she, winking and tilting her cheek on her shoulder, acknowledged that those few brushstrokes had been enough to catch that little something of charm and personality possessed by her features. Triumphantly we carried the portrait home.

It was time. The guests were beginning to arrive. The portrait was hoisted up on the large wall of the drawing room, in line with that of madame's husband, Spiridion Valsamakis. It too was by Gervex's hand. Madame Amelia's husband was ceremonious and taciturn. He exhibited an admirable eloquence of smiles. For lack of more distinguished

51

qualities, he was said to be "good as bread." The triad was complete. Between mama's portrait and papa's, hung Gervex's masterpiece: *Greek Maiden Seated at the Foot of the Parthenon.* For this large composition in which the ruins of the Acropolis served as backdrop, the beautiful and delightful Maria Valsamakis had posed, dressed as a libation bearer and with her hair wreathed in Attic roses. Steadfast relations have always prevailed between the Acropolis of Athens and the French Academy, as attested by Renan's *Prière sur l'Acropole* and other manifestations of the kind. Fifteen years old at the time, Maria Valsamakis has since progressed in that vocation of which she has given the most persuasive proofs, and now victoriously treads the boards.

The rooms were soon packed. There were even Aglae and Sébasté, the thin, solemn sisters of that Basil Zaharoff who had earned the nickname of "munitions king." In the refreshment room the pyramid of pastries miraculously disappeared and just as miraculously was resupplied. In a surge of passion now raging, now subdued, the talented daughter of the house declaimed some stanzas by Jean Moréas dedicated "To Immortal Greece." Madame Amelia wept, as did Monsieur Spiridion. When the recitation was over, a violinist from Patras launched into the "Meditation" from *Thais,* and was bowing a long F sharp when the attention of his listeners was broken by a tramp of footsteps and the noise of chairs being moved. The audience opened to form two wings, and from the far end of the drawing rooms I saw a bearded figure with glasses advance, dispersing smiles around him. I thought of the unknown didaskalos who many years before had led the chorus of rustic children in that remote little schoolhouse in Thessaly.

"Who's that gentleman with the beard and glasses?" I asked someone standing next to me.

"Who's that?" he replied, looking me up and down. "That's 'our' Venizelos!"

Gemito's Second Life

Any affinity between Vincenzo Gemito and Joan of Arc would seem impossible. Still a common fate unites the Maid of Orleans with 'o scultore pazzo. Both were mistreated by life. Both have earned posthumous rehabilitation. I have periphrastically called Gemito 'o scultore pazzo, the mad sculptor. The periphrasis is not mine: it is by a Neapolitan magistrate. Until a few years ago the vox populi had another name for him. As for the "elite," those who have no need for anomalies and eccentricities to characterize an artist, they treated Gemito, Ximenes, Calandra, and Apolloni to the same contempt. Nor is that all. Even today when the "elite" are repenting and with cries of wonder are discovering Gemito's true worth, I have heard one of the most intelligent painters in Milan assert that Gemito's drawings are banal. These errors in judgment are less gratuitous than they may seem. They are even justified. Gemito's worth finds its place in that category of values that impressionism has made people forget. After a brief triumph, the values imposed by impressionism are in crisis. We are witnessing a new transfer of powers.

The veil woven with trembling hand by the artists of sensibility is being rapidly torn asunder, and behind the rents the old, eternal values are reappearing, radiant and severe.

Gemito's drawings have a tone, an eloquence, an effective way of scanning and "articulating" the sign, all silenced by impressionism. Impressionism evaded precise lines. For the tonic it substituted the harmony of the ninth. Line was evanescent, seismographic. I have watched some followers of impressionism draw. Having traced the line, they hastened to smudge it with the eraser until only the

53

faintest suggestion of it was left. And over the trail of this ghost, they repeated the line with a trembling hand: to make the drawing vibrate. Gemito's drawings take us to a higher world, the only acceptable one. Faced with Gemito's drawings, the tiresome determinations of those who abuse criticism—realistic or literary, human or illustrative—are overcome and fall silent. An artist of superior caliber, Gemito had the faculty of transfiguration. The muddy figure of the Gypsy Woman *(sepia of 1910) becomes a tragic character. The* Peasant Woman *of* Genazzano *takes on the majesty of a goddess. The breath of art has passed over her. The mortal creature becomes immortal. Under Gemito's pencil, man assumes a grave and monumental appearance.*

Gemito was more of a sculptor in his drawings than in his statues. In his drawings he starts from the point, from the one, from the intimate, and dwells on it endlessly. His drawings extend beyond the paper. As a sculptor, Gemito dominates the material with all the grandeur of his soul, all the strength of his hands: he isolates it, reduces it to the necessary minimum, no longer with a view to lyrical perfection, but to a material one. Gemito's statues are the pastimes of a demiurge.

Much has been done to rehabilitate the Italian nineteenth century, comparing it with the French nineteenth century. Why then these comparisons, and only with France, that bête noire? *So far as I know, no one has thought of the only two artists who "illuminate" the Italian nineteenth century, the only ones who do not fear comparisons, the only ones in whom the strength, serenity, and profound and solemn poetry of the Italian soul still shine: Giovanni Carnevali and Vincenzo Gemito.*

As a justification for the present conditions of Italian art, there is talk of struggle, of suffering, of the contortion of form so as to put art back in the service of life and humanity. Gemito lived in a world of mummies and stuffed parrots, and yet he never felt the need to contort, macerate, or debase himself: there is no trace of it in his works. Before these works one may speak not simply of the nineteenth century, not simply of Italian art in a general and limited sense, but of Italian art in the broader sense of Mediterranean art.

One of the most dismal memories of my childhood has to do with a dumbwaiter. This melancholy food elevator had for years relinquished all activity. It lay inoperative inside its dark shaft, where huge spiders, friends of gloom, had spun their webs, which swelled at the breath of mysterious and underground winds. My curiosity as I turned the rusted key was all the more urgent because seasoned with disgust and fear. Two ropes traversed the shaft horizontally, one for going up and the other for going down. With the precautions of a miner and the spellbinding terror that some reptile would suddenly coil itself around my hands, I pulled the ascent rope and the dumbwaiter came creaking up from the depths of the basement. The two shelves were always empty, except one time when a scorpion that looked like the caduceus of Mercury was running in a circle on the upper shelf like a madman in his cell, and the moment I caught sight of it I immediately let go of the rope and the dumbwaiter fell back with an awful crash to the bottom of the shaft, along with its frightful tenant. And yet in its years of splendor this dumbwaiter had brought the preparations for sumptuous banquets up from the basement: glazed capons studded with truffles, pheasants cleverly reconstituted in their entirety as iridescent fowl, shining roast suckling pigs, a newborn baby still bearing the marks of the birth canal . . .

Dumbwaiter and revolving door of the orphanage: why do these two images always merge in my mind?

16 July 1852. All day Naples has been celebrating the feast of the Blessed Virgin of the Carmine, and now it is sleeping it off like a drunken mermaid. The *guappi* have gone back into their strongholds, and the fireworks have just been extinguished over the city's prostrate body. Still dim and as though seen across water, the shadow of Garibaldi is beginning to appear on the screen of the future. The Market quarter, which by day swarms like a full net that has just been pulled from the sea, lives at this hour only by a lingering stench of wet fish and the dripping of a fountain. Over the deserted fish market looms the square shadow of the Ospizio del l'Annunziata, in which all the abandoned orphans of Naples, otherwise called "children of the Madonna," secretly enter, and from which no less secretly emerge all the Espo-

sitos who little by little scatter all over the world, bringing to the most remote peoples the agile language of their fingers and the ancient art of not letting themselves be made fools of. The name of the nun standing guard behind the revolving door is Maria Egiziaca Esposito, because the nuns charged with receiving the children of no one at the entrance to their asylum are by an exquisite delicacy themselves chosen from among the children of no one.

A hand has knocked; and while the plop-plop of two slippers hurries away in the night, the door creaks and when its rotation is completed reveals a tiny bawling creature, in which is concentrated the entire physical entity of one who will not only be a profound and subtle artist, but will constitute one more highly unusual case of man transferred from one epoch to another, the delegate so to speak of fifth-century Greece to nineteenth-century Naples.

In the actual physical misery of that little creature something mysteriously ambiguous shines, the reflection of a love mingling the mortal and immortal. And with the rag in which his loins are wrapped, and the blood that forms a ruby on the lobe of his pierced ear, he is taken to the director of the establishment, whose name, since everything in this drama of nativity is prearranged like a mise-en-scène, is Passante. The newborn baby is given the name Vincenzo Genito—i.e., generated—and entered under the letter G in the register of the asylum as number 1191.

On that same day three other "children of the Madonna" entered the Annunziata, and all, in accordance with a pre-conceived routine, were given the same surname of Genito: Vincenzo Genito, Giuseppe Genito, Maria Giuseppa Genito, Nicola Genito. But next day, that same ineffable presence that was to watch over Gemito in every act of his life, ruffles the clerk whose job it was to enter the orphans' names in the register, and he, by an inspired error, alters one consonant in the surname. Thus emerges the fine Neapolitan surname Gemito, which like Sospiro, Speranza, and Oriente, is both a man's badge and a poetic expression. When later they were to remind Gemito of the mistake in his name, he would frown and reply, "My name is Gemito. Gemito means grief!" For Gemito too, like all profound artists, had a taste for etymology.

At this point the conjecture arises that was also expressed by Gabriele d'Annunzio in the preface to his *Ode to Verdi*, that "in the youth from the Campania lived again the religious soul of the Athenian statuary designed to capture the attitudes of the ephebes and canephorae in the Panathenaic procession."

To tell the truth, not even for Gemito did things go as smoothly as the easy optimism of the aesthetes would have it. But no one will deny that he worked "from memory" and that an obscure remembrance inspired his life from afar. He sought teachers who would initiate him into the mysteries of art, but gradually abandoned them *sans tambours ni trompettes*. What Gemito was looking for in the second half of the nineteenth century, he who was mindful of other centuries and other climes, neither Naples nor Italy could give him, nor could Europe or the world, which was veiling itself in impressionism. The only useful work for Vincenzo Gemito was to train his little harpsichord-player hands, or rather to stretch them in order to reawaken in them their ancient agility, lulled but not destroyed by the inaction of death. As for the rest, that mysterious inspiration that illuminates the mind and guides the hand, Gemito was as closed as a deaf-mute to the voices that surrounded him, and gave ear only to the voice from a previous life that reminded him of the majesty of Alexander, the gravity of the ancient philosophers, and the flash of nude bodies on the seashore. His mind was like a paralytic who little by little rediscovers movement. Only in this way can we explain the presence of an ancient culture in this man, completely wrapped in the darkness of ignorance and living testimony to the theory of ideas.

Let there be no mistake: Gemito's life represents a priceless example of eternal return. His very madness is confirmation of his condition as a transmigrator. Especially if one thinks of madness as a way of transmigrating from form to form within the same life, as a strange but laudable freedom assumed by man to take a stroll outside himself. No one has obeyed his own inner will more than Gemito: no one has been more indifferent to outside will. And only by obeying that will older than himself, which held sway over him and of which he himself was perhaps not clearly aware, was Gemito able to carry out, with no uncertainties or anxieties, his work composed of profound and metaphysically justified lines, in open contradiction with impressionism, which with increasing intensity was enveloping Italy, Europe, and the world, the superficial and merely physical manner that was attracting the major artists and most generous hearts.

Gemito's nonimpressionism has thickened the ambiguity around him. They have placed him among the academics, they have enrolled him among the *pompiers*, they have confounded him with Ximenes, Apolloni, and Calandra.

There is as much spontaneity in Gemito's line as in Manet's brushstroke, with the additional fact that Gemito's spontaneity goes to the origin of things and remains there, while Manet's albeit touching spontaneity is scarcely a fleeting glance.

Providence, whose vast designs wholly escape us, we recognize instead in such particular moments of life as when the birth of little Vincenzo Gemito is made to coincide with the death of little Francesco Bes. Francesco's mother, Giuseppina Baratta, was mourning the loss of her little one, who after a sojourn of only eight days in this world had returned to his Maker, and the milk from her swollen breasts dripped into her lap, ran down her legs, and made a puddle at her feet. This fountain of nourishment therefore applied to the Ospizio dell'Annunziata, and so that that sustaining river would not flow in vain she chose from among its many waifs the one who had been given the name Vincenzo Gemito, and began to raise him as her own child. Giuseppina Baratta's husband was the Frenchman Joseph Bes, a kind of liquid man, who had been a friar in a provincial monastery, a supplier of foodstuffs to the Bourbon court, and finally a house painter, and who spoke Neapolitan with a French r and lived in a state of constant drunkenness. His footsteps in the house where Vincenzo was growing up like a reed were the unsteady and absentminded ones of a peaceful lunatic; until one day, unsteady as always, he died, and all that remained to Gemito of that first putative father was the trembling image of a figure reflected in water.

In the meantime Garibaldi marches across Sicily, routs the Bourbons, and triumphantly enters Naples. Emanuele Caggiano, a veteran of the 1861 campaign, has taken off his red shirt, hung it on a nail in his studio in Foro Carlino, and as he roughs out in marble the statue of *Victory* destined to adorn the Piazza dei Martiri, he perceives four sharp eyes spying on him from the half open door.

"Who are you?" asks the Garibaldian sculptor, with his solemn beard of a drawing-room Moses, glaring at the two street urchins.

"I'm Vicienzo," replies the older of the two, "and this is Totonno."

Totonno was Antonio Mancini, and this was the beginning of the friendship between Antonio Mancini and Vincenzo Gemito, which was to end only with death.

Gemito asked the sculptor if he could stay with him "to learn art," and since Caggiano accepted, "Vicienzo" kissed his hand, because Neapolitan respect required it and because for him that hand was an instrument of miracles.

The friendship between Gemito and Mancini was a splendid and "lifelong" one, with Mancini under Gemito's thumb. Nevertheless, after Gemito in 1884 failed to repay Mancini a loan of seventy lire, the two friends went for forty years without seeing or speaking to each other.

"Totonno" was an innocent who in 1924 was still afraid of meeting "Vicienzo." Their financial relations aside, the friendship between the two is a touching and amusing poem. Does anyone recall René Clair's *Les deux timides?* The friendship between Gemito and Mancini is the story of Bouvard and Pécuchet as artists.

An extraordinary cortege crosses the center of Naples. The band marches at its head, followed by elephants, their castles filled with Moors and dancing girls, then apes dressed as

men, their tails outside their checkered frock coats, berib-
boned ponies dancing the polka, a troupe of clowns, lions
yawning behind the bars of their cages, tightrope walkers
under their open umbrellas, acrobats glittering with spangles,
dwarfs with shoes longer than themselves, and finally Monsieur Guillaume, owner and director of the circus who doffs
his red top hat to right and left to greet the crowd massed on
the sidewalks and leaning out the windows.

The Guillaume circus settled into the Teatro Bellini, which
was connected with Caggiano's studio by a dark corridor, and
Gemito found himself on familiar terms with this world of
marvels.

The marvel of marvels was the "octopus man," a discon-
nected sort of creature dressed in slippery leather, whose
limbs were transformed into tentacles and who with horrible
contortions would climb up the rungs of a ladder. "Vicienzo"
tried to be an octopus man too, on a very tall ladder that stood
in his teacher's studio, but he fell down and lay on the floor
like a bloodstained plaster cast. For four days the boy hung
between life and death, and when he recovered and returned
to Caggiano's studio, he ran into the *Victory* on its way out.
Could Gemito remain in the place from which Victory had
departed? "Vicienzo" himself departed, leaving the sculptor
a small portrait of his dog, whose name was Medoro and who
had a pointed snout like an anteater.

To the end of his life Gemito preserved the childish forms
of pride: imitation and emulation. He had apelike ambitions.
As a boy, he had tried to perform the "octopus-man act," and
we have seen the price he had to pay for that piece of
mimicry; in 1901, on the threshold of old age, Edoardo
Scarfoglio having told him one day that Succi* had gone for a
month without eating, Gemito swore to do likewise and
began fasting.

Gemito had never been a serious eater. He fed himself
intermittently and as though what he introduced into his

---

* Giovanni Succi (1850–1918), renowned subject of experiments in
fasting. (Tr.)

digestive tract was of no concern to him. He ate bread, nuts, greens, and fruit. As for meat, he did not wish even to smell its odor. He was primarily carpophagous, and in this too he manifested a profound affinity with apes and a genuine Greek essence.

Aesthetes have accumulated a store of ambiguities and falsehoods about the true quality of the Greek spirit. The Greek spirit consists less of spiritualism than of animal refinement. It is found much more in the ass than in the ephebe, in the goat than in the canephora, in the ape than in the parthenos. And these three mammals combine and mingle to form the mysterious essence of Vincenzo Gemito.

Also in his extraordinary strength, his unseeming and concentrated strength, his *strength of an olive tree*, Gemito was Greek.

But there is a great difference between eating intermittently and not eating at all. Twenty days after his platonic challenge to Succi, Gemito was unable to move, and amid his beard and ruffled hair, his sharp nose and pointed cheekbones looked like three little dead birds in a nest of straw. His daughter and son-in-law were very worried and called a doctor, who, recognizing that oral nourishment might be dangerous, prepared an alimentary clyster. As the doctor approached the bed holding the clyster like a flamethrower, Gemito opened one eye, pointed a finger at this Aesculapius, and in the faintest of voices but heavy with menace said: "You worm, you want to do this to Vincenzo Gemito?" Having said these words, Gemito got out of bed, and being too much of an artist to act directly, he picked up a chisel from the table, rested it on his knee, and bent it like tin.

The friend of Gemito's who told me this episode at first gave me a version *ad asum delphini*, in which the clyster was replaced by a hypodermic needle, and only my suspicions and curiosity succeeded little by little in freeing the original version from the veils of this incomprehensible modesty. I might mention in this connection that all the biographies of Gemito I have consulted present him as a "bizarre artist in search of his own ideal," but strictly omit the facts—sometimes tragic, sometimes comical, but all of them just as necessary to the historian as a knowledge of anatomical structure is to the doctor—that make Gemito's life the natural continuation of his art. I cannot understand my colleagues' terror of the truth, nor their concern to conceal the drama and its depth under an artificial optimism that lacks even the charm of the eighteenth century's rosy hypocrisy. On the other hand, I can see why so much of our literature smacks of bland and regurgitated food.

Ever since the now remote death of the "liquid" Bes, Giuseppina Baratta had remained anandrous, that is to say, without a man, which is like saying a lock without a key. After much hesitation she made the decision to take herself another man, and in an exquisite gesture to her adopted son, who had in the meantime become a bearded man, she chose one who resembled Vincenzo Gemito like a brother. He was that "Masto Ciccio" who became not only Giuseppina's husband, not only "Vicienzo's" foster father, but his damned soul as well and perpetual model.

In depicting "Masto Ciccio," Gemito had the illusion of doing a self-portrait. Among the drawings in the Minozzi Collection, one shows a seated man tying his shoe. The caption says that this man is getting dressed in a hurry in order to take a statue to the Duchess of Aosta, but no one will ever know if it is the "father" or the "son."

Furthermore, Masto Ciccio, by the "antique head" he had on his shoulders, aroused in Gemito memories of his previous life. Gemito's wholly authentic *Greek Philosopher* is Masto Ciccio's head in bronze.

By her earthly life, Giuseppina Baratta redeemed the age-old sins of stepmothers.

The same scene that had taken place in Caggiano's studio was repeated in the studio of the sculptor Lista. One morning in 1864, while Lista was working on one of those marble lions that now lie at the foot of the obelisk in Piazza dei Martiri, there was a knock at the door, and when the sculptor went to open it and asked the boy standing on the threshold what he wanted, the latter replied, "To learn art." And in order to

show Stanislao Lista that he had already had some practice
in drawing, he took out of his pocket the stub of a red pencil
(he preferred to draw with red pencil, "which doesn't allow
for second thoughts," and to open the way for writers who
today impose the same discipline on themselves by composing directly on the typewriter) and copied a plaster relief
hanging on the wall with such fervor and care that the
sculptor was dazzled.

Gemito was diligent, affectionate, obliging. Every week he
carried the sculptor's tools to the blacksmith. He didn't mind
playing second fiddle, kept the studio in order, and continued
to draw.

One day he asked Lista's permission to do his portrait and
modeled a small bust in clay. Urged by the maestro to
translate it into marble, Gemito confessed that he hated
marble because "it didn't yield to the fingers."

This hatred for marble accompanied Gemito for the rest of
his life. In 1886 he was commissioned to do a statue of
Charles V. This meant completing on the façade of the Royal
Palace in Naples that series of eight large statues lined up in
the poses of madmen about to descend from their niches,
throw the city into turmoil, set fire to the ships in the harbor,
and reopen the gates of Lake Avernus.*

Gemito did the model in Paris, during his second stay in
that city, and brought it back to Italy wrapped in rags like the
mummy of a child, with that maternal tenderness that he put
into the transporting of his own works, clutching it to his
breast and covering it with his overcoat to keep it from
catching cold.

In Naples the model was entrusted to the stonecutter
Pennino, so that, enlarged to the desired size, it could be
reproduced in marble. Gemito did not go to see the statue
during the work, he did not attend the unveiling, but a few
days later he arrived alone in Piazza Plebiscito, and seeing
that the marble Charles V held his right hand in a different

---

* Near Pozzuoli, and thought in ancient times to be one of the
entrances to hell. (Tr.)

position from the plaster Charles V, he ran to collect stones and with the fury of a Balilla,* shouting and cursing, began to stone the image of the emperor on whose realm the sun never set.

Two carabinieri, stern and gloomy under their black cocked hats, were standing guard nearby. With long strides they approached the "mad sculptor" and laid a hand on his shoulder. And Gemito, who usually showed an invincible intolerance for authority, calmed down quickly this time: under the uniforms of the carabinieri he had recognized Castor and Pollux, sons of the divine swan.

If Gemito threw stones at the children of his spirit, he cannot be said to have treated the children of his flesh any better. In Paris, where he stayed twice, in 1877 and 1886, Gemito had struck up a close friendship with Meissonier. For Gemito men were symbols or, so to speak, "points of departure": beyond the painter of battles he saw in Meissonier the whole Napoleonic saga, including Napoleon III, known as Lulu.

During his second stay in Paris, Gemito had given signs, I won't say of insanity but of deep depression, and shortly after he arrived back in Naples with his little Charles V tucked under his overcoat, he received a worried letter from Elise Besançon, Meissonier's wife, in which she wrote: *"Ne m'écrivez qu'un mot, si vous souffrez trop pour enchaîner votre pensée dans une lettre, mais dites-nous comment vous êtes. À quoi se passent vos heures? Et ce que vous rêvez. Votre femme et votre amour d'enfant doivent vous faire du bien au coeur . . ."*

From which one can assume that Meissonier's wife, Elise Besançon, had a limited range of vision, for had she been able to see from Paris what was happening in Naples, she would have seen Gemito take his *amour d'enfant* by her little legs, whirl her around like a sling, and bash her against the wall, with the sure and violent gesture used by fishermen to break the tenacious vitality of octopuses.

But even in this act, in which trite and frivolous people will

---

* Boy hero of the 1746 Genoese uprising against the Austrians. (Tr.)

see nothing but a sign of madness, Gemito showed himself to be Greek, or rather Saturnian.

The friendship between Gemito and Meissonier was a great one, but "compromising" for Gemito. A romantic friendship, beset by clouds and winds like the landscapes of Salvator Rosa, and full of confessions.

Meissonier too is a victim of the defective vision of those who read only the large letters on the oculist's chart, see nothing but enlarged forms returned to their rudimentary state, creatures afflicted with acromegalia, and believe precision, attention to detail, and a love for the particular to be prerogatives of the *pompiers.*

In the Louvre, they have looked neither at the *Musketeer Gazing through Half-closed Shutters,* nor at *Jean-Jacques Rousseau Escorting Madame de Warens Down a Flight of Stairs,* or if they have looked at them, it is with a big slice of ham in front of their eyes.

Giuseppina, who in her crushed frontal bones preserves the memory of that contact long ago with the wall of her father's house, was born of Gemito's union with Anna Cuttolo, a beautiful and docile model who had posed for Domenico Morelli, Volpe, De Santis, Caprile, Vetri, and others, and whom the Neapolitan painters, as in the song, called "Cosarella."

Even in his loves Gemito had the divine and bestial qualities of the woodland deities. Having tied the nuptial bond with Cosarella, Gemito carried her home like a spider carrying a fly, and for two weeks he was not to be seen. Previously he had been married to Mathilde Duffaud, a Bovary exiled to Naples, a Frenchwoman with heavy eyelids, fragrant perspiration, and whose consumption made her life even more precious.

In the spring of 1881, in a poetic little villa in Resina, Mathilde Duffaud's life flickered out. *Loin des yeux loin du coeur.* Gemito, who when his women were alive entwined himself around them like a vine around an elm tree, quickly forgot about them when they were dead. And this inability to love anything that is not present and tangible also shows the amazing and impassive quality of the Greek.

As for Cosarella's death, it had an even more surprising effect on Vincenzo Gemito.

Anna was a loving slave to Gemito. She loved him, helped him, and took care of him during his eighteen years of madness. She held all the parts of her body motionless before his eyes, so that he could draw her endlessly, in pencil, in red chalk, in charcoal. The only thing she couldn't do was to clean him, perhaps because she herself felt no compelling need for cleanliness. Then around 1906, a malignant tumor, like a black worm, began to undermine that beautiful body in its most secret parts.

In the Galleria Minozzi in Naples, in which Achille Minozzi collected and Ada Minozzi Limoncelli preserves more than three hundred of Gemito's drawings, one can see behind glass a large sheet of paper on which Gemito drew Anna in pencil squatting on the floor with a ragged blouse over her shoulders, four days before her death. Who can show me a more faithful image of human misery?

Four days later Cosarella dies, and Gemito not only forgets her immediately, but after having been insane for eighteen years, suddenly recovers his wits.

In his limbs Gemito concealed the strength of a vampire bat. He would wrap his legs around a column and for hours live like a stylite, as comfortable as in an armchair.

One day he and a beautiful Neapolitan were sacrificing to earthly Venus. The husband suddenly arrives and Gemito has just enough time to dash out on the terrace. The husband searches the room, goes out on the terrace, *finds no one,* and goes away. The adulteress runs to the terrace and looks over, expecting to see her lover's shattered body four floors below, when she hears a disembodied whisper: *"Se n'è juto?*—Has he gone?" Gemito was underneath the terrace, clinging by his hands to its two marble supports.

One day Edoardo Scarfoglio explained to him the function and importance of the pores. Gemito had a sudden revelation of filth. He didn't pause to think twice, and he who for thirty years had refrained from all contact with water, set off on the run and didn't stop until he had reached the Villa Nazionale.

And there, in the presence of strolling mothers pushing their babies in carriages, lovers walking arm in arm, aristocratic ladies seated in landaus like creatures of feathers and lace, beggars, and the municipal band, which was playing a selection from Verdi's *I Lombardi alla prima crociata*, the enemy of ablutions began taking off his clothes in order to plunge into the sea. But once again the sons of the divine swan intervened, those two stern, gloomy, and inseparable young men in cocked hats, who accosted the sculptor and just as he was, with his underpants at half mast, carried him bodily to the police station. The intervention of the carabinieri was salutary this time as well. During his enforced leisure at the police station, Gemito pondered, and discovered that along with beneficial air the pores also allowed the entry of germs and death. Better to keep them closed with a good patina of filth. In which Gemito found himself in agreement with the sponge fishermen of the Polynesian archipelago, who dive into the lagoons of the atolls even when the water is poisoned by the putrefaction of coral and is fatal to everyone except the sponge fisherman protected by his impenetrable layer of dirt.

We insist on collecting even the smallest critical element, however indirect and remote it may be.

The same phobia about water is shared by Picasso and Giorgio de Chirico, that is to say, the three artists of our time, including Vincenzo Gemito, in whom the strict, profound, and lyrical sense of line is most manifest. And what is line if not the sign of clarity or, so to speak, of plastic *cleanliness*? A strange contradiction. The artist's eye is as curious and demanding as the eye of a jealous woman: it makes its way through the chiaroscuro, amid the spots of impressionism, and reaches the origin of the thing, its secret mechanism. Only then is it placated, because it discovers that there has been no betrayal. Picasso refuses to go in the water: he is afraid of dissolving like soap. "Besides," he says, "there's no need to wash, one should just be careful not to get dirty." As for Giorgio de Chirico's contacts with the element that according to Thales is the primordial element *par excellence*, they happen rarely or only after long family persuasion, sometimes backed up by threats.

Gemito had lived one life in pre-Socratic Greece, another in the Italy of the Renaissance. He aspired not only to Cellini's completeness, but to his infernal rites as well. He knew that in Christianity the pagan gods are devils, and in the devil's friendship he hoped to rediscover that of "his" god.

He had conceived a new and "diabolical" way of casting, in which the wax rods are placed inside the statue instead of outside, and with this very risky method he proposed to cast the *Water Carrier with Dolphin*.

Before the operation has begun, a priest friend of Gemito's enters the foundry. To avoid misunderstandings, the sculptor warns him: *"Nun è ccossa e Ddio, ma è ccossa de e ddiavolo."* Then he puts two lire in his hand and looking at him with eyes as piercing as daggers, orders him: *"Zi prè, cheste so ddoie lire: dimme na messa all'inferno!"* And to please the devil's friend, the "uncle priest" concentrates in a corner of the red-hot foundry and amid the glare of the furnace simulates a black mass.

While Gemito was in Stanislao Lista's studio, the Institute of Fine Arts in Naples announced a competition for a statue of Brutus. Gemito entered the contest but his model failed to win, despite all the praise and efforts at persuasion on the fifteen-year-old sculptor's behalf by various members of the jury, especially Domenico Morelli.

During those days Cesare Correnti, minister of public education, arrived in Naples.

Correnti looked at the models, approved the judges' decision, but commissioned Gemito to reproduce his *Brutus* in marble. To poor Vicienzo it was like someone treading on his corn.

Out of vexation he attacked the marble directly and without first "roughing it out," and when his teacher warned that he would not be able to go on that way, Gemito threw down his mallet and chisel, went away, and never came back.

There was in him that element of haste, of the wild and erratic, that one also finds in Shelley and naturally in young girls: not a consistent glow, but a light that suddenly goes on, and just as suddenly goes out.

He disappears like a fish returning to the bottom. He disappears after two vain attempts to learn art, to receive the secret by transmission and from the hands of men. He takes to the wilds, this slithering fifteen-year-old, or rather to the wilds of which there are so many in Naples. And when he reappears, we find him in the same setting where Masaniello had planned the uprising against the Duke of Arcos.

La bella Napoli is built on the same landscape as Lake Avernus. Houses and gardens are deliberately situated to disguise the frightful holes, horrible caverns, and shuddering tar pits in which the souls of the damned lay in mythological times. In one of these caverns, where the nuns of the convent of Sant'Andrea delle Dame had once stored the beans for their frugal daily meal, Gemito holed himself up to work among the snakes and scorpions, bringing with him all the beggar children of Castelnuovo, who served as his models. And from that underground labyrinth of the pious order founded by Claudia, Giulia, and Lucrezia Palascandolo, virgins from Sorrento, Gemito's first statue, the *Gambler*, emerged one morning in 1868, and went on to be displayed in a room at the Promotrice di Belle Arti, where Victor Emmanuel saw and admired it, and wanted to acquire it for his collection in the Royal Palace of Capodimonte.

The King! It was written that the first work by Gemito worthy of the name should strike the eye of a king. This first contact with the monarchy reawakened in Gemito great memories of the past, mysterious recollections of his previous life, the time when kings were the handsomest, strongest, most valiant men, and he himself, incising his works with the same bold precision with which Nature incises the spirals of conches, lived in the light of Alexander.

The analogy between Gemito's drawings and those of conches is another critical element.

For Gemito there was nothing grander or more august than the king. As for his relations with God Almighty, they were those between a legitimate sovereign and a usurper, between

Louis XVIII and Napoleon. "I am God Almighty," Gemito used to say, and he allowed no objections. And if of all the explanations that have been given of Gemito's "madness," and especially of the great crisis that kept him shut up in his house for eighteen years, the most scientifically exact is the "French disease" contracted in the very capital of the "French disease," the most reliable psychological explanation is the *idée fixe* that had lodged itself in Gemito's head, that only the king in person could confirm the commission he had received from the palace in Naples for a table centerpiece.

When he arrived in London, Gemito went straight to Buckingham Palace. The horse guards explained to him that if he wished to see the king, he ought first to apply to his own ambassador. A similar response had been given to Friedrich Nietzsche at the door of the Quirinale. Gemito went away thinking that to him, Gemito, Alexander of Macedon would have been more accessible. Camaraderie between artists and sovereigns is an illusion of artists.

For the execution of the table centerpiece, Pompeo Carafa, the king's chamberlain, had provided the sculptor with space in the Royal Palace of Naples. An ineffable joy illumined Gemito's soul. He no longer had any doubts about his own worth, now that the works that came from his hands had been consecrated by the sovereign's approval. The shadow of Alexander, his head tilted sideways on his shoulders, stood out more sharply against the dark background of memory. What difference did it make if the "space" in the Royal Palace was a dark, bare little room in the basement of the Royal Stables? When Vincenzo Gemito entered that hole, it was like a poet ascending the Capitol.

Gemito took over the "space" and set about conceiving sylphs, dryads, and reclining personifications of rivers, which all together symbolically foreshadowed that "history of Italy" that the centerpiece was supposed to illustrate in the splendor of its precious metals. Meanwhile, as they passed back and forth before that constantly closed door, dark suspicions accumulated under the cocked hats of the carabinieri on guard. At night, suspicious himself and obsessed by fear that the precious metals entrusted to him for the centerpiece might be stolen, Gemito, lantern in hand and resembling King Lear in the forest, would patrol the long empty corridors and vast deserted rooms. And one night King Lear ran into the carabinieri. In the darkness Gemito did not recognize in those two gloomy, brawny youths the sons of the divine swan, nor did they for their part recognize in that wandering ghost *'o scultore pazzo*, whom they mistook for a thief. They gave him a sound thrashing and Gemito, strong as he was, was able to appreciate how heavy is the hand of Authority. Next day, awakening from the sleep and stupor into which the nocturnal fray had plunged him, Gemito was mad not only *de jure* but *de facto* as well.

Gemito escaped from the insane asylum by the classical method of tearing a sheet into strips and using it as a rope. He walked across Naples barefoot and in a nightshirt. He arrived home like a fury, and since his woman and his putative parents, out of their minds with fear, wanted to take him back to the asylum, he, still more out of his mind at the idea of being put back among lunatics, knelt on the floor, kissed the tiles, and swore that if they would just let him be, he would never go out of the house, and not only the house but the studio. He kept his word and stayed there for eighteen years.

For eighteen years he stayed in the little studio on Via Tasso, sitting on the floor, under the grated window. At night he huddled in a corner, on a scrubbing stone, and slept with his legs doubled up. By day he drew, then tore up the paper, the same way that members of the lower animal orders eat their own offspring. When they told him to come out and resume his work on the table centerpiece, he replied that he was waiting for the king since only the king could confirm his commission for him. One day they told him the king was dead but Gemito burst out laughing. Who were they trying to fool?

Only a personage of royal blood could free him from this monarchical fixation. And one day, tall and solemn, Elena of Aosta entered the mad sculptor's studio. Elena spoke. "Gemito," she said, "make a little water carrier and take it for me to Her Majesty Queen Margherita." Gemito didn't have to be told twice: with delicate and caressing hands, he molded the little figure of a water carrier, girded its loins with a pair of underpants that could be taken off or left on at will, cast it in silver, put it under his coat like a puppy, and took it to Rome. Gemito's meeting with Margherita of Savoy is illustrated on the cover of an issue of the *Domenica del Corriere* in 1909, by that excellent iconographer of the Third Italy who goes by the name of Achille Beltrame.

Gemito made a third trip to Paris in 1924. The *Ville Lumière* inspired him to thoughts of elegance: he carried a small comb in his vest pocket and every so often spruced up his beard. But Meissonier was dead, his friends of former times were dead or dispersed, and Goupil was asking a thousand francs a day to rent him one of his show windows on the Avenue de l'Opéra.

Gemito had checked into the Hôtel Favart, opposite the Opéra Comique. He had chosen a fine room on the first floor. He had been commissioned by a Milanese collector to model a head of Medusa and was searching for a model with long hair. But in 1924 women wore their hair *à la garçonne*.

One day Camillo Antona Traversi announced to him that in the corps de ballet of the Folies Bergère he had discovered a dancer, Mademoiselle Adolphe, who had very long blond hair. An appointment was made for the Café Napolitain, and when Mademoiselle Adolphe, so that there would be no mistake, loosened her abundant head of hair before Gemito, he threw himself on his knees and exclaimed in adoration, "Mademoiselle Adolphe? No! Mademoiselle Soleil!"

Work on the Medusa went on for a month. Gemito was running out of money. From the first floor he moved to the second. Then to the third. Then to the fourth. Then to the fifth. Finally he moved to the sixth, which the French call *mansarde*, from the name of the architect Mansard. That was as far up as he could go.

From the *mansarde* of the Hôtel Favart Gemito went directly to Villa Scoppa. He went back to his Neapolitan habits. He slept in his frock coat and with the rosette of the Legion of

Honor that France had given him in 1906. He lived with his daughter Giuseppina and her husband, Giuseppe De Cristoforo.

Gemito behaved toward his son-in-law like Monsieur Bergeret toward his adulterous wife: he ignored him. Not that he was angry with him or even hostile, but though living under the same roof and running into him at all times, and perhaps secretly loving him, he did not speak to him, did not look at him, and had he been able to, he would have walked right through him.

To his grandson he gave the name Alessandro, and since an Alexander needs a Bucephalus, with his girlish hands he carved him a magnificent wooden horse, huge, jointed, and truly worthy of a king.

The only good souvenir he had brought back from his last trip to Paris was a collection of those small clay pipes known as *Jacobs*, which Gemito filled with shredded Tuscan cigars, and which when smoked methodically and with concentration, taking alternate puffs and sips of water, are refreshing in the summer.

He died in 1929, at the age of seventy-six, which is not all that old considering the longevity of madmen. He died speaking of Alexander. From the top of the Vomero a voice cried out: *O panmegas thethneken!* But like the voices in the time of Augustus that from the coasts of Epirus at night announced the death of the god Tammuz, neither was this voice understood. From the Parco Grifeo the cortege slowly descended between the rows of eucalyptus trees. The sea shone in the sunlight, the stores had closed their shutters and lighted their lamps. As they arrived at the shore, all of a sudden the pallbearers felt the coffin to be lighter on their shoulders. There was a ripple of confusion among the official personages. A gentleman in a top hat raised his hand and pointed to the gulf: escorted by two dolphins, Gemito was on his way toward the seas of Greece.

Guillaume Apollinaire

The story of a life begins with the date of birth. In the case of Guillaume Apollinaire this first appearance is denied us. Apollinaire's birth-register data is wrapped in obscurity, and his birthplace is equally obscure. This is how Apollinaire himself wanted it. The childish zeal with which he guarded "his" secret was just as touching as his fear of its being revealed. Let us preserve this legendary, antediluvian element surrounding the life of Guillaume Apollinaire.

When I knew him, Apollinaire lived at 202 Boulevard Saint-Germain. You climbed the six flights of stairs that are *de rigueur* in every Parisian house. As far as the fifth, the house had the lawful and pug-nosed look of any *habitation bourgeoise*. A gray striped runner accompanied the polished wooden steps, and on every landing three doors loomed in an image of Calvary. From the sixth floor you took an extra little stairway: the poet's door was set flush with its top step.

How different the rich man's doorbell is from the poor man's! The latter rings immediately and gaily, the former resounds distantly and in alarm. At the slightest pull, the rabbit's foot hanging on Apollinaire's door set off a rustic peal, which was prolonged while the visitor was treacherously scrutinized from the peephole. Between the first ring of the bell and your entrance into the flat, you lived the agonies of someone condemned to a firing squad. The peephole drilled not only the center of the door, but the wall behind you. If you were a petitioner, the door remained insensible to the monologue of the doorbell; if a friend, the door opened magically as in Alcina's palace, into a vestibule where the almond-shaped eyes of Congolese idols kept watch amid the first documents of cubism and monstrous, full-breasted tropical fruits. Then came a further little staircase that led up to the top deck, the poet's study, which overlooked an urban landscape where the dome of the Invalides emerged from the gray of the *mansardes* like a golden balloon.

I still have equally precise summer and winter memories of Apollinaire "at home." With each change of season he performed an "internal" move, transferring himself from the top deck to the floor below and vice versa. His friends, painters and writers, helped him to move. Bed and armchairs teetered on the shoulders of cubists. Apollinaire directed the operations, and lent a hand insofar as his asthma and bulk allowed.

One day I found him wrapped up in woolens, sitting next to the roaring stove. André Derain, who was present, asked him whether all that heat didn't make him lose weight. *"Vous voyez bien que non,"* Apollinaire replied regretfully. Fat was his enemy and in November 1918 it snuffed out his heart.

In summer, in his airy study, Apollinaire worked in his underpants. He sat at his desk, smoked a clay pipe, and wrote "La vie anecdotique" for the *Mercure de France,* art reviews for the newspapers, and the fantasies and oddities that helped him with some difficulty to make ends meet. Between puffs on his pipe, he took sips of cool water, an infallible method for mitigating the summer heat. Facing him sat his "secretary." This word suggests the successful writer, the man of letters who has arrived and cares nothing about expenses. This illusion will be strengthened when one adds that the "secretary" was a baron and descended from an English royal dynasty. His name sounded like that of the Plantagenets. In truth, and aside from being penniless, the "baron" was a mental infant who was unable to formulate a sentence of more than five words. Apollinaire repaid the "baron" for his secretarial functions by giving him lodging in a storeroom full of incunabula, African statues, and clysters from the time of Molière, and providing him with a noonday meal and free tickets to the Bal Bulier. The meal was prepared by the "baron" himself and eaten in company with his patron and friend. His culinary skill was limited to chicken livers with rice. Apollinaire asserted that the baron's cooking was *délectable*. I had occasion to taste it, and for once I disagreed with my friend.

Frugality formed part of Apollinaire's daytime discipline. In the evening this scholar of gastronomy, this athlete of the table, this priest of the "physiology of taste" recovered himself at the tables of his friends. His convivial life was perfectly organized. A list of names marked on a weekly schedule reminded him from one day to the next of the designated table. Apollinaire was not only the dinner guest, but the inspiration for and often the maker of the dinner. No one else was allowed to toss the salad. When there were Italian specialties he went personally into the kitchen and literally put his finger in the pie.

The baron was a kleptomaniac. He would go to the Louvre wearing an ample cloak, and the minute the guard's back was turned snatch the first object that lay at hand and carry it off. Unbeknown to Apollinaire, the storeroom where the baron slept had become a depository of tanagras, small Egyptian idols, pots from Minoan Crete, necklaces from Sidon. One day the custodian of the Egyptian rooms caught the baron thrusting a statuette of Anubis under his cloak. He was tailed by a detective, who discovered that the thief lived in Apollinaire's house. When a patch of bare wall was found where the *Mona Lisa* should have been, the police rounded up all thieves known to specialize in art, and jailed the baron as well; they also jailed Apollinaire, whom they held responsible for his secretary's exploit. The poet was put into the lineup and his mug shots were published in the newspapers. He was in prison for a week. His jailers doused him with nenuphar water, which calms the heat of the senses. This imprisonment inspired Apollinaire to write one of his most moving poems, "À la Santé."

I met the "baron" in 1917 in Macedonia, where he served as

a military courier. Shortly before he had been a guard in a camp for infected prisoners. I met him again in 1924 in Paris. He was managing an arty cabaret and invited me to come and see it. I got to the Caveau Rouge one evening at ten o'clock. The baron was not there and a nervous individual with curly blond hair informed me that *la baronne* didn't begin her managerial functions before two in the morning. The nervous individual introduced himself to me also as part of the management: he was *la marquise*. A place where the male managers bore aristocratic female titles—I got out of there in a hurry. Later I heard that the baron had been hired as a tutor by a family in Spa.

One day I ran into Apollinaire when he was on his way to the police station to renew his foreign resident's permit.

Everybody knew that Apollinaire was not French by nationality, but for him to confess it to me himself was for me a rare proof of trust. He was very reticent about the "mystery" of his origin, and this mystery weighed on him like a sin. He did not have the heart to recall examples from English epic poetry that recognized greater virtues in illegitimate sons than in legitimate offspring.

Apollinaire was born in Italy. *Le Poète assassiné* is in part autobiographical. Croniamantal is Apollinaire. And this confirms Apollinaire's Italian youth, and his adolescence on the French Riviera.

From his Polish mother Apollinaire had received the surname Kostrowitzky. She had been a great courtesan who even when the last trace of her beauty had faded, worked in gambling houses as a "decoy." Sometimes there was no answer to Apollinaire's doorbell. Later we would learn that our friend had gone to see *sa maman*. These absences coincided with changes in the seasons, when the "decoy" moved from the gambling houses on the Riviera to those on the Atlantic coast, with a stopover in Paris for a few days' rest.

War, which accelerates the pace of time, heightens men's lives, and brings together and resolves the "knots" of History, was also to resolve the involuntary sin that weighed on Apollinaire's humanity. By volunteering for the French army,

Apollinaire finally earned the right to French nationality that had hitherto been denied him. He fought first as a noncommissioned artillery officer, then as an officer in the infantry. He earned his stripes on the battlefield. Wounded in the head, he was admitted to the Italian hospital in Auteuil, and trepanned by Doctor Palazzoli. From his hospital bed, under the cap that covered the hole in his skull, Apollinaire thought back on the "prophetic" portrait of him painted by Giorgio de Chirico in 1913: that portrait in which the silhouette of the poet stands out in the shape of a target against a deep green background, the skull pierced at the same spot where three years later he was struck by a splinter of shrapnel.

Like Caligula, Apollinaire was terrified of lightning. He had little faith in the poet's laurel. When lightning flashed, he hid his face in his hands and cried, "Uhi ahi ahi!" His voice was out of proportion to his body: it sounded as though a tiny little man were hidden inside him, this big burly man. He spoke in short bursts and let the sentence trail off. His laugh was childish. He countered arrogance with an invincible ignorance. Somebody starts telling him about Racine. Apollinaire opens his eyes wide, which gives him an owlish look, and repeats, "*Racine? Vous avez bien dit Racine?*" And looking more and more amazed he gets him to explain who Racine was and what he had done. He was nourished by a vast knowledge of culture, as varied as the clouds, Alexandrian, and with a tendency toward mystagogy. He was highly versed in demonology. He had the world at his fingertips. The misfortunes, vicissitudes, and asperities of life had polished him like a pebble in a stream. Fate, among countless experiences, had also allowed this vagabond and knight errant to essay that of amanuensis to a stockbroker. His knowledge had been enriched by cold exposure to the field of finance and the stock market. He was tolerant and wise. His visual perspective was out of the ordinary. He looked at men and things sometimes through a telescope, sometimes through a microscope, and both of them brought "reality" to what for others is fog and emptiness. He had resolved on his own what the cabalists had tried to resolve by "solar dust," and to him the invisible, the landscapes of the air, were visible: no longer a dangerous faculty since supported by a grave and profound human seriousness. This abnormal being ardently, touchingly, aspired to the norm; he aspired to the love of his *maman*, of a woman, of his friends. This *fantaisiste* aspired to reality, or rather to *surreality*, as he used to say, and with more right than others who later usurped and polluted this term. Patiently but anxiously he marched toward a higher life, a higher norm, a higher poetry. Like the Good Patriarch, Apollinaire also died within sight of the Promised Land. Latin by blood, "classical" to the marrow of his bones, he harbored for everything barbaric an aversion that was not only instinctive but rational, cultural, and "civilized" as well. As the war raged on, he remembered his wandering life:

> *Pauvres Hôtels de l'Allemagne*
> *Où j'ai vécu pendant deux ans,*
> *Votre souvenir qui s'éloigne. . .*

When the face of Death, which had leaned forward and almost touched him, began to move back and fade; when Apollinaire started getting up from his hospital bed; when "pierced" but alive he returned to his acroteric flat on Boulevard Saint-Germain, it seemed that the "jinx" was over, that the destiny of this pure man and angelic poet, who had dubbed himself *"le mal-aimé,"* had changed course. A loyal and loving woman appeared on the scene and became his wife. Finally Apollinaire had a home of his own, a table of his own, peace and security.

The autumn of 1918 came, and for him, an autumnal poet,

> *J'aime les fruits, je déteste les fleurs,*

that autumn was both dawn and twilight.

Giuseppe Ungaretti is on a short leave in Paris. Before rejoining his unit at the front, he asks Apollinaire what he would like him to bring him from Italy on his next leave. Apollinaire says he would like a bundle of Tuscan cigars. A few days later the Armistice is signed and Ungaretti returns to Paris, climbs the seven flights of stairs four at a time, then the extra little stairway . . . It was a very hot day, and Apollinaire's fat was beginning to decompose. A posthumous insult, Rostand also died on that very same day. Two poets' funerals proceed on foot through the streets of Paris. The city is draped in flags, brass bands cross each other's paths at the intersections, people dance in the street. The "Polish woman," with painted face, follows her son's coffin in her flounces and feathers. Friends think it their duty to comfort her. She laughs and bristles. "My son a poet? Say rather a good-for-nothing. Rostand—now there was a poet!" Within a year she herself is dead, and in Mexico Albert de Kostro-witzky also died, the brother to whom Apollinaire, across seas and continents, had sent touching appeals in the form of "oceanic letters." His earthly fate was over. But the ineffable life of Apollinaire continues and revitalizes.

> *Le printemps tout mouillé, la veilleuse, l'Attaque!* . . .
> *Il pleut, soldat, il pleut, mais il pleut des yeux morts.*
> *Ulysse, que de jours pour rentrer dans Ithaque!*
> *Mais, Orgues, aux fétus de la paille où tu dors*
> *L'hymne de l'avenir est paradisiaque.*

Antonio Stradivari

Torrential rains swelled Lake Tana, which in turn swelled the Blue Nile, the Blue Nile joined the White Nile, and both descended to fecundate the lands of the pharaoh. As he did every year, the pharaoh waited for the periodic fecundation to be over, and when the waters had receded into the channel, he emerged from his palace to stretch his legs and take a walk in the countryside, which shone like the skin of a seal. As he walked, the pharaoh felt himself pierced by the sweetest of sounds. He looked around: he was alone. At his feet lay the remains of a tortoise . . .

When those who attend the Sunday concerts at the Teatro Adriano in Rome melt with pleasure at the technique of a Hubermann or a Veczey, may they forget for a moment the delights of those sounds and think back gratefully to that pharaoh. For the remains of the tortoise, whose dried tendons on contact with the wind emitted those sweetest of sonorities, were the ancestor of the violin.

As everyone knows, the word "viola" comes from the Low Latin *vitula* and goes back to the classical *vitulari*, which means "to rejoice," "to dance," or more precisely "to gambol like a calf" (Lat. *vitulus*).

Before arriving at "viola", *vitula* became softened into *vidula*, then passed successively through *viula*, *vivuola*, and *violla*.

L'us men harpa, l'autre viula
L'us flautella, l'autre siula

81

> *L'us mena giga, l'autre Rota*
> *L'us is mots e l'autr'els nota*[1]

The viola is a woman. It took an Italian to give the viola a son. This worthy was old Testori or Testator the Elder, who around 1450 "having improved its shape and drawn from a small violina or violette a beautiful and majestic sound, desired to give this miracle of art a masculine name."

It was long believed that the Greeks and Romans knew only instruments to be plucked by hand or with the plectrum, but this was an error. Not only did they know the use of the bow, but the invention of this most precious auxiliary to string instruments can be credited to the poet Sappho.

The lyre itself, which as the *lyra mendicorum* or "rustic lyre" had the shape of a tortoise, was played with a bow. Apollonius of Tyana, who taught eloquence and rhetoric in Athens in the time of Nero (A.D. 60), wrote that Orpheus held his right foot in position to beat time while drawing his bow over the lyre.

As for the use of the barbiton or theorbo, it is typically Roman. Ovid says: *Non facit ad lacrimas barbytos ulla meas.*

In writing of Antonio Stradivari, whose life was not one of events but simply of sweet and drifting sounds, one must try to reconstruct the tenuous web of arcane analogies and ineffable coincidences with a spider's lightness and skill.

Let us throw nothing away. The *sordino* for dancing was the *linterculus* of the Latins. And the *linterculus* was so named because its sound box was shaped like a little boat. Here is the coincidence: Cremona itself was likened to a boat plowing an emerald sea, and the comparison was suggested by the oblong shape of the city, delineated by stout bastions and with the Torrazzo in the middle as the mast, which the mists in certain seasons shrouded with fantastic sails.

---

1. Giraud de Cabrera, *Roman de Flamenca.*

Magna phaselus, the envious said about the prosperity of Cremona.

Antonio Stradivari was born of famine and pestilence. Let me explain. From 1628 to 1629 a terrible famine devastated Cremona. Then in 1630, riding a nag dappled like the skin of a frog, a scythe on its shoulder and a wooden mallet in its hand, Plague made its entry into the capital of violinmaking. Anyone able to escape did so. Why should Alessandro Stradivari have lingered in a city where the black death went knocking from door to door? Friendship perhaps . . . But Gerolamo Amati, his wife, and his daughters had already fallen under the scythe of the terrible horseman. And so Alessandro Stradivari took his wife and children and went far away, to that unknown place—city? town? village?—where on a date equally obscure the child was born who from maple wood, varnish, and four taut gut strings was to draw the voice of grief and love.

The very name—Stradivari—is "bowlike," and makes ideas reverberate. In various spellings, the surname Stradivari had been borne since the twelfth century by more or less well-known citizens of Cremona. Stradivari is the plural of Stradivare, the Lombard variation of the word *stradiere,* meaning "toll collector."

Strade varie: different roads.

The great secret of the Stradivarius violin is that unlike the Amati, Stainer, Guarnieri, and all other makes past, present and future, every Stradivarius is unique of its kind.

In what year did Alessandro Stradivari return to Cremona? At what age was little Antonio placed in Nicola Amati's workshop? Why was this "traditional" profession chosen for him when none of his relatives or in-laws had ever been a violinmaker?

Not a musician himself, but a faithful ally of musicians, Stradivari lived on Borgo Santa Cecilia. Antonio's early years are hidden in peaceful obscurity. And when the veil is slightly rent, a date appears in the hole, or rather through the "ff" of one of the first violins created by Antonio Stradivari: 1666.

In that year Stradivari was probably still in Nicola Amati's workshop.

Two years earlier, a blast from a harquebus had attracted a crowd of dismayed citizens into Piazza Sant'Agata (today Piazza Garibaldi). Among them was a young man holding a violin handle in his hand, as though it were a question mark with which he was going to propound riddles to the passersby. What had happened? At first the only answer to the alarm and curiosity was that question mark in the young violinmaker's hand. A man lay on the ground, his face blackened and bloody, and a beautiful woman, whose grief made her even more beautiful, stood over him, wringing her hands and tearing her hair.

How do you say *coup de foudre* in Cremona dialect? Three years later, the man with the question mark married Francesca Feraboschi, widow of Giacomo Capra, who three years before had killed himself in Piazza Sant'Agata, with a shot in the head from the harquebus.

We reject as false the absurd opinion expressed by Napoleon that "marriage kills love." But though it does not kill love—indeed it nourishes it, causing it to bloom even more vigorously—it is no less true that marriage brings about a profound change in a man's life, and constitutes the transition from a time of experimentation, of strumming so to speak, into one of full and positive activity. Having married the suicide's lovely widow, Stradivari understood that it was time to stop dreaming and start catching fish, and to this end he left the parish of Santa Cecilia and moved to that of his young wife, to a house that after due consideration was dubbed the *Casa del Pescatore*, the Fisherman's House.

Antonio was twenty-three years old, Francesca twenty-six.

One of the supposed portraits of Antonio Stradivari, the one that turned up in Paris with the Vuillaume heirs, is from about this age. A youth with rather curly chestnut hair, sprouting moustaches, wide-open round eyes, and a dreamy look, is shown in the act of playing a viola da gamba. Another viola, not da gamba and drawn with anatomical precision, displays its big numbfish face on the wall.

Hill, Stradivari's biographer and exegete of the abovementioned portrait, does not realize that what he mistakes in musicians for poetic reverie is simply a fog that curtails the gaze instead of prolonging it, and prepares the way for that hyenalike turbidity that makes the musician's eye look as though scorched with terror. As for the appearance of the half-open mouth, from which Hill deduces that the supposed Stradivari is singing, to us it is an indication of adenoidism.

In 1870 a note worth fifty centesimi, issued by a bank in Cremona in the name of a workers' society, bore a small round portrait of Stradivari with a beard. Needless to say, there is not the slightest resemblance, even making allowance for the beard, between this monetary portrait and the adenoidal one of the Vuillaume heirs.

Another presumed portrait of Stradivari was once owned by Cavaliere Pietro Anelli of Cremona, later passed to a junk dealer in Genoa, and was ultimately bought by the violinist Sassi of Alessandria.

A few years ago, a violinmaker discovered another "presumed" portrait of Stradivari in the house of a priest in the Valle d'Intelvi. It is an oil portrait on canvas, 86 cm. high and 64 cm. wide. It depicts life-size to just below the waist of a corpulent man of about sixty, with long gray hair parted in the middle, an intelligent, beardless face, aquiline nose, thick eyebrows, fleshy mouth, round chin with a dimple, and oval-shaped eyes (the adenoidal individual's eyes were round). On the right an inscription: "1702 Antonio Stradivarius Cremonensis," and on the back of the painting the name of the artist, Gregorio Lazzarini, who was born in 1655 in Venice and died in 1740, and was compared by some of his willing contemporaries to Raphael. There is the usual opening in the form of a window, framing the Torrazzo and the upper part of the Cremona cathedral.

Aside from these "presumed" portraits, in which, however, for better or worse, one recognizes a certain wish to

Operatic Lives

create a likeness, we have a so to speak "ideal" portrait of Antonio Stradivari, and which for the violinmaker of Cremona is what Lionello Balestrieri's *Beethoven* is for the titan of the symphony: a poem in color.

The author of this poem is the painter Hamman, not to be confused with *Hammam*, the original name of the Turkish bath, now closer, however, to the exclamation *hammán!*, the equivalent to our *misericordia!*, or "good heavens!" Because of a poster displayed all over Italy advertising the festivities in Cremona in 1937, Hamman-Misericordia's painting, duly complete with the Torrazzo and the cathedral by moonlight, has been generally preferred to the others. In this picture the famous violinmaker was looking with a thoughtful and rather worried eye at the instrument he was holding in his left hand, while pressing his mouth with his right like someone seized with the impulse to vomit. The anatomical details of the hand were somewhat overdone in the rendering, and from a distance it was easy to mistake this hand for a beard surmounted by a pair of moustaches, which created an odd resemblance between the supposed Stradivari and Wilhelm II in his exile in Dorn.

What hopes can we have after so many serious disappointments? There seems to be a mysterious ban on revealing the physical physiognomy of Antonio Stradivari, for the purpose of confining us solely to his metaphysical and sonorous physiognomy. So it is worthwhile to imagine Stradivari as a kind of "Stradivarius," hips narrowed by the bouts, f-holes open to the breath of harmony, small head curled in a scroll, and pegs adjusted to the four winds, the strings functioning as the nervous system.

In addition to other happy results, the celebration of the second centenary of Antonio Stradivari's death had the happy one of bringing forth from the shadows many "Stradivarius" instruments whose existence was unknown: priceless violins, duly nasal in sound, and all equally supplied with the famous label: "Antonius Stradivarius faciebat anno . . ."

In Ferrara, Arsenio Bergamo, a butcher, discovers that an

old fiddle bought years before in a coastal village of the Po is a "Stradivarius" of 1734. In Narni, Signora Elena Morselli, a housewife, discovers that the violin left to her by her grandfather and which she has hitherto considered a dud, is a magnificent "Stradivarius" of 1717. Similar discoveries take place in Novara, Cremona, and Brescia.

Hope courses with dreamlike speed up and down the peninsula, and turns into a fever in those houses where some old piece of junk slumbers in the attic.

Speak up, violin, is your name perhaps Stradivarius?

The widow of the man who had shot himself gave Antonio five children, one too many as compared to the strings of the violin. A little girl registered with the name Emily shows that the sad mania for English names is much older than we thought.

The Stradivaris resided in the Fisherman's House until 1680. In that year, and for a sum of 7000 imperial lire, equal to 100,000 of ours, Stradivari bought from the Picenardi family the house marked no. 2 in Piazza San Domenico, which has become no. 1 in the present Piazza Roma.

Three floors and an attic. On the roof opened the *seccadour*, so called because that was where the laundry was hung to dry. In the summer months Stradivari worked in the loft and one by one placed the freshly varnished violins in the *seccadour*. Small strips of parchment bristling with nails can still be seen on the beams, where Stradivari hung the more delicate tools of his trade. In a wall cupboard, curled shavings of maple and fir were stored, locks of hair snipped from the head of an archangel.

The workshop was on the ground floor. If some ardent Stradivarian were to undertake a pious pilgrimage to Cremona, and on tiptoe enter that workshop consecrated by fifty years of harmonious creation, he should not be surprised if instead of concentration and silence, at the end of which the vellumy voice of a violin mysteriously sparkles, he finds worthy citizens of Cremona in shirtsleeves, their Tuscan cigars tilted and cues held behind their backs, noisily playing billiards. And yet in that interior, before those armored cars for caramboling, squat-legged and covered with green felt, made their entry in 1888 on the orders of Signor Soresini, café owner, Cremona saw Antonio Stradivari hunched over his tools; there gentlemen and friends, artists and patrons hied themselves to enjoy the spectacle of his skill; from there emerged the throbbing instruments, the thoroughbreds of the "golden period," the finest names of the Stradivarian stable: the "Ernst," the "Pulcella," the celebrated "Viotti," the grandiose "Vieuxtemps," the imposing "Parke," the admirable "Delfino" of the Munro Collection, the famous "Allard," and that matchless "Messia," with which Stradivari, seeing it so proud and robust in his hands, did not want to part.

On 20 May 1698, at the age of sixty, Francesca Feraboschi leaves Antonio Stradivari and goes to rejoin Giacomo Capra.

Stradivari, as well as being a prominent citizen and man of means, leans toward that strange temptation that we might call "making a show of the corpse," and orders a sumptuous funeral for his wife. In the overall expenditure of 560 imperial lire, only 12 lire go for "gravediggers with cloaks."

In August of the following year, Antonio Stradivari marries Antonia Maria Zambelli, who being more attentive than her predecessor to her husband's art, gives him four children: the strings of the violin.

With the celebration of his second marriage, the story of Antonio Stradivari's life enters into shadow and silence; in other words, Antonio Stradivari's history becomes entirely absorbed by his work. Nothing is manifested outwardly except in the regular dates of his "creations": "Sasserno 1717," "Maurin 1718," "Lauterback 1719" . . .

Later, and as a sign of pride, the violinmaker's age is added: "made at age 83," "made at age 89," "made at age 91," and so on.

Eighty years, every day of which, without interruption, with the "natural" movement of a river, Antonio Stradivari works. Will anyone stop him?

Ninety-two *aetatis suae.* Ninety-three. Ninety-four . . .
Over his eyes, over the landscape of almost a century, fell
the shadow of evening. His hand, when left unsupported,
was seized by a tremor like the hand of an alcoholic.

Antonio worked. But sometimes the sheet of maple buckled
in the cutting, sometimes broke when sawed. The f-holes
relinquished the sprightliness of seahorses, the once beauti-
fully curled scrolls lost their pride.

They say that Mrs. Harding, wife of the former president of
the United States, in order to save her husband from scandal
and dishonor, administered a powder to him that produces
the final sleep.

Seeing Antonio on the brink, not of scandal—for what
scandal could possibly blemish that model of a craftsman?—
but of disgrace in the face of his spotless craftsman's honor,
the Grim Reaper was moved to pity: he covered his eyesockets and grinning teeth, and appearing in Cremona at the
violinmaker's window, said to him, "Antonio, come home."

The Grim Reaper's invitation conveyed a precise meaning:
it was a question of home. I have a brother-in-law in Piedmont,
a hale and hearty young man, who one day said to me, "I can
do without a house of my own, but I'm buying a plot in the
cemetery if it costs the shirt off my back."

My Piedmontese brother-in-law and Antonio Stradivari
share an identity of views on the benefits for the dead man in
having a tomb of his own. It reminds one of the funerary
houses in Cerveteri, with their sleeping quarters for the
family, adjoining room for the servants, weapons, flat cakes,
and water jars. There has been obvious progress: Stradivari
didn't care about food and weapons; for him lodging was
enough.

Antonio Stradivari had been making arrangements for his
"house of the dead" since 1729. It had not been built
especially for him: he had bought it second hand. And when
the Grim Reaper took him by the hand and led him out of the
workshop where year after year Antonio had silently fed the
springs of song, they crossed the street, entered the opposite
church of San Domenico, sought out the Chapel of the Holy

Virgin of the Rosary, entered the crypt of the noble Villani family, which Antonio Stradivari had bought eight years before from the heirs of Francesco Villani, and there Antonio lay down.

I'm about to cause my Piedmontese brother-in-law considerable pain. In 1869, the church of San Domenico was crumbling. By way of contrast, that distressing spectacle gave rise to proud and glowing schemes in the minds of the town councillors of Cremona. Thus emerged the first idea for those leafy gardens of Piazza Roma, where around the bandstand the belles of Cremona, languidly hanging on the arms of their attentive sweethearts, listen to the "Dance of the Hours" by another great fellow citizen of theirs: Amilcare Ponchielli.

Listen to the sorrowful voice of an eyewitness, Giovanni Battista Mandelli:

"The demolition of San Domenico was making rapid progress. The apse, tower, and chapel had already fallen. Then came the turn of the Chapel of the Rosary. Malosso's cupola and Cattapane's ceiling were attacked with picks. What havoc! I can still see Aurelio Betti, the photographer, aiming his camera at the various fragments as they came crashing down. The authorities were gathered around Stradivari's violated tomb. There was Mayor Tavolotti, Dr. Robolotti, Professor Bissolati the librarian, and Professor Fecit. 'Too much confusion,' someone said, 'it's pointless to go on looking.' "

These words having been spoken, workmen came and took away the bones of the dead by the cartload. Only the tombstone was saved, which, with the name Antonio Stradivari inscribed on the front, has been in the Museo Civico of Cremona ever since.

The varnish of Stradivarius violins is inimitable.

On the instruments of the "golden period," the varnish attains perfection, wavering between red and a yellowish tinge. It is transparent, warm, and resonant as a summer sunset. The varnish of the Stradivarius has been no less "studied" than the medium of Pompeiian painting or Van Dyck's tempera. "Tell me how you varnish and I'll tell you who you are," has been the battle cry of those who believed and continue to believe that the "secret" of the Stradivarius violin lies hidden in the varnish. In 1923, Ferruccio Zanier, a violinmaker from Trieste, starting out with the idea that oil was not the base of the varnish first used by Gasparo da Salò, and which gives Italian violins their celebrated mellow and nasal sound, but a Persian resin called "gum ammoniac," obtained after repeated tests a varnish apparently similar to that of the Stradivarius.

Why was the Stradivarius not reborn? Zanier's theory was harshly attacked by Isaia Billé, double-bass teacher at the Conservatory of Santa Cecilia and student of violinmaking. Supported by Professor Pacifico and armed with copious material about Stradivarius varnishes, Isaia Billé, with an anxiety to which we cannot remain indifferent, awaits the hot summer sun for definitive proof, the dog days of August.

Will the secret be revealed? Even the sun, cooker *par excellence,* plays a role in the "secret" of the Stradivarius.

For us the Stradivarius "secret" is too scattered, too diffuse to be isolated in one part of the violin and extracted from there: be it the varnish, be it the quality of Lombard or Croatian woods, be it the combination of various kinds of woods (almost always maple and fir), be it the proportions of the various parts and the very dimensions of the instrument (the body of the violin is 35–36 centimeters long, has a maximum width of 21 centimeters, a minimum width of 11, and a thickness of 6; it is fragile and very light in appearance— barely 240 grams—but can sustain a pressure of 12 kilograms), be it the cut of the f-holes, the rounding of the bouts, the length and shape of the handle, the curvature of the scroll, or the position and perforation of the bridge.

No line, no detail is "repeated" from one Stradivarius to another. *"Facies non omnibus una—Non diversa tamen."* A vague similarity imparts a family resemblance to the 1,116 Stradivarius instruments scattered around the world, including violas and cellos: not the guitars, which have all disappeared with nothing remaining but a perforated ornament in the shape of a rose. It is in this constant "invention," this constant "inspiration," that the Stradivarius secret is hidden: the miracle of hand craftsmanship.

Oddly enough, the individuality that distinguishes one violin from another is not repeated in the violas, much less in the cellos. Antonio Stradivari's violas are first-rate instruments. Some are majestic in appearance, such as the "Tenore," known as the "Toscano," an even larger instrument than the Gaspare da Salò and the Amati.

Stradivarius instruments in which the effects of Nicola Amati's training can be detected are called *stradivari amatizzati.*

In his cellos Antonio Stradivari set the definitive standard. While his violins leave room for improvement, the cellos say: *nec plus ultra!*

The "Aylesford," the "Archinto," and the "Duport" are particularly famous.

At the Tuileries, Duport was performing a solo *pathétique.* Enter Napoleon with boots up to his thighs and roweled spurs. He listens with obvious pleasure, and when the piece is over grabs the cello, sticks it between his legs and says, "Show me how you hold this instrument."

The unfortunate cellist, struck dumb by fear and respect, finally succeeds in stammering "Sire" so desperately that Napoleon immediately hands him back his instrument.

One can understand why only a mulatto woman could have put up with Napoleon's love, and why Maria Luisa, as a "good European," relinquished the joys of the imperial ardor.

Did Stradivari know how to play the violin? The hunting dog does not eat the prey. A good chef tastes the dishes but does not feed on them. Do these analogies help us to make a distinction between Stradivari the player and Stradivari the nonplayer? Stradivari tasted the sound, he savored it, but he did not feed on it.

Antonio Stradivari

On the other hand, he was an impeccable draftsman, and of this we have irrefutable testimony. The Arisi brothers, priests, intellectuals, and contempories of Antonio Stradivari, assert in their writings that the embellishments, arabesques, flowers, fruits, and cupids that adorn "decorated" Stradivarius instruments with such grace, neatness, and perfection are by his hand.

In 1874, with the "Delfino" in mind, Charles Reade wrote in the *Pall Mall Gazette* that, in his opinion, the height of beauty was the effect of light and shadow produced when the velvety outline of a red Stradivarius becomes rounded, and the varnish on the bottom wears away in the shape of a vague triangle. We, looking at that faded triangle, recall the celebrated jaws that have pressed, suffered, and agonized above the Stradivarius violin; the adorable little jaw of a young lady violinist, on which the burning contact left a light strawberry-colored mark . . .

A Stradivarius should be looked at from the back. The Arisi brothers describe the care with which Stradivari chose the woods for the bottom panels, sometimes in a single piece, sometimes in two. He preferred the broad grain of the wood arranged like the rippling effect of waves on the bottom of the sea. Thus emerged those splendid violin backs, which have the streaked markings and feline grace of panthers.

Do violins suffer? Pearls, they say, come back to life on the skin of the wearer. At night Spanish dancers take their castanets to their breasts, lest they *se constipan* and their sound "die." The suffering of idle violins, "showcased" violins, violins laid out like the decorations of one's poor colonel uncle on a velvet cushion, violins suspended like high-priced sausages under bell jars, violins tightly enclosed in their little red, orange, or brown jackets and with their bows alongside them like the swords of dead knights—the suffering of violins that no longer feel the support of a heaving shoulder or convulsed breast, do not feel themselves grazed, caressed, or dominated by the fingers of a Sarasate, a Joachim, or a Kubelik, do not feel themselves swept by the

93

melodious currents of a Bach, a Mozart, or a Beethoven—the suffering of violins may not arrive at the suffering of Niobe, but some such process of petrification, or at least of chilling, must take place in the bodies of these poor little things.

Lest their sound "die," those who are worthy of them should take their Stradivarius violins to their breasts.

Jules Verne

One evening in January 1910 I was dining in Paris at the home of a high magistrate. He had one of those double-barreled surnames of a reactionary from the time of the Dreyfus affair: it was Binot de Villiers. He was pompous and deaf. His wife, *la présidente*, had been crudely carved out of wood. Dinner dragged on. Yawns were more frequent than the spoonfuls of *potage impératrice*. Almost all the guests belonged to the courts. Their mastiff faces rested on enormous starched collars. In cavernous voices they formulated childish little thoughts. Their ladies belonged to the species of guinea hens, but wore evening dresses and fanned themselves with the feathers of their elder brother the ostrich. As the only young man, I had been placed next to a girl dressed as a dragonfly, who was experiencing a fit of spastic rhinitis. The minute I turned to her to murmur something innocuous, such as "Do you like flowers?" or "Have you been to hear *Firebird?*", she went red in the face, stuck her head under the table, and smothered a series of sneezes in her napkin. We arrived at the dessert course. It was a pudding in the shape of an automobile tire, accompanied by a chocolate sauce offered by the second waiter in a silver sauceboat. I don't remember how it happened, but I accidentally knocked the waiter's arm, and the sauce, thick and dark as cloacal liquid, spilled all over the splendid Brussels lace that adorned the tablecloth. I tried to explain that among us Italians chocolate on the tablecloth was a sign of good luck, I performed the gesture of dipping two fingers in that mess and wetting the back of my neck. In vain! The sycamore-bark face of *la présidente*, the owlish stupor of the judge, and the silence and consternation of the other guests left no room for hope. We retired to the drawing room for coffee, and while I held my cup with infinite precautions in dread of new disasters, a gentleman short in stature and with Mongolian cheekbones came over to me, and having expressed his satisfaction over the deft way I had extricated myself, added, "These bourgeois types don't deserve any other treatment."

"But I was as embarrassed as a thief," I objected.

"*À d'autres!*" rejoined my interlocutor, who meanwhile had introduced himself as Monsieur Pierre Roy, *artiste peintre*. "I could see immediately that you were a different sort."

To return the compliment, I praised Monsieur Roy's shirt, which with its marbled front and flowers in relief, was the most ridiculous and inappropriate shirt I had ever seen.

"It's beautiful," the *artiste peintre* acknowledged without false modesty, "but unfortunately it's the only one I have left from poor Verne."

"Jules Verne?"

"My uncle. When he died, that wonderful man left me his shirts."

It's strange, how attached some men are to articles of apparel. Medardo Rosso was crazy about shoes, Verne about shirts. In 1852 he wrote to his mother: "Often a shirt sleeve stays in the sleeve of my jacket. You tell me to change the front, but where am I going to get the back? On one of my shirts only the top part is left. Why keep calling it a shirt when it's no more than a collar?" He was also *"nato con la camicia,"** which, had he been Italian, would have given him material for countless puns. Like other "great men," Jules Verne was also a shameless punster.

---

* Literally "born with a shirt"—i.e., "born with a silver spoon in his mouth." (Tr.)

His birth occurred in Nantes, on 8 February 1828, on the stroke of noon. There was nothing to indicate that the newborn baby was to become an exceptional eater. His father, Pierre Verne, a notary, went to his office in a *dame blanche*. Painted white, drawn by four white horses, driven by postilions dressed in white livery, the spotless omnibuses of Nantes were furnished with bellows organs, which with the movement of the wheels ground out the more evocative airs from Boieldieu's *La dame blanche*. As for little Jules's mother, her name was a current of air: Sophie Allotte de la Fuye.

A half century earlier Nantes had boasted a powerful class of shipbuilders and merchants, owners of fleets on the Loire and lands in the Antilles. The "Santo Domingo planters," as they were nicknamed by the populace, had built in the heart of Nantes a private quarter, an Arabian Nights city, palaces supported by caryatids, aviaries resounding with birds from the islands, bearded plants, and flowers frightening as fireworks. When Verne as a boy wandered along the canals of that river port, and his eyes looked rapturously at departing brigantines and steamships, the "Santo Domingo planters" had been dead for some time and their wealth dispersed, but a glimmer of the old splendor still persisted amid the ruins of the private city, and a colonial aroma lingered in the air.

On the evening of 10 November 1848 Jules Verne arrives in Paris in time to see the National Assembly's celebration of the proclamation of the new Constitution end amid the smoke of torches, while in the middle of the Place de la Concorde, which is decorated like a cathedral, Alphonse de Lamartine proclaims the religion of oppressed peoples. It is adieu to Romanticism. The Romanticism of weeping willows and of the not yet discovered Koch bacillus dies, and a heroic Romanticism, akin to the *Odyssey*, is about to be born: that of the pioneers of progress and the wonders of science, and from which Jules Verne will derive poetry in abundance.

The new arrival ventures into literary salons. Those of Madame Jomini and Madame Mariani are gardens of crystal, unsuitable for the lumbering steps of a lover of gross puns. "Ah!" young Jules murmurs one day to a girl whose ribs are tortured by her whalebone stays, "if I could only go whale-fishing on those *côtes!*" But in the salon of Madame Barrère, Verne meets the Chevalier d'Arpentigny, a celebrated chiromancer. Dumas *père* is an enthusiast for chiromancy. In the chevalier's wake, Jules Verne crosses the threshold of the giant mulatto, and is allowed to partake of the flaming omelettes and heavenly mayonnaises that the author of *The Three Musketeers* prepares with his big chocolate-colored hands. From the intimacy of food they pass to that of literature. On 12 June 1850, the Théâtre-Historique offers to the judgment of the public *Les pailles rompues*, a platitudinous comedy in verse by Jules Verne and Alexandre Dumas *fils*. This silly trifle is followed by others: *Colin-Maillard, Les Compagnons de la Marjolaine, Monsieur de Chimpanzé.* Driven by an unworthy illusion, by a false estimate of himself, Verne, who is destined to sail the high seas, in the meantime navigates the theatrical swamp. Comos and Tragos have so bewitched him that he, from whose head Phileas Fogg with his muttonchop whiskers and checkered suit is about to spring like Minerva fully armed, becomes the secretary for the Théâtre-Lyrique. He thinks he has arrived. Not only that, but the future moralist and austere writer, he who only in passing will allow the figure of a chaste wife or exemplary sister to appear in his heroic books, composes such cheap licentious comedies and vaudevilles that his notary of a father, seated amid the refrains of the *dame blanche*, replies with embarrassment to passengers who ask for news of his Jules's theatrical successes, "But I know nothing about it. My son is studying law."

Many watches have been stolen since the world began, but none with the results of the watch stolen one evening in 1852 from Jules Verne's bedside table. Next morning the victim goes to the police. "Did your watch have an escapement?" "Unfortunately!" Inspiration strikes his brow, along with the involuntary pun. He leaves the police station and gropes his way home. Wheels and ratchets revolve in his head. Little by little from among the gears rises the lean figure of Master

Zacharius, watchmaker from Geneva and inventor of the escapement. Zacharius has discovered in the watch mechanism the secret of body and soul. Who can now forbid him to compete with God? In vain does his daughter, the gentle Geranda, try to cure this disturbed mind. Master Zacharius dies at the height of his aberration, and the clocks that surround the madman's death throes with their endless tick-tock suddenly stop.

Along with the clocks of the demiurge *manqué*, Verne's "low vein" also stops. The *deus* has revealed its presence in the breast of this descendant of magistrates and dreamers. How did the mysterious visitation occur?

One evening Verne was in his bedroom. The window was open on the glittering boulevard. Along with lights and voices, in through that window came a lady dressed as a Bible seller for the Salvation Army, with bonnet, spectacles, and her arms loaded with compasses, sextants, and spherometers. She stopped before the writing table on which Jules Verne was composing one of those hybrid spectacles, half music and half prose, and staring at him sternly, said, "Jules, enough of these stupid things!"

The lady was skinny and ugly, but even had she been the most appetizing of women, her virtue all the same would not have been in jeopardy in that bachelor's bedroom, for Jules, though having offered out of pure ostentation to go whale-fishing on the ribs of virgins from Nantes, in truth, and like other "great men," was more prone to the joys of fantasy than to those of love.

Verne rose from his chair. "*À qui ai-je l'honneur?*" he asked.

"I am Science," replied the visitor. And from that day the austere lady became for Jules Verne what Troy had been for Homer: a source of inspiration.

Jules is happy. He goes down into the street so as to give vent to his joy. Paris is drenched in light. "Are these lights for me?" he asks a passerby, who looks at him dumbfounded. "They're for our emperor's wedding," he replies. In that spring of 1853, Napoleon III, fondling his corkscrew goatee and sharpening his moustaches to pinpoints, had brought

Eugénie de Montijo to the Tuileries, the beautiful Spaniard with a bowed neck, a bovine sweetness in her eyes, and a pair of tresses on her alabaster shoulders. "Our emperor . . ." the lover of Science repeats, and his face darkens. The more appealing he was to emperors, the less appealing they were to him. When Verne died, Wilhelm II wrote from the seashore to his widow: "I should like to have followed his dear remains. I still remember the charm of those marvelous books." Instead of his own august person, the Kaiser sent as his representative to the writer's funeral an embassy councillor with the same name as the composer of *Martha:* von Flotow. An intentional choice? Anything is possible with Kaiser Bill. Like Isidore Ducasse and Marcel Proust, Verne was crazy about music. To provide an outlet for his passion, he had, as a student, paid twenty-five francs for a hundred-year-old piano that had belonged to Grétry. Who can forget Captain Nemo's sublime, heartrending improvisations during the underwater stops of the *Nautilus?* Who can forget the Wagnerian harmonies that strike the astonished ears of Lord Glenervan and his companions in the night of the Australian forest?

The Crimean War itself helped save Verne from theatrical sin. In September 1854 the first wounded arrived from the Crimea, and with the gestures of sowers scattered cholera germs on the fertile fields of Paris. Within a few hours, Seveste, director of the Théâtre-Lyrique, of which Verne is the secretary, makes his exit from the world. With the director dead, the secretary also dies "to the theater." Even friendship takes a different turn. The good goddess whose name is Philia takes him away from his stage fans and throws him into the arms of Jacques Arago, the blind traveler. Do not the blind retain the third eye, that "inner" eye that man, according to the Stoics, bears at the top of his brain and with which he sees his dreams? More fortunate than ourselves, the blind see their dreams even when awake. Standing before an audience of astonished eyes, Arago is back from having guided a band of gold seekers, whom pun-loving Paris has nicknamed

Jules Verne

the "Aragonauts," on the Colorado plains. To Jules Verne the blind traveler offers his extraordinary geographical memories, the colossal lianas of America, that endless creeper of the raft that will guide the sons of James Dacosta through the Brazilian jungle. Still formless and opaque, the Novel of Science gradually takes shape in his mind. His immense idealism, which will ultimately lead him to the most prickly misanthropy, still stinks of milk and has barely the consistency of pap. Under these conditions, but already staring at a dream "on the other shore," Verne writes, and in verse to boot, an "Italian comedy" on the "incorporeal and intellectual" loves of Leonardo da Vinci and La Gioconda. Destiny emerges from chaos. The design proposed to us by this reckless man exceeds that of Balzac, of Homer, of Dante: a walk through the cosmos, no less.

From the moment Jules Verne glimpses the face of his destiny, his steady concern is to give literary form to the "epic of science," and to remove whatever obstacle may interpose itself to this design.

Even love?

Even love. Verne has hitherto considered love the most poetic adventure of life, but now he understands that it too is an obstacle to be left behind, perhaps the most serious one. In order to settle this irksome necessity once and for all, the novelist of science marries Honorine Hébé Anne du Fraysne de Viane. Does he fool himself into thinking that with all these names he is setting up a harem? Be that as it may, the bride whom Verne takes home is already a "practiced" one, who in addition to herself brings him a pair of grown-up daughters ready in their turn to be brides. When Honorine four years later gives birth to a little boy, Verne after due consideration is able to say, "My wife has three children, I one." Was Honorine for Verne what Cosima was for Wagner, and what every wife of a great man deceives herself into thinking she is for her husband: an inspiration and a collaborator? "Silent husband," Honorine calls hers. And one day, finding themselves both on board the *Saint-Michel*, and Verne

101

as usual lying face down on the deck, his wife scolds him: "Jules, the only way you ever look at the sky is with your backside." Poor Honorine! She did not know that for the supreme purposes of poetry, it is precisely with the backside that one ought to look at the sky.

Around the naive and bearded heroes of the nineteenth century, triumphant mechanization was weaving a mythology of pistons. Papin's steam was the new cloud of Jove. Verne believes in the majesty of science, and has a blind faith in man. "Everything I invent, everything my mind imagines will still be less than reality, because the day will come when the creations of science will exceed those of the imagination." These are the apothegms that like steel columns support the mind of this apostle of discovery, this Mazzini of geographical maps, this champion of Esperanto. For his marvelous navigation, in the course of which 104 bound works illustrated by Riou, Benett, Bayard, and Neuville will rise from the ocean bottom to the light of the aurora borealis, nothing is missing from Jules Verne's equipment: not even that necessary block of stupidity, which is for the artist of strength what ballast is for a ship. Verne does not doubt. He is not gnawed by introspection. He is a simple genius, armed with practicality. A Giuseppe Verdi of geography. But how can you navigate if you do not surround yourself with the very solitude of the sea?

A false and hypocritical legend of goodness has grown up around Jules Verne. Chiefly because of Edmondo De Amicis, another individual "deformed" by legend, the names of Philemon and Baucis have been applied to Jules Verne and his wife. Do we wish to deny this legend? Anyone wanting to find the likes of Jules Verne should take as a model that Bongiovanni, astronomer of Ferrara, who spent his life atop a tower of the Castello Estense, and consented to receive his wife and daughter only once a week, from eleven o'clock to noon on Sunday. As far as eating was concerned, the novelist of geography copied Menelik, because Jules Verne too, in imitation of the "king of kings" but not for the same reasons of "dietary modesty," took his meals in solitude.

Humanitarianism swelled him like a hot-air balloon. Even his work was to be consecrated to the good of humanity. Supreme reward, on 7 July 1884, in one of the eleven thousand rooms of the Vatican, a room gilded and painted like a tabernacle, the "humanitarian mission" of his work was to be recognized and praised by an old man light as smoke and white as an enormous snowy locust. "Celestial vision," writes a nephew of Jules Verne in his travel journal. "Emerging from his audience with Leo XIII, my uncle bawled like a calf." Meanwhile the family affections of this "calf" are getting progressively cooler. Jules Verne encloses himself more and more in that idealism that is the supreme achievement of the bourgeois soul. The more he extends his love to the distant circles of humanity, the more those close by remain deprived of it.

The book that triumphantly opens the series of Extraordinary Voyages owes its origins partly to Edgar Allan Poe's "Balloon-Hoax," as well as to Verne's friendship with Félix Tournachon, known as Nadar and by anagram Ardan in the *Voyage from the Earth to the Moon,* who was the first to raise photography to an art form and on 4 October 1863, on board the *Géant,* sailed into the sky from the soil of Paris. Was it Nadar who influenced Verne, or Verne who influenced Nadar? Truth, as always, is controversial. From their meeting emerged the first draft of that prophetic novel whose final version bears the title *Five Weeks in a Balloon.*

The name of the man who in his capacity as publisher is destined to share Jules Verne's fortunes is Hetzel, and a fearful man he is, in more than one respect. First of all, Hetzel is the Germanic name of Attila, as it appears in the Swiss version of the *Nibelungenlied.* Moreover, Hetzel is not only a publisher but also the author of refined novels, signed with the pseudonym Stahl, which in German means "steel." Nevertheless, when on a foggy morning in the autumn of 1862, Jules Verne, with the manuscript of his first "scientific" novel in his pocket, goes to knock on the door of this steely Attila, the latter receives him in a bedroom padded like a pincushion, lying on a bed over which precious Flemish tapestries dangle from the canopy, and resembling more a sultana validé, or Turkish queen mother, than the indomitable king of the Huns.

Jules Verne and Hetzel were made for each other. The publisher commissions the writer to supply him with two novels a year, forty novels in twenty years.

From that moment Jules Verne becomes the Saint Nicholas of the children of both hemispheres. He also acquires little by little the appearance of Saint Nicholas: cotton wool beard, tufted eyebrows, the step of a dancing bear. For forty years and more, this scientific and imaginative Saint Nicholas will arrive punctually at the year's end party, his sack full of beautiful new volumes, bound in red and with a gold fillet on the spine. And while the Nativity bells ring and the snow spreads a soft grandmotherly semblance over the tragic face of our mother earth, the radiant face of Adventure glows in the frost-chilled windows, and inside the rooms padded with rugs, to the murmuring heat from the stoves, an immense sigh of happiness, an expansive wind, swells the hearts of thousands and thousands of little readers.

And yet, the most impassioned of these, a "grown boy" on whom the space between nose and lip has already been shadowed with down, lies in wait one evening in March 1886 near Jules Verne's home in Amiens, and when his idol emerges from the darkness of the street, fires the contents of a large revolver at him.

The poet of adventure falls face down on the sidewalk, and the would-be assassin slinks away at the end of the street. The veil of mystery falls on this absurd and sinister scene. Will the reasons for the incomprehensible attempt on Verne's life ever be disclosed? A voice whispers: "Keep silent! Keep silent!" And it would perhaps be more disappointing to know them than not to. There are reasons that *do not live up to expectations,* reasons *devoid of reason.*

While they carry the "children's friend" into the house, his shoe dangles as though empty and suspended by its lace. The navigator is reduced to flotsam. To while away the time during his immobility, the weaver of adventures on land and sea composes hieroglyphs, cryptograms, and "eight hundred" crosswords. "In the lameness to which I'm forever condemned, I will console myself thinking of Mademoiselle de La Vallière, Talleyrand, and Lord Byron." Thus he jokes about his broken foot. But what will become of the seafaring life he loves so much?

Legend has also woven its cobwebs around Jules Verne the voyager. One represents him as an "armchair traveler," another as a kind of marine centaur. As usual Truth, the sister of Banality, is somewhere in between. The sea is this misogynist's great love. The summer of 1854 is inauspicious for him: biliary disorders, headaches, ridiculous duties at the Théâtre-Lyrique, a facial paralysis that makes his cheek look flabby and lowers a small curtain of eyelid over one eye. Still, from the depths of such misery, a cry of joy bursts from Verne's heart, and reaches his mother in Nantes in the form of a letter: "Saturday evening I took the train: I saw the North Sea!" The shining seas of the south are not excluded from Verne's thalassophilia, but his real friends, his "secret advisers," are the sad, dark, boundless seas of the north. In 1869, his first great voyage: Scotland, the Hebrides, Fingal's Cave. Then a journey in America on the *Great Eastern,* the huge paddle boat that gives him the idea for *A Floating City.* Later, when his royalties begin to accumulate, Verne buys the first of his pleasure vessels, the first of his three *Saint-Michels:* the first little more than a rowboat, the second a sailing yacht, the third a steamboat, on which he will circumnavigate the western Mediterranean.

As soon as he is back on his feet, limping and more grumpy than ever, Verne returns to Nantes, seeking the mild shadow of his mother, the notary ghost of his father. In ports, ghosts collect on the pier. Also moored to the pier is the *Saint-Michel III.* With one last hope in his body, Verne climbs the special ladder that the captain has had made for his employer's damaged foot. The ship heads out to sea. At the first pitch the sea wolf takes a tumble. All is over! The great voyages, the endless cruises will no longer happen except by virtue of the imagination. The insatiable navigator gives up the sea. He gives up Paris, which in its way is also a sea. In Amiens, where he has retired, he gives up a house that is too large and where too many people, too many friends, too many admirers have landed as though in a port. He is reduced to a house barely sufficient for himself and the briny dreams that, like the waves of the sea, pound without letup day and night in his head. The *Saint-Michel III*, its prow sharp as a pencil, will go to satisfy the seafaring moods of the Prince of Montenegro.

The Frenchman is greedy for honors. Verne himself, believe it or not, was not immune to this insane appetite. In February 1870, Ferdinand de Lesseps requests the cross of the Legion of Honor for the author of the *Extraordinary Voyages:* the homage of the man who joined the Mediterranean and the Red Sea to the one who, by means of a submarine passage, joined these same seas in a literary sense. Just as Napoleon III is about to sign the decree, Mars tears the pen from his fingers, and urges his horse at a gallop in the direction of the Rhine. At the end of this thunderous ride, evil tidings begin to rain down on the capital: Reichshoffen, Forbach, Sedan. The government falls. Before laying down his ministerial arms, Emile Ollivier submits for the empress's signature the decree that had remained in abeyance. It is one of the last documents signed by Eugénie as "regent." France loses two provinces, but the rosette will gleam in Jules Verne's button-hole.

Appointed to coast-guard duties by the military authorities, the new member of the Legion of Honor mounts guard over the Loire, on board the *Saint-Michel II*. He is silent, gloomy, lost in thought. Of all the Olympian deities, Mars is the one least to his liking. The boasts of his compatriots inspire in him bitter reflections. On the war Verne will not say a word. And he keeps his promise. One of Jules Verne's leanest books, the *Adventures of Three Russians and Three Englishmen*, takes place in the 1870s, and in it the war is scarcely mentioned.

His life becomes increasingly detached from the lives of other people. His mind rises gradually to the supreme solitude of the *Sphinx of the Ice*—epic conclusion of Poe's *Narrative of Arthur Gordon Pym*—to the rampant green madness of the *Aerial Village*, to the hermeticism of *Golden Volcano*, *Lighthouse at the End of the World*, and *Invasion of the Sea*.

By a necessary fiction, Jules Verne, or rather the simulacrum of Jules Verne, the *nume* of the extraordinary voyager, goes through the motions of an absurd life lightly tinged with politics. This Jules Verne in disguise is elected on the Socialist ticket to the town council of Amiens, deals with urban problems, enters into correspondence with the Archduke Luigi Salvatore of Tuscany and with a mysterious Demetrios Zanini, a millionaire who proclaims him a "future Solon" and offers to let him legislate a "renewed world"; he takes on the posts of financial comptroller for theaters and inspector of traveling circuses. A double life. A life of the highest poetic creation, and a stunted life of exemplary citizen that continues until 20 March 1905. But at dusk on this day Jules Verne is offered a new and supreme opportunity to detach himself once and for all from the world of other people.

Jules Verne is in bed. His paunch makes a balloon under the quilt. His eye is submerged between its drooping eyelid and swollen bag of yellowish fat. In the middle of the silvery bushy beard and hair, his face is a bare patch of flesh yellowed by diabetes. His hands rest on the covers, the right one moves slowly as though writing. The iron cot sags under his weight. Phileas Fogg's papa is a bear playing dead, in a comedy of trained animals.

Enter Madame Guillon: leg-of-mutton sleeves, a wood dove on her head, a half veil with black dots on her nose. "Jules! Jules!" cries the dying man's sister, and gives vent to sobs that make her nose swell. Jules does not stir. Enter Suzanne, Valentine, his son Michel. Enter Hetzel himself, the publisher. The bear plays his role to perfection: he recognizes no one.

All of a sudden the door opens by itself, and from the darkness of the anteroom in comes a walking stick. Huge, knotty, studded. It comes thumping forward. Behind the walking stick comes a delegation from the Boys' Imperial League: four angelic schoolboys, the tadpole tails of their Eton jackets covering their little round backsides; and the eldest, speaking for them all, says in a nasal voice: "Good day, Mister Verne. This is the stoutest walking stick we could find in all of London. We've taken up a collection to buy it, and we present it to you so that you may have something to lean on for your future pilgrimages."

The bear on the cot grunts with pleasure as though he had seen food arriving, but goes on playing dead. So then not even death brings that total solitude to which from the depths of life he had aspired? The delegates from the Boys' Imperial League leave, but are soon replaced by the members of the Amiens town council, relatives close and distant, friends, admirers, priests, lighted candles, and flowers as fat as beefsteaks and replete with nauseating odors.

There is no salvation. Jules Verne gets out of bed, barefoot and in his nightshirt, like an ill-clad God Almighty. In a last farewell to those present, he hikes up the nightshirt, grasps the walking stick of the Boys' Imperial League by its neck and brandishes it like a club, and then leaves the funeral chamber with broad footsteps that remain impressed on the flowered carpet, like the paw prints of a ground sloth in the clay of the Pliocene.

Meanwhile in Monaco, in the dormitory of a college of Marist friars, a "boarder" named Guillaume de Kostrowitzky, but who later as a poet will take the pseudonym Guillaume Apollinaire, looks out the window and shouts:

"Jules Verne—what a style! He uses nothing but nouns!"

It is the new generation's salute to the old poet as he departs.

Lorenzo Mabili

The physical figure of Lorenzo Mabili lives again in one of my childhood memories.

It was 1906. My father had died the year before. Our house was closed, its furnishings scattered, and at summer's end we sailed from Patras on the *Romania*, owned by the Navigazione Generale Italiana.

I was leaving the land where I had been born and had spent the mythical part of my life, and was on my way to another land, one with which so far I had only an imaginary acquaintance, although I felt bound to it by ties of blood and thought.

My first contact with Italy was on that ship, among those sailors who from the captain to the lowest cabin boy all spoke Italian, that is to say that same language that we back in Greece had spoken only within the four walls of our home. It was like a second birth and more real than the first. I felt that a new life was beginning for me.

The *Romania* stopped at Corfu. We went ashore to look up Lorenzo Mabili, who had been a close friend of my father.

The house was a labyrinth of small stairways, dark corridors, and large bare rooms. To temper the persistent summer heat, woods and streams shone transparently on the lowered rush blinds at the windows. The furniture was sparse and looked dead. None of us dared to profane those corpselike seats and defunct armchairs. A man in a consul's uniform, with two expressionless eyes and a pair of unlikely red moustaches, looked down on us from the middle of the wall.

They had told me the house belonged to Mabili, all that remained of a considerable inheritance. But they had fooled me. The real owner of that house was silence. A silence that was not even broken by the sudden appearance of Mabili himself, who was suddenly there in our midst without my realizing where he had come from. He was smiling at us sadly, as though offering us his condolences. He was expansive but only to a degree. At first I suspected some grudge between him and my family, but shortly I noticed that this circumspect look of affliction was his natural expression. I had heard much praise of Mabili's good looks. "Mabili," my father had said, "is an Apollo." And since I knew that Mabili was a poet, I reasoned that a resemblance to this god was the natural condition of every poet. But he was an aged Apollo, overweight and poorly dressed as a man. A little gold still shone in his beard. His eyes were blue, very gentle, and remote. His speech was slow and as though impeded by asthma. His words were kept waiting. And when he decided to bring them out, you could tell it was not the word he'd been thinking of, but another. It was as though he were at confession and having trouble confessing his sins. The conversation was halting. Even when not reciting his own lines, a poet talks about poetry. Or so I believed. But poetry was a key that none of us dared press. When it was said in our home that Mabili wrote poetry, it was like saying that Mabili was a thief.

"And Esther?" my mother asked, after a pause in which the conversation had fallen to the floor and threatened not to get up again.

"She's coming," Mabili replied, and added, "Poor thing!"

Later I understood the reason for this commiserative expression, when Esther with silent little steps entered that tomblike drawing room.

Esther was Mabili's sister. She wore the uniform of old age with honor. Her white hair was parted in two side tresses; she wore a pleated dress and on her bosom several strands of small black pearls.

By one of those understandings inexplicable by ordinary

reason, Esther and Lorenzo had sacrificed their lives to each other. Neither had given any thought to marrying, or to creating a family on his or her own. Faithful to their sterile pact, Esther had arrived at old age, and Lorenzo was on its threshold. As well as being a sister, Esther to Lorenzo was a mother and in part a wife. In both of them there was something closed, something ineffably silent. The void awaited them at the end of their solitary days, and nothingness. They were still sustained by a thread of hope. I go back nine years and transcribe a letter from the time of the war between Turkey and Greece in 1897. Lorenzo Mabili was a volunteer in the Garibaldi Legion.

Arta, 4 April 1897

My Esther,

Once more I send you greetings before going on to where it will no longer be possible for me to write you: the mountains of this territory and the poor villages along the border.

I think of you and your solitude and my heart aches. I know that if you lose me you lose everything, even what reminded you of our poor mother. I know all this and weep. And my heart is torn at the thought that I have been unable in my life to repay you even a fraction of all the good you have done me.

Who knows? Perhaps we will still be able to live together, happy in a happy country, honored in an honored country.

Nine years after this letter, Lorenzo Mabili was alive in my presence and burdened with sorrow. He had returned from the mountains of Epirus and from the poor villages along the Turkish border, but his wish to live happy in a happy country, honored in an honored country, had not come true.

In the afternoon, after a luncheon worthy of the house in Emmaus (never as at that table have I understood so well the sanctity of bread), we took a carriage to the Achilleion. Esther had tied the ribbons of her bonnet under her chin and put on lace gloves that covered her hands halfway. Lorenzo wore a boater too large for his head. (Apollo in a boater! It was a subject for *Simplicissimus* and Bavarian cartoonists.) We visited that villa that had once housed an empress's melancholy, the villa that had been one of the Kaiser's favorite residences, the villa that the government of Mr. Theotokis kept from being transformed into the Monte Carlo of the East.

From the height of a terrace where Aeolian harps softly throbbed, Lorenzo pointed to Pontikonisi out there in the middle of the sea: Mouse Isle. "Pontikonisi," said Mabili, "inspired Böcklin to paint his *Island of the Dead.*" Later, in my wanderings through Europe, I became convinced that there are as many sites that inspired Böcklin's *Island of the Dead* as there are beds where Napoleon I slept.

We came to the statue of Heine. Before this monument perpetuating the memory of the poet, Mabili's eyes shone, and his face was illuminated by a radiant smile, the first and last of that day. Then, without another word, we descended to the port as the sun was setting.

When our goodbyes were over, Lorenzo said, "How lucky you are to be going to Europe!" And he turned to look westward.

As the *Romania* got underway, I watched those two human beings with neither future nor hope grow smaller on the pier: she in her bonnet of a trained poodle, he in his oversize boater.

Next morning I woke up for the first time in Italy.

The Greek refers vaguely to the lands that begin at the Italian shore of the Adriatic and extend to the coasts of the Atlantic as Europe or the West. Despite the truth of geography, the Greek situates himself outside this continent. Europe or the West exercises on him a singular fascination. Any Greek who has the means to take a trip to "Europe" is a favorite of the gods. There civilization shines with its greatest splendor. Lucky is the Greek who suffers from dyspepsia and can go to Vichy to take a cure. Lucky is the Greek who has an abscess and can go to Vienna or Berlin to have it operated on.

There the most refined pleasures are to be found, the most exquisite joys.

The admiration the Greek feels for "Europe" is not reciprocated by Europe in equal measure. Still less does Europe reciprocate the devoted love the Greek feels for the "poetry" of the West. When we talk among ourselves of the new Greek poetry, the only name that comes to mind is Jean Moréas. Europe knows Moréas because he lived and died in Paris, threw in his lot with the Parnassians, renounced the name Papadiamantopoulos, and adopted a sonorous pseudonym that through French phonetics reminded him of his native province—the Morea.

A pity! The new Greek poetry deserves to be known in its own house and in its mother tongue. I, who had the good fortune to be born in Greece and to live in Greece during the years when one collects one's most vivid and lasting memories, can say that poetry is as much a natural faculty to the Greek of today as it was to his brilliant ancestors. If then the fame of the new Greek poets does not match that of Anacreon, this is due less to its poetic quality than for those imponderable reasons that sometimes succeed in smothering the greatest possibilities. But apart from itself, the new Greek literature is also interesting in philological terms. Among us the question of language has not yet been resolved, but by a tacit agreement no one speaks of it any more. In Greece, the question of language is still today a problem so alive and kicking that it sometimes requires the intervention of the evzones to resolve it.

Anyone who says "new Greek language" is speaking of something that exists virtually but not in fact. The Greeks have not yet succeeded in reaching an agreement on what their language ought to be. They have a sacerdotal and administrative tongue that draws directly on the Byzantine of the Gospels, and save for a few morphological and syntactical variations still imitates it, both in the rigidity of its articulations and the archaism of its words. It is the language of the liturgy, of public officials, and of purists. They call it *katharevousa*, that is to say "the pure." *Katharevousa* not only wears formal dress, it is a starched language as well. Its spelling bristles with spines. I don't know if this custom still holds, but up until twenty years ago there were grammarians in the Parliament in Athens whose job was to act as scribes and correct the deputies' prose. Those able to write without errors in spelling could be counted on one's fingers. These clever scribes resolved the countless difficulties of accentuation by putting the accents and aspirates in a little clump at the top of the page and letting the reader distribute them as the case might be.

Alongside this thorny language, which is less an instrument of knowlege than an obstacle to it, there has grown up with weedlike spontaneity the popular language or *maliara*, that is to say "the hairy." It is a corruption of *katharevousa*. Young and unprejudiced, *maliara* has welcomed and made room for all the neologisms and barbarisms that the "pure" language had repudiated as unworthy of itself. It has put a good face on many Turkish and Slavic words. It has given favored treatment to Italian, Venetian, and Genoese words. It has turned the morphology of its surly mother topsy-turvy. It has broken the skeleton of conjugations. It has stripped the declinations of their ancient authority. It has left the nouns from the nominative to the vocative in peace. It has appointed prepositions to govern the set of cases.

Maliara is a colorful and highly effective language. It allows for a variety of composite words equal if not greater than German. It is rich in synonyms. It offers such possibilities for puns that *argot* by comparison has the gravity of a court language. And for a naturally witty and caustic people like the Greeks, there is no need to demonstrate the importance of puns. *Maliara*, in short, is a flexible and light-hearted language, certainly no less and perhaps more so than Homer's Ionic and Plato's Attic. An admirable instrument for a literature that does not reject subtleties, nuances, and a variety and multiplicity of meanings, and which has no fear of that divine game, the double meaning.

And yet this language, so beautiful, so varied, so "Greek," is still today a disjointed organism. Up until a few years ago there was no dictionary to collect it nor grammar book to administer it. It lacked the consecration of poets, the authority of linguists, and the dignity of texts. Greek children in their classrooms did not learn this language of their lives, but the strategic Attic of the *Cyroanabasis* and the administrative one of the *Cyropaedia*. To give *maliara* a secure grammar and official vocabulary was a task that belonged to the Academy. And there is an Academy in Greece. It is not to be found in the gardens of Akademo but on University Street, in white modern Athens. A sumptuous headquarters was planned for it, built in unadulterated neoclassical style by a Bavarian architect and preceded by two columns of Parian marble, one of which supports the statue of Apollo Musagetes, the other the statue of Pallas Athena. Gaudy frescoes adorn the main hall, and these too are the product of the brush of one of those classicizing Bavarians who came down into Greece in the wake of King Otho. But the Academy of Athens is, or at least was in the time of Lorenzo Mabili, like an oyster shell completely lacking the body of the mollusk. In the more than fifty years that this building had stood there with its marbles and frescoes, the twenty prominent men needed to populate it honorably were not to be found. Still there was no lack in Greece of grammarians and philologists who would have been able to give the "hairy" language the necessary structure. But would they have been able to dedicate themselves to anything except polishing the body of that mummy, *katharevousa?*

The singular stubbornness of partisans of the "pure" against accepting the "hairy" as a living and at the same time literary language is to be attributed less to philological snobbery than to age-old sentiments of nationality and religion. Orthodox Christianity is not only a faith and a religion, it is also the most direct expression of national sentiment. Religion and State merge in the Greek mind into a single concept. This unity is justified by history. During the centuries of Turkish rule, it was religion that kept national sentiment alive in the minds of the Greeks. Subjected to the authority of a barbarous and infidel people, governed by its government and administered by its administration, the Greeks were left with nothing but the Church. This was the house of God, but it was also municipality, school, and archive of tradition, the hearth on which the flame of Hellenism burned. And the priest was not only confessor and God's minister, but a teacher of both language and history, a depository not only of the sacred wisdom of the Gospels but of the likewise venerable wisdom of secular learning. It was in the cells of monasteries that the 1821 uprising was organized. These were less retreats of peace and prayer than political clubs, citadels built on the heights and inaccessible to the control of the pasha. In the heart of Thessaly, in a certain locality known as "the Meteora," some of these rocky monasteries still rise, which cannot be reached except by curling up in a basket and being pulled up by ropes and pulleys. Under the sign of the cross and the shadow of holy buildings, national sentiment was identified with religious sentiment. The language itself became not only an instrument of culture but of worship. This language was not only the language of Byzantium and of the final spendor of Greece; above all it was the language of the Gospels, and thus doubly venerable. The face of History had changed. For more than half a century Greece had been independent. What did it matter? For those "who did not forget," the language of Byzantium and of the Gospels was still an untouchable and sacred language.

I think it was around 1903 and 1904. I was a small boy. One day I went for a carriage drive with my mother. The streets of Athens were more lively than usual. All of a sudden a crowd of demonstrators comes running from the end of the street. Shots echo. The citizens take to their heels, the iron shutters of the shops come down with a crash. A deputy had proposed in the Chamber that the Gospels be translated into the "hairy" language. What sacrilege! Revolution had broken out.

The reaction came from the University. The leader of the purists at that time was a professor of philology named

Mistriotis. A kind of Greek Angelo de Gubernatis.* He wore the uniform of the teaching profession ostentatiously, including a greasy frock coat and a stovepipe hat that was losing its nap. His nose was porous and shaped like an eggplant.

Although gouty, he was an enthusiastic walker. He was also a mystic of carpophagy. Fruit constituted his sole nourishment, and Mistriotis selected it for himself between noon and one o'clock, on his way home from the University to the wretched quarters where he lived, a stubborn old bachelor and scholar. He would hover over the baskets of the fruit sellers, feel the peaches with an expert hand, and bring them close to his quivering, riddled nose. He pressed the figs for the joy of seeing them ooze, bent an ear over the cantaloupes, and thumped the watermelons, listening to them the way a doctor listens to the patient's pleura. His great fear was that the fruit might be watery. Awed by this well of knowledge, the fruit seller ignored his fussiness and called him "Mister Professor." But he used the wrong case ending. Mistriotis flew into a rage. He rebuked the ignorant fruit seller, and after reciting the entire scale of the classical declination for the noun "professor," he went away satisfied with his cantaloupe under his arm.

This duet between the professor and the fruit seller is a miniature example of the bitter dispute that divided Greece into two linguistically opposed factions: the "pure" and the "hairy." Needless to say, the more intelligent and lively part of intellectual Greece sided with the "hairy." For their part, the most able writers strove to furnish this language, which had neither past nor tradition, with the necessary patents of nobility. One of the most fervent apostles of the vernacular was the poet Lorenzo Mabili. He called himself an "ultravernacularist." His proselytism crossed the borders of Greece. Thus he wrote to Professor Eliseo Brighenti of Cesena, phil-Hellene, student of the new Greek literature, and editor of an anthology of new Greek poets:

---

* Italian Orientalist, editor, and literary historian (1840–1913). (Tr.)

Corfu, 22 September 1907

Dear Sir,

I am sorry that you have been unable to come to Corfu. We would have discussed the interesting question of language. I would certainly have succeeded in convincing you that, as in Hamlet's madness, there is a bit of method in the way we ultravernacularists think. While as it is I fear that you have already dismissed us as incurable fanatics, incapable of reasoning.

As his name attests, Lorenzo Mabili was not of Greek origin. In Greek his name is pronounced *Mavílis*. Lorenzo's grandfather was a Spaniard named Mabili y Buligny. The government of the Catholic king had sent him to head the consulate in Corfu. When he reached retirement age, Mabili y Buligny did not return to Spain but settled in Corcyra for good. Corfu is the island of the Phaeacians, and a Phaeacian poet once said:

> *Whoever has drunk the water of Corfu*
> *Never returns to his native soil.*

The consul's wife was a remarkable beauty and celebrated as such even in this land rich in beautiful women. But the Countess Mabili y Buligny was not only exceptionally beautiful, she was also pious and knew that physical beauty is short-lived.

She would never allow a painter or sculptor to do her portrait, and not even the daguerrotype, that extraordinary invention of her time, succeeded in overcoming the repugnance she felt toward iconography. Lorenzo's father was a lawyer. He married a Greek woman named Joanna Capodistria Sufi. They had two children: Esther and Lorenzo. He was born in Corfu on 6 September 1860. Even as a boy he devoted himself to his studies. His teacher was a certain Politas, who was know on Corfu as a distinguished man of letters. Following the poet Dionysios Solomos, he took a keen interest in the problem of language. He went to Germany, and took a degree in philosophy at the University of Erlangen. During the fourteen years he spent in Germany, he translated Virgil, Schiller, Uhland, Burger, Byron, Shelley, and Tennyson into "hairy" Greek. He studied linguistics and Sanskrit. He penetrated the mysteries of Hinduism. He devoted himself to philosophy. He was a Kantian to the point of exhaustion. In one of his poems, "Mysteries of the Unknowable," he says goodbye to pure reason:

My hopes are spent. Farewell!
The fantasy of golden wings has fled.
All that survives in me is that torment
That the Erinyes have placed
In the depths of my troubled mind
So that it be both my demon and my god.

He changed models and went from Kant to Schopenhauer. His sonnets are imbued with a cold resignation, a quiet pessimism. In "The Windmill" he invokes the happiness of nonbeing. In others he celebrates his island, woman, love, friendship. A steady lament increases the harmony of the line. His voice is directed more to the dead than to the living. Like Leopardi, Mabili too thinks that life is an intolerable burden for man. "Disintegration" reflects this philothanasia:

Happy the dead who forget the bitterness of life.
When the sun sets and shadows spread over the earth,
Don't mourn the dead, however great your pain.
This is the hour when the dead are thirsty and go
To the crystalline spring of oblivion.
But should a single tear trickle from the eyes of those
Who are still alive and remember them,
The water grows cloudy,
And if the dead drink this cloudy water,
They too, passing through the fields of asphodel,
Remember their former pain.
If you cannot help crying,
See that your tears fall not on the dead but on the living:
They would like to forget but can't.

From that time on, however, and even through the necessary shadows of the still prevailing Romanticism, his love for his homeland shines brightly. One of his first sonnets, written in 1878, is dedicated "To the Motherland" and in the manner of Petrarch invokes:

Greece, O my mother, why as at other times are you not still
Erect, tall, crowned with laurel and adorned with the gifts of
*   immortal Victory?*
When will the hour come when your lifeless face
Will shine again and you will illuminate this desolate, or
*   courageous, land of yours*
With hopes? Arise, O my country! May your brow
Shine again in the heavens.

In 1888, and in the expectation that a war of liberation would restore to Greece that portion of territory that still lay under Turkish domination, the poet's heart was filled with fond hopes. But hopes they remained. In 1890 he celebrates the sun, the sea, the light of his homeland:

O my country, a sun like yours shines in no other place.
Oh, how the sea and fields throb in its light!

His was a rational patriotism. After Kant, after Schopenhauer, a third philosopher came to inspire the poet: Fichte. Like Fichte, Mabili too thought that love of country is not only a natural sentiment but also man's first duty: precepts of the educated man, who serves as an example to the people. Just as Fichte identified the "German people" with the "maximum good," so Mabili identified the "maximum good" with the "Greek people." Just as for Fichte, the "German idea" represented "goodness, the holy, the just," for Mabili "goodness, the holy, the just" were represented by the "Greek idea." He thought besides that Hellenism was about to become a luminous political example to all peoples. The modern history of Greece, its long servitude, and its rebirth were to Mabili reassurance of the lofty mission reserved for the Greek people.

120

He had precise knowledge of the grandeur and difficulty of art. He did not like to talk about himself or his work. He kept revising his sonnets for years and only rarely decided to have them printed. Whatever time he did not devote to poetry he gave to the study of philosophy. He dreamed of doing for Greece what Dante had done for Italy. At least this is how it looked to people who were close to him. Mabili never confessed his great secret to anyone. He left some fifty sonnets, admirable for their beauty of form and nobility of concepts. Translations from the Mahabharata, Dante, Goethe, Leopardi, Foscolo. A sonnet, "Love and Death," in imitation of Leopardi. Another entitled, in the manner of Dante, "Angelic Butterfly." Two sonnets in German and a "farewell," Many critical essays. A copious correspondence. In 1915 the magazine *Grammata* in Alexandria undertook the publication of his *Works*. He had a prodigious memory. He knew by heart the Homeric poems and the *Divine Comedy*. He was a formidable chess player. He could take on seven opponents at once, without looking at the chessboard. He was a superlative billiard shot. His name is inscribed in the gold book of the billiard room in the Café Luittpold in Munich. He was a pure man, an exemplary citizen, a perfect idealist.

After his student period in Germany, he lived a solitary life in his house on Corfu. Although invited, even urged to do so, he did not take part in the unstable politics of his time. He refused tributes and honors. After the military revolt that purified the politics of Greece, he agreed to represent his fellow citizens in the Parliament in Athens. From his seat as a deputy he fought for the acceptance of the "new" language. To a colleague who called *maliara* base, he replied, "There are no base languages, only base men!" Next day he had to defend his philological faith with the point of a sword.

He took part in the war of 1897 and was wounded in the arm. At the outbreak of the Balkan Wars of 1912 he was fifty-three years old. He enlisted in the Garibaldi division. He fought in Thessaly, in Macedonia, in Epirus. He was promoted to lieutenant on the battlefield. The volunteers fought at Drisco, in the environs of Ioannina. Mabili dreamed of witnessing the liberation of Epirus. The battle of Drisco was a bloody one. On the evening of 28 November 1912 the order comes to retreat. Lieutenant Mabili is against it. He persuades the commander to go on fighting, "if only to save the honor of the forces." At dawn the battle begins again. Almost all the officers are dead. Lieutenant Mabili advances alone toward the top of the mountain. A bullet goes right through his head. They transport him to a little country church that has been turned into an emergency hospital. Before going in he turns to look at the battlefield. A bullet strikes his mouth. Mabili turns back to his comrades. His mouth bleeding, he says in Italian: "I expected many honors from this war, but not also that of giving my life for my beloved Greece." Thus died the poet Lorenzo Mabili.

A monument to the "poet and patriot Lorenzo Mabili" stands in a public square on Corfu. Esther is dead. They buried her with her black pearls and her half gloves of lace. "To live happy in a happy country, honored in an honored country." The poet's dream did not come true for that tired, sober body of flesh that I had seen him drag among the columns of the Achilleion, but for his cold body of marble.

Verdi, Man of Oak

Music is a secret society. Musicians recognize each other by covert signs just as freemasons once did, and a musician from Pretoria arriving in Valparaiso, or one from Stockholm arriving in Chicago, is sure to find brothers waiting for him at the station to give him food and lodging and supply him with money.

A musician carries his own environment along with him, the proper air for his lungs, the temperature that best suits his organism and which is usually high, since contrary to what most people think, the musician is a cold-blooded animal.

Musicians can be recognized by their pallor and cold sweaty fingers, and by the moist cloudiness of their eyes, which resemble celluloid balls full of watery milk.

All musicians have cold, pale fingers, but especially flutists. Depending on whether the articulation is simple or double, the flutist goes *te te te* or *te ke te ke* into the mouthpiece of his instrument. If women were not so jealous of their secrets, it would be interesting to know what the kisses of flutists taste like.

Musicians can also be recognized by their odor. An odor characterized, as the case may be, by the smell of sweaty fingers on ivory piano keys, or of old resin on the violin bow, or of the saliva that trickles into the tubes of brasses.

Musicians are marked by strange deformities: the spot like a kind of strawberry mark under the jaws of violinists, the calluses on the gentle fingers of harpists, the bowlegged gait

123

of cellists, which though resembling that of horseback riders, can be distinguished from it by unmistakable signs.

I have a sister-in-law, a graduate of Santa Cecilia, who spent her childhood and adolescence at the piano, and if she absented herself for so much as a minute from that species of big black credenza, sporting a cannibal's dentures in its middle and thrusting two small yellow candelabra upward from its glossy breast like atrophied arms, her mother, from the depths of the kitchen where she was preparing those rubbery stuffed octopuses that I too had to swallow repeatedly during the period of my engagement, would shout at her, "Delia, your fugues!"; and as a result the poor girl's feet became so flat that she was eventually obliged to wear arch supporters inside her shoes.

In the conservatories, which is to say the schools where the secret art of music is taught, an air of initiation prevails, a Templar atmosphere, an Eleusian breeze, not to be found in other schools; and anyone who is not initiated into these mysteries barely perceives the confused sonority when on a maternal autumn afternoon padded with soft kindnesses, or a troubled spring morning shot through with fatal anxieties, he passes along the wall of a conservatory through the sounds that stream from the windows, and in which polonaises by Chopin and Hungarian rhapsodies by Liszt, chaconnes by Bach and pluckings on the fourth string by Wieniawski, chromatic scales on the clarinet and solos on the English horn are all entangled.

Add the secret language of music, its script, indecipherable to anyone who is not an initiate, the signs for quavers and demisemiquavers, the keys, the sharps, the naturals, the fugues for several voices and the canons, the partita and the counterpoint, and you will see the justification for all that is abstract in musicians, their absent looks, their unsociable behavior, as well as their complicity among themselves and their detachment from the rest of humanity.

Similar to the kind once led by alchemists, the home life of musicians is also peculiar and secret, amid metronomes, tuning forks, and large sheets of paper printed with staves.

The fascination of music lies in its mystery.

One day the people of Crotona assembled in the public square, whence they converged on the house used for meetings by the Pythagoreans, theosophists who dressed in white linen and abstained from eating beans, and set fire to it. This we learn from Vincenzo Cuoco's *Platone in Italia*, one of the few authoritative accounts in Italian historical writing, but which neglects to add that the Pythagoreans formed a sect of musicians, who not only studied and evaluated the kinds of music made in this world, but also measured those made by the stars in their celestial revolutions.

What sort of figure would little Peppino Verdi, the country lad from Le Roncole, hamlet in the township of Busseto, have cut among such moonstruck metaphysicians?

A minor writer and director of the Comédie-Française, Jules Claretie was a complete imbecile, with a pronounced facial asymmetry, but nevertheless he "wrote" a physical portrait of Giuseppe Verdi that is a perfect likeness. It was 1867 and Verdi was in Paris for the rehearsals of *Don Carlo*, which was being staged at the Opéra, or rather at the *grande Boutique*, as Verdi called it.

"Verdi is tall in stature and of a nervous gauntness," Claretie wrote, "his Atlas shoulders seem to be holding up mountains. His long thick hair falls over his temples in massive locks, his shining black beard is starting to look grizzled under his chin. His cheeks are furrowed by two deep wrinkles, sunken face, heavy eyebrows, very mobile eyes, wide, bitter, scornful mouth, proud virile appearance, harsh and disrespectful attitudes."

Where have we seen Giuseppe Verdi?

Once, many years ago, I was on my way from Parma to Borgo San Donnino, which was not yet called Fidenza, where I would catch the local train for Salsomaggiore. It was a slow train that stopped at every wayside station, and at each stop slow, inexorable men "tall in stature, of a nervous gauntness, with Atlas shoulders that seemed to be holding up mountains" got on and off. As they sat on the train, their knotty hands resting on the bundle they carried with them, composed as the statues of pharaohs, there was no way of telling what they were thinking or if they were thinking at all, what they were looking at or if they were looking at anything. Their unbuttoned shirts disclosed the bark of their necks, streaked by long sinews, and the parchment of their chests. You don't ask whether an ilex is clean or dirty. And if a few smells came from those bodies that had been baked by the sun and washed by the rain, it was the very smell of the earth. One, in crossing the compartment, stepped on my foot, but he did not stop, he ignored my agony, and behaved as though I didn't even exist, and it was as though an oak tree had passed over my poor foot.

Now, not only the man who stepped on my foot, but also his fellows who were getting on and off the train between Parma and Borgo San Donnino, were all equally Giuseppe Verdi. Except they hadn't written *Don Carlo* or had their portrait penned by Jules Claretie.

In the Museo Teatrale of the Scala, in the center of the room devoted to Verdi, there is something that looks like a small kneading trough resting on a pair of trestles and open on a red keyboard, as though this little wooden quadruped liked to feed on chewed-up bricks.

This curious instrument, enclosed for safekeeping between glass partitions, also suggests a pirogue from the lacustrine period preserved in a museum of paleontology, but before this idea can lodge itself firmly in our heads, we read the little card resting against the glass: "Verdi's first spinet."

Has this spinet ever emitted a sound, from that horrible mouth stained with the blood of devoured bricks? There is reason to doubt it.

This spinet was bought by Carlo Verdi, who kept an inn with stables at Le Roncole near Busseto, as a present for his son Peppino, because whenever an accordian passed along the highway, that instrument that has the voice of a broken heart, Peppino ran out of the house like a little lunatic and set out in pursuit of the accordion player.

At what moment in his life was the love for the accordion extinguished in Verdi's heart? We do not know, but in any case in 1857 this love was still present, for to give a popular tone to Gabriele's barcarole in the first act of *Simon Boccanegra,* Verdi wrote it with an accordion accompaniment. Critics of the time blamed the accordion in part for *Boccanegra's* lack of success, and Verdi twenty-three years later, still remembering the disapproving remarks of the likes of Mazzucato, Locatelli, and Achille Montignani, replaced the accordion with a harp in the second *Boccanegra.* This replacement exposes Verdi's "development." The accordion was an expedient. It was, in the score of *Boccanegra,* what the piano is in the score of *Petrushka:* an unexpected sound "outside the orchestra." By replacing the accordion with a harp, Verdi killed this expedient, drowning it in the vague orchestral sonority of nineteenth-century opera. And he thought he was refining the score, like those who write "reached" and think they are being more elegant than if they had written "arrived." But at the time of the second *Boccanegra,* Verdi was already under the baleful influence of Arrigo Boito, who for his part, under the name of Tobia Gorio, had already refined Piave's libretto.

So much evil has been spoken of poor Piave! Now listen to this quatrain from the first *Boccanegra* and see if it isn't worthy of Metastasio:

> *Ogni letizia in terra*
> *E menzognero incanto,*
> *D'interminato pianto*
> *Fonte è l'umano cor.*

Not Euterpe, because Euterpe protects musicians belonging to the secret sect, but a strong and healthy god, devoid of hysteria and endowed with a calm and prodigious intelligence, saved Verdi from other "refinements" of this kind.

In Milan Francesco Maria Piave lived for many years in that Galleria De Cristoforis that was like a dead-end street in Baghdad, and where swollen red papier-maché lungs and hearts crowned with rose campions glowed in the windows of the firm of Paravia. Perhaps he lived in that very same house in which we ourselves lived many years later, that boarding house "for artists" where vocalizing issued from every room, and where if it rained at night you had to lie in bed with an umbrella.

As evidence of Piave's stupidity, people have quoted such lines as "*Il balen del tuo sorriso,*" (The flash of your smile), "*Raggiante di pallor,*" (Radiant with pallor), "*Sento l'orma dei passi spietati,*" (I detect the track of relentless footsteps), "*Il raggio lunare del miele,*" (The lunar ray of honey). And to think that if one day we should seek an equivalent of Rimbaud, Hölderlin, or Nietzsche the poet, we should have to drag out poor Piave!

Piave's end was Nietzschean as well. One day paralysis struck the unfortunate librettist, neglected poet, and wretched Jove whose imagination flashed higher and more strangely the darker the sky of his stupidity, and nailed him for eight years to a chair. And when Verdi went to 7 Via Solferino to visit this little Prometheus nailed to a straw chair, Piave roused himself as best he could with only one part of his body, and whimpered like a dog who again sees his master but cannot speak, cannot move because he is chained up.

Piave, not Boito, is Verdi's true librettist. He was the "Verdian" librettist *par excellence.* In Piave there was the intelligence of stupidity, in Boito the stupidity of intelligence. Look closely and you will see that Verdi's strangest, highest, most memorable moments are in music what "*Il balen del tuo sorriso,*" "*Raggiante di pallor,*" and "*Sento l'orma dei passi spietati*" are in poetry.

When Piave fell out of his chair dead, Verdi wrote to the Countess Maffei: "Poor Piave! He was a good man!" "Good man" is more a synonym for "poor devil" than for *kalokagathos.* What wouldn't we pay to have a single sentence, a single word, a single hint that revealed in Giuseppe Verdi an intelligence equal to the flashes of light that run through his work!

Peppino's spinet didn't work. They had to send for a specialist to repair it, and he, when he had finished the repairs, pasted a card inside the chest of the aphonic instrument reading as follows: "I, Stefano Cavalletti, replaced these jacks and leather quills, and I installed pedals as a gift, just as I also replaced the said jacks gratis, seeing how willing young Giuseppe Verdi is to learn to play this instrument, which for me is payment enough. Anno Domini 1821."

In the very years when a great people was being reborn to independence, Verdi was being born to music. This suffices to explain Verdi's "patriotism."

Had he been one of those "other" musicians, who when you call them don't answer, when you look at them don't see you, and in whom that witch Music has dried up all human feeling, Verdi at this time, under his broad-brimmed hat and in his double-breasted jacket, would not appear among the leading figures of the Risorgimento, alongside Cavour, Mazzini, and Garibaldi, while all around, on a boundless field, under a blue sky populated with saints in red and gold armchairs, thousands and thousands of hurdy-gurdies repeat close by, then farther away, then still farther away, and finally in the remote distance: *"Va pensiero sull'ali dora-a-a-te. . ."*

Broad-brimmed hat and double-breasted jacket are kept in the museum of La Scala, and at first sight, placed as they are, the hat on top, the jacket below, and between hat and jacket the empty space for the head, they give the impression of the Invisible Man caught and imprisoned behind glass. It takes no effort to understand that there is nothing diabolically musical about these garments; they are simply the hat and jacket that the Good Rustic, the Man of Oak, before emerging from them as a naked soul on 27 January 1901, left on the chair in his room in the Albergo Milano.

There is a stark and tragic document of Verdi's death: the drawings made by Hohenstein of the head of Verdi as he lay dying, and under which a notation of the time and date marks the passage from life to death:

20 hours	25-1-1901
9:30 hours	26-1-1901
10 hours	26-1-1901
16 hours	26-1-1901
20 hours	26-1-1901

And there it stops.

Verdi's music does not lie in the fingers of anyone who tries to play it on the piano. The exception is *Falstaff* in its piano transcription. But is that to Verdi's credit or that of the excellent maestro Carignani? Certain instances of diminished seconds, as in the accompaniment to the Doge's words *"Tu piangi"* in *Simon Boccanegra,* are astonishing, as though they were not his.

Even his life did not have the chemical, abstract, astral quality of the cabalistic life of musicians. His music is to be sung, which means it is direct and natural. He got along well with sopranos, tenors, and basses, fat mammals with beautiful rings on their fingers and their brains permanently lulled.

Such was the health and "peculiarity" of his destiny. A rustic, Verdi did not enrich his soil with chemical fertilizers, but with good natural manure.

Not even he knew himself. And judging his music by *musical* standards, he gave it barely ten years of life.

And yet other music will die while his will go on living. For unlike the other kind, it is not sterile and detached from the world, but worked and reworked with a rustic's strong coarse hands, and kneaded with the very elements of the earth: the good and evil of the earth, its love and hatred, its gentleness and cruelty, its stupidity, its indifference, its madness.

Men of higher mind, more extraordinary in their thinking, sometimes ignore Bach, ignore Mozart, ignore Wagner, but they pause amazed and fascinated by the madness of the Universe: the madness of Giuseppe Verdi.

Life and Death of Cayetano Bienvenida

Ronda, in Andalusia, is small in the number of its inhabitants but large in fame. Toreros are divided into *rondeños* and *cordobeses*. The difference is similar to that between Spartans and Athenians. The *rondeño* is masculine and devoid of affectations. The "Cordovan" is the so-called *torero señorita*, who embellishes his killer's sport with the flourishes of a dancer. The *rondeño's* Spartanism is not limited to form, but bears on the technique of bullfighting. Thus in the *verónicas*, the little steps and passes that the torero performs around the bull in order to tease and irritate it, the Cordovan puts his right foot forward, which allows him to make a rapid retreat, while the *rondeño* "burns his bridges" by putting his left foot forward, precluding any possibility of retreat.

Ronda's houses are clustered in the shadow of the crumbling "Castle of the Jealous Moor," which from the side of the mountain where it clings like a snail in the sun looks straight down into the sinister gorges at whose bottom the Tagus foams. Everywhere else vultures defecate on humans; in Ronda humans defecate on vultures, which fly in circles below the *miradores* of the town.

It was in this center of the sternest bullfighting tradition that Cayetano Bienvenida first saw the light twenty-five years ago, if one can use the expression "saw the light" for a birth that took place in the gloomy Calle de las Sierpas, where day and night have the same dark face. His mother, Amparo Triana, brought him into the world at exactly twelve o'clock

131

noon, the sacred hour of the corridas and which in the Calle de las Sierpas is determined more than anything else by the acrid smell of frying that comes temporarily to reinforce the permanent stench of the latrine. This coincidence of hours reveals the hand of Destiny, for it was also at noon that Cayetano died.

One is born a torero. Those so predestined become conscious of their vocation in early childhood. At the age of seven Cayetano felt that *le gustaban los toros*. He was not the only one. Eluding the watchful eyes of their parents, Cayetano Bienvenida, Pablo Atarfeño, Paquito Rodriguez, and others would leave Ronda before noon and betake themselves to the *ganaderias*, the stock farms where the young bulls are raised and where adolescent toreros learn to dodge the animal, vault over it with a pole, and pretend to kill it with a stick—in short to perform initiatory corridas.

Arriving in the vicinity of the *ganaderias*, the boys would climb trees and hide in the foliage, and when at noon the herdsmen went away to eat, they let themselves drop from the tree like ripe pears and began to *capear* with their jackets.

Did these "'civilian" corridas outside the magic circle of the bullring fulfill Cayetano's ambition? After his exertions at the *ganaderias*, Cayetano would go home and throw himself down on his cot, and there, amid splendid families of bedbugs that came climbing up the wall with papa bedbug in the lead and the lastborn at the end as a kind of nethermost red dot, the future torero dreamed of Madrid, the bullfighting capital, acclamations in the sun and the pungent smell of blood on the sand, just as Odysseus on the beach of Ogygia dreamed of rocky Ithaca and the reclaimed delights of being a husband and father.

At the age of fourteen Cayetano felt himself to be a man and his resolution was made. One night he sneaked quietly out of the house, and descended the crags and ravines to the road leading to Madrid, his light steps resounding in the silence of the night. He walked for days and weeks. An automobile had stopped at a road intersection, and they asked him who he was and where he was coming from. He replied, "I'm from Ronda and my name is Cayetano." And on hearing his own name so clearly, and alongside that place of origin, Cayetano saw himself inscribed in the great book of fame.

In Madrid Cayetano frequented the bullfighting centers and especially the Calle Alcalá, the place where contracts are drawn up. Calle Alcalá was for the torero in search of a contract what the Galleria in Milan was for the aspiring actor. And like theatrical seasons, corridas too are organized by impresarios. Once the terms are agreed to, the parties go to the café for the signing. There, on green velvet divans, engaged in endless card games, and surrounded by beer steins full of *café con leche*, the toreros conjure up outstanding memories, episodes of unusual courage, mad and reckless acts, before the throng of *aficionados*, who with cries of admiration comment on the stories like an ancient chorus.

Cayetano was seventeen when the capital was thrown into an uproar by the name of the great Marcial Alanda. Cayetano spent the last two pesetas jingling in his pocket for a seat *al sol* (the seats in the shade being the expensive ones). The bull went circling around the man, who stood motionless as a statue in his plaster-of-Paris suit. The *banderilleros*, waving scarlet capes, attracted the bull from afar, then moved to the left, forcing the bull to follow them. In the meantime, Don Tancredo changed position. Having completed the circuit, the bull found itself facing him again but in a changed way. It stared at him perplexed, then galloped forward, suddenly stopping a yard away from him, hooves in the sand. It seemed less like a corrida than one of those insipid affairs presided over by the former president of the French Republic Gaston Doumergue in Provence, with debilitated bulls as gentle as cows. A small white dog, last trace of a glorious past, slowly followed the bull, curled itself up on the sand, and licked its own belly. The series of watercolors of bullfights presented by Goya to Carlos IV illustrates the Moorish custom of launching packs of dogs into the arena to be massacred by the bull, a foretaste of blood that the public much enjoyed. The dogs in their turn were the survival of the original corrida, which was run in the country with lances (the corrida was originally a hunt), and in which *palenques con burros*, "barriers of donkeys," were set against the fury of the cornered bull, becoming themselves the victims of horrible carnage. Gradually the corrida has been mitigated, and today the *picadores* wear iron kneeplates under their pants and the stomachs of the horses are protected by padding. The "true" corrida is still practiced at Medina del Campo, where once a year, with the participation of all the inhabitants, a "free" corrida is held, with infuriated bulls being released in the streets of the town and some thirty deaths each time.

The public was calling for *las banderillas de fuego*, which ignite the bull's combativeness. Pablo Atarfeño, who had joined Cayetano in Madrid and was sitting next to him, urged him: "Now's the time! Jump in! It's now or never!" And all of a sudden, in the sun-dazzled arena surrounded by two orders of vaguely Moorish arches, a cry went up: *"El espontaneo!"* Cayetano had "jumped." It is not unusual for amateurs to throw themselves "'spontaneously" into the arena. While Cayetano circled around the bull, approaching it with *pasos de muleta*, and two guards tried to grab him by the seat of the pants and pull him away, the crowd all of a sudden stood up like newly sprouted grass and shouted to them to let him "work." The bull, grazing him with its horn, tore his jacket. His pants in shreds and half a jacket on his shoulders, Cayetano felt himself sliced in two by fear. He started running toward the *burladero*, the wooden partition concealing the door of the *barrera*. But instead of jumping behind the *burladero* to get away, he ran right into it. The animal was on top of him. It picked him up like hay on a pitchfork and tossed him in the air. Crumpled up in the fetal position, Cayetano turned a triple somersault and fell back almost soundlessly to the ground.

At the infirmary the impresario rolled back his eyelid, certain of finding the eyeball exposed. This gesture rekindled the dying boy's awareness, and in a quavering voice he asked: "If I come out of this, will you let me do a corrida of my own?" The doctor, who looked like a hairy butcher, answered yes, thinking the minutes were numbered anyway. Three months later and to the sound of stately marches, Cayetano Bienvenida, nicknamed *el niño de la Palma*, "the child of Fortune," because of his miraculous escape from death, triumphantly entered the bullring at the head of the *cuadrilla*, covered with glittering spangles, sequins, and braided cords, the *coleta* at the nape of his neck and his backside resplendent with sunlight.

It was a triumph. By decree of the *inteligente*, the technical director of the corrida, the president to whom the corrida was dedicated offered the new torero the ears and tail of the bull. That same evening, Cayetano, surrounded by his retinue of *zanganos*, made his entrance into the Villa Rosa amid the ovations of *flamencos* and *bailadoras*. He ate, he got drunk, he cleaned his teeth with his fork and his ears with a toothpick, he put a glass of Amontillado on the tip of his shoe and drank it by lifting his foot. La Romerito, famous for treating men like dogs, took a carnation from her hair and threw it in his face. It was the dead of night when Cayetano came reeling out of the Villa Rosa, surrounded by his hangers-on and carrying the beautiful Romerito folded over his arm like an overcoat.

On the eve of the great corrida in Talavera de la Reina, for which the impresario had guaranteed him fifty thousand pesetas, Cayetano left his house and set out for the station escorted by forty *zanganos*. There was an ugly surprise in store for him in the street. An old man, whom he recognized as Alonzo Triana, the brother of his mother Amparo, stopped him and asked for a hundred pesetas.

"Where am I supposed to get them?" asked Cayetano. Frowning, he took out five pesetas and gave them to his uncle, who took them, looked at them dully, then threw them on the ground and spat on them.

"*Vamos!*" said Cayetano, and started walking away with his forty *zanganos*. The old man, who had remained standing in the middle of the street, shouted after him, "Watch out, Cayetano, the bull's going to kill you tomorrow at Talavera."

When he arrived in Talavera, his Uncle Alonzo's words were still ringing in Cayetano's ears. He had sent a telegram asking for a room with bath. They took him up to a tiny room with no bath. Cayetano came back down furious. "I am Cayetano from Ronda," he yelled, "and I want a room with bath!" The manager and the desk clerk tried to calm him down. When he was finally given a room with bath, Cayetano had all his luggage dumped in the tub. "That's what I think of your bath!" he said, while the manager stood wringing his hands in the doorway.

Next morning the impresario came to warn him that the bull was squint-eyed and had a low left horn. Cayetano, who was lacing his shoes, uttered a curse: he had laced one shoe backwards.

"What are you afraid of?" the impresario asked him. "Aren't you *el niño de la Palma?*"

The *cuadrilla* entered to the sound of the band, lined up under the president's box, and saluted by waving their hats. When the preliminaries were over, those who were not taking part in the corrida jumped over the *barrera*, leaving the arena to the *picadores* and *banderilleros*. At the low, harsh blast of a trumpet, the small red door of the *toril* opened.

The bull took its time coming out. While Cayetano stared spellbound at the dark hole of the *toril*, his Uncle Alonzo's words came back to his mind: "Watch out, Cayetano . . ."

The bull was squat and sluggish. It moved uncertainly, like a gouty banker. The similarity was enhanced by the one-eyed effect. The games of the *picadores* and *banderilleros* passed like a sigh, and Cayetano found himself alone facing the animal. Then to him it happened as to Achilles with the horse; it seemed to him that the bull spoke and said to him: *"Cayetano, yo vengo por ti."*

Cayetano shivered. But what was he afraid of? Wasn't he *el niño de la Palma?* He began to circle around the bull, like a seamstress trying a dress on a lady customer. But when like a good *rondeño* he went down on his left knee for the *media verónica*, the bull tore his *taleguilla*, then followed through by driving its low horn into his eye.

A red sun welled up in Cayetano's eye. They stared at each other: two one-eyed beings face to face.

Cayetano went on wondering: "Can anything bad happen to the child of Fortune?"

It was noon. Lying in its brief shadow, Cayetano held his forefinger and little finger against his chest.

He died bearing this sign of exorcism.

Collodi

I

There are more than two hundred translations of *Pinocchio* spread around the world. This pearl of our literature has been rendered in all spoken languages and many dialects. The most recent version is by Professor Malherbe of the University of Stellenbosch. Though he is the namesake of the famous reformer of French poetry, Professor Malherbe has translated *Pinocchio* into Afrikaans, the language of the Boers. If our Collodi has not achieved glory, then what indeed is glory? Now listen to this.

On Sunday, 10 July, I and my friend Giorgio, head of the Accademia di Belle Arti and owner of a three-speed Balilla auto, left Florence by the Porta a Prato. After driving through Pescia and taking the road to Lucca, we stopped at an intersection. Stalled at the same intersection was a young man sheathed in white like a thief in a public bath, who having raised the hood of a stupendous racing car, was rummaging around in its intestines with a surgeon's hand.

"Could you please tell us the road to Collodi?"

The young man raised his head from that mass of metal guts, and gazed at us with two magnificent velvety eyes.

"Collodi?"

"The village of Collodi, which is also the name of the author of *Pinocchio*."

"Pinocchio?" he repeated, wrinkling his handsome brow. "I don't know, I'm a stranger here myself."

"We should recognize Collodi by its smell," says my friend G.

Friend Giorgio is right. After making a right turn by olfactory inspiration, and shortly finding ourselves amid mangy dogs, plucked hens, and scattered urchins playing in the middle of the road, we recognize Pinocchio's village. Collodi lies slantwise on the ridge of a hill, like a many-colored cloak on a green velvet pouf.

The cloak is an expensive one. The major part of Collodi consists of the "historical park," which in the shape of a reading desk displays its vegetal architecture and the scribbles of its flowerbeds, and when the castellan is in a good mood allows its waters to rush down by a series of stepped terraces.

Will we let ourselves be seduced by these eighteenth-century extravagances?

"No! no!" shrieks a staccato little voice on our left, in which we recognize the tone of the Talking Cricket. We turn to look, and on the façade of a house tinged with the pink of the feeblest dawn we read:

"In this house—there lived for the first years of his childhood—later returning often—drawn by maternal memories—Carlo Lorenzini—well-known journalist—volunteer soldier in his country's battles—urbane and witty writer—renowned in public education—who with the pseudonym of Collodi—made the name of this village famous—the people of Collodi—with the agreement and approval of the town hall of Pescia—P.P.—Born 24 November 1826, died 26 October 1890."

For collectors of literary curiosities, we should add that this plaque was dictated by Rigutini, Collodi's friend and drinking companion.

"What was Rigutini's first name?" I ask. And my friend Giorgio replies, "Fanfani."

Baron Eckermann nourished an admiration for Goethe that went beyond the bounds of decency. Others dote on Giovanni Pascoli; we, modestly, pass directly from a firm friendship with Homer to an equally firm one with the books of Collodi.

On tiptoe, as into the room of a sleeping friend, we enter the house where Carlo Lorenzini "lived for the first years of his childhood." For a long time this house made an effort to keep up its dignity. Such is obvious. Then one day it "gave up." Today spiderwebs festoon its small green door, and a grime-blackened rope serves as a handrail to the steps hollowed out like rowboats.

The Lorenzini house now belongs to the Balbanis. The Balbani family is waiting for us upstairs. From the nurslings to the grandmother they are all dressed up to have their picture taken. In a twinkling, they have also summoned their relatives from all over the village. My friend Giorgio comes along behind me, holding the tripod of his Leica as though selling children's skeletons. The smile of the Balbanis lacks spontaneity. They recognize this themselves: "If you only knew how many times people have come to take a picture of this house!" We gaze tenderly at the console, the portrait of Umberto I, the paper flowers, all the things "he looked at as a boy." From the terrace you can see the slope of the village, the Villa Garzoni set on the hill like a white sideboard to serve a giant, and the paper mills with their closely hanging rows of festoons that tomorrow will be paper, will go out into the world, and wrap thousands of sausages.

We go in the kitchen. It is painted red like Fire-Eater's kitchen. The hearth is in a niche and full of shadow. The flies fly in spirals. In one corner two terracotta basins half set in the wall are ready for the laundry. They are the "curiosity" of the house and the Balbanis show them off with pride. We are thinking: "Inside there Carlino's little shirts and underpants were boiled with ashes and egg shells." From the window you can see a cultivated hill, a balcony with flower boxes, a millstream formed by the waters of the Pescia river and which drives, as one of the Balbanis says—he smokes his cigarette elegantly and hasn't opened his mouth during the whole inspection tour except to offer this bit of industrial information: "It drives a grinding machine over there."

"And this furniture, these objects, were they his?" We

point to the copper pots on the wall, and the table, which looks as though it had escaped a fire.

The man doesn't answer. In his stead the old woman shrieks, "Those are my things! I bought the house myself from Lorenzini's mother. Empty. There's nothing of Carlo Lorenzini's left here."

"Maybe these," remarks one of the younger Balbani women, and so saying opens the doors of a wall closet.

Irony has taken up residence in Pinocchio's house, even though Pinocchio is no longer there.

Since we have been unable to find the wandering spirit of Carlo Lorenzini in the house where he lived as a boy, will it be easier to find it in the park of Collodi?

It costs four lire each to enter. Your four lire entitle you to visit the park, but not the villa, which is out of bounds to the ordinary visitor. But are we ordinary visitors? Once we have stated our qualifications, the custodian, who had been bareheaded, quickly disappears into a kind of vegetal storeroom, and comes out again with his head covered by a visor cap inscribed with gold letters: "Historical Park of Collodi."

If Bouvard and Pécuchet were to come this way, they would find that their ideal had taken on the form of reality.

In this park, as in others scattered throughout Italy, the vegetable kingdom is reduced to the conditions of a poodle clipped to look like a lion. The uniformed speak of "bad taste." How can I put it? Bad taste, intolerable in ordinary folk, becomes majestic insanity among men of higher caliber. Discretion, which passes for an expression of good taste, is in reality the refuge of the weak. You must show off when you can. But few have the right to practice bad taste. One who did was the Marquis Paolo Garzoni, feudal lord, councillor of state and war, who in the middle of the seventeenth century ordered the construction of the Collodi park.

The Collodi Garzonis go back to the fourteenth century. They lived in a house set on high ground, which has been restored several times and still stands to the right of the palace. Around the seventeenth century, upstream from the palace, they built a small villa, all swags and floral cornices, fresh and rosy as strawberry ice cream, with a clock in front that acts as an eye, and a little bell tower on top that acts as a cap. To give the sumptuous garden a proper creator, the name of the Lucca patrician Ottaviano Diodati has been suggested. Among the loops in the middle of the central flower bed, laid out on the ground with pebbles like a children's game, lies the Garzoni coat of arms: *Probus et providus esto*. To right and left masses of boxwood trimmed in the shape of dadoes, cubes, shells, and spheres, present the melancholy appearance of wild beasts trained to silence and immobility. Elevated in front, a row of terracotta figures play peek-a-boo from inside the niches of a thick wall of vegetation.

We go up to a terrace with a balustrade, on which some earthenware monkeys are depicted in the attitudes of soccer players. From here the ramps of the cascades begin and ascend to the "Baths," dominated by a gigantic statue of Fame with a trumpet.

Ever so timidly we enter the Baths. Intimacy and mystery have remained intact in these doll-sized bathhouses. We hesitate to push the doors, lightly graced with ornamental paintings, for fear that behind them the rosy nudity of some tiny lady, lingering there for three centuries but still alive in all its coral details, would shine forth again. Here is the tub for ladies, there the one for gentlemen, and above the wooden partition the common roof.

Who is playing music?

We tilt our heads back on our shoulders, like chickens looking upward: the musicians' loge is full of cavaliers. They are trimmed with gold thread and scrape away on Amati and Gasparo da Salò violins, so as to bathe with music the naked little ladies who gurgle and splash below in the fortunate water.

Who said our glowing faucets, our showers with flexible tubes, were the *nec plus ultra* of hydrotherapeutic civilization? Again we lift our chicken eye to the loge . . . Alas! The evocation of those torture-chamber instruments has extinguished the music and dissolved the gentlemen behind the bare music stands.

We ask the custodian, "Did you know him, did you ever see him?"

"Who?"

"Carlo Lorenzini . . . Collodi . . . the author of *Pinocchio.*"

"Of course! I learned to read and write from his sister, Teresina Lorenzini, who taught school down there in the village."

"But him?"

"Him?. . . well . . . sure . . ."

He never saw him! But the hope of a tip compels custodians of the most beautiful gardens in Italy to lie.

Being an accountant is more than a profession, it is a physiological condition. In the owner of the castle of Collodi, who comes toward us with his hand extended and a smile on his lips, we are stunned to recognize one of the purest examples of the "accountant" type.

After the last Garzoni family inheritance had been dissipated, castle and park became the property about fifteen years ago of a certain Bibi, a wood dealer from Carrara. From Bibi they passed to the engineer Malvezzi, from Malvezzi to Commendatore Dante Giacomini, and from Giacomini to the accountant Signor Angelo Furbi.

Judging by the number of its owners over a span of fifteen years, the suspicion arises that Collodi Castle exercises on its so to speak "illegitimate" castellans an influence similar to that of the famous Cullinan diamond, which did not tolerate masters.

The accountant does the honors of the house, and tells us the effort and expense it has cost him to put the castle and park, left in such a sad state by his predecessor, back in shape.

We pass through the galleries enlivened by bright still lifes in fresco, and through the rooms, this one inhabited by a canopied bed, that one by a timid blond spinet, still another by a suit of armor, its laughing mouth gaping like a money box.

What's this?

We look closer: in one corner of a dressing room, white and solitary as a swan, a bidet! An eighteenth-century bidet!

It has the usual violin shape, but the material is different. This one is of marble, and carved from rim to base from a single block. A bidet fit for a queen, or a goddess.

It remains to be seen what Italian name goes with this very Italian instrument of ablutions. Can we trust the dictionary that gives the word *"bidetto"*?

"A princely abode," exclaims the accountant, cleaving the air with his hand. "But uncomfortable for anyone accustomed to modern living."

"All too true, sir. But what about you?"

"I'm fixing up a small modern apartment for myself."

He opens a door: the workmen's labor is visible, the smell of paint stings the nostrils.

A woman is leaning out the window, her elbows on the sill. The sun, setting beyond the mountains of the Val di Nievole, kindles a halo in her golden hair.

When Moses went up to Sinai to meet the Lord, the latter called to him from afar, "Go in that cave, Moses, and do not look at my face as I go by unless you want to die." For greater caution the Lord placed his hand over the opening of the cave, and did not withdraw it until he had passed. When Moses stuck his head out, he saw the enormous back of Sabaoth, receding amid flashes of lightning.

Was that woman afraid that if she turned around, we standing behind her would be struck down?

The castle and park of Collodi, broad and extensive, separate the upper and lower village. By a centuries-old concession, and in order to shorten their walk, the people of Collodi are allowed to use the ramps and cross the castle grounds under the portico.

We arrive at the open space in front of the entrance. Three little old women, like three silent magpies, are perched on the low stone wall opposite. Are they looking at the fertile valley, with its abundant water and cultivation? Are they catching their breath after the climb? Who knows?

The accountant steps forward.

"I've told you time and again you can go this way but not stop."

"But we . . . for all these years . . ."

"Don't talk to me about years! I said I won't have it!"

And to us, standing behind him and trying to look elsewhere: "You see? It's indecent! It looks like a public market!"

The three old women, black and bent as remorse itself, resume their climb.

"And the cascades? What, you haven't seen the cascades? Quick, Giovanni, the cascades!"

To go down and see the cascades, we skirt the labyrinth of reeds, and pass in front of the theater of greenery with its stage of myrtle and prompter's box of boxwood, where the actors in the spectacle are leafy tubes with arms and legs, who exchange green dialogues.

Giovanni has placed wicker armchairs at the foot of the waterfalls, and we settle ourselves comfortably.

At an ineffable blast from Fame up above, blowing her earthenware trumpet, a silvery light appears at the top, shines, descends into the second basin, extends to the third, the fourth, the fifth, and forms a bubbling liquid stairway that would have fooled Tobias himself. Simultaneously two jets spurt from the center of the side basins, first in two modest bursts as though tossing up a couple of eggs for target practice, then making a great leap and immobilizing themselves at a decorous height.

> *Waters that from narrow enclosed places*
> *In secret prisons underground*
> *Released to the light happily emerge*
> *Celebrating with countless playful effects.*

Thus sang Francesco Sbarra in his *Pompe di Collodi*. But here *pompe* means "pomp", not "pumps."

All of a sudden our aquatic enjoyment is interrupted by a

145

horrible thought. Just like ourselves today, a friend of ours some years ago had come to visit the park of Collodi. When the tour was over, they asked him if he wanted to see the cascades.

"Let's see them."

"And the jets?"

"Let's see the jets too."

"And the water effects?"

"Sure, let's have the water effects."

When it was over, they presented him with a bill for eighty lire worth of water.

The accountant is searching for an image that will illustrate this hydraulic splendor. "One might say . . ."

His youthful and assured voice reminds us just in time that as guests of the most liberal of castellans, such ugly surprises will never befall us.

"One might say so many panes of glass . . ." the accountant says.

We admire in silence.

II

The owls are waking up in the Collodi park. At twilight Giovanni the custodian sidles up to us like an assassin, and whispers in our ear: "I've got him! The engineer Frateschi was more than a friend to Carlo Lorenzini, he was a brother. I've sent for him. Here he comes now." From the end of an alley a heavy shadow advances at a snail's pace. "He's deaf," the custodian warns us.

The custodian hasn't told the whole story: Lorenzini's friend is also blind. He extends a big wrinkled glove—his hand. His eyes, veiled in white, are turned upward searching the sky for God. The skin under his right eye droops over his cheek and forms a black drop at the level of the nostril.

We enter a dark storeroom, the engineer's office. In the yellowish light from the electric bulb it looks like something between an alchemist's foundry and a junkshop. From the shadows on the wall, Margherita of Savoy smiles amid her pearls. Frateschi seats himself like a block of stone at the desk. His turkey-claw fingers delicately extract some pieces of paper from a dusty folder. "We don't care about documents," we shout, "just tell us about him!" Frateschi goes on extracting pieces of paper. The custodian leans over the deaf man's huge ear, cups his hands, and launches a sound track inside: "Tell these gentlemen what you know about Carlo Lorenzini!" Frateschi drops the piece of paper, gives the custodian a frightened look, then turns his melted eyes to the ceiling. The quavering sounds of his voice spread in the silence.

"Lorenzini liked to have a good time, he was a loudmouth. One day he went to listen to some music in the cathedral. The church was full of peasants. One of them steps on his foot. Lorenzini goes and stands next to him, pretending to be looking at something or other, and bam! stamps on the peasant's foot . . ."

Silence.

"Lorenzini went to a dance. A lady was singing. Lorenzini came into the room with his hands over his ears. Lorenzini's brother, who was a serious person, goes up to the lady. 'You must excuse him, signora, my brother is a boor.' "

Silence.

"Every five years they hold a May festival in Pescia. Lorenzini hired the diligence from Florence all for himself and went to the celebration."

Silence.

"One day I go to see him in a little office he kept. 'What are you doing?' 'I'm writing the story of a puppet . . .' "

Silence.

"I'd suggested that all the schoolchildren be asked to contribute two pennies to raise a monument to him here in Collodi. They told me it was forbidden to take up collections in the schools . . ."

One of us shouts at the top of his lungs: "Don't go on! You haven't even had Lorenzini born yet! Tell us about his birth!"

Frateschi shakes himself like someone waking up with a start. He makes a gesture as though driving away a ghost. After a final silence, he begins speaking again.

The Marquis Ginori and the Marquis Garzoni were great friends. Between Doccia, the Ginori residence, and Collodi, the Garzoni residence, the two marquises and their families repeated that quadrille figure that consists in separating into two groups, with one group moving toward the other, crossing, and beginning the same maneuver again in the opposite direction.

The Marquis Garzoni had a cook named Domenico Lorenzini, and the Marquis Ginori a chamberlain named Orzali, who in turn had a daughter named Angiolina. One day Domenico met Angiolina in the Collodi park, and the cook caught fire like an *omelette au rhum*.

Domenico did not, as the song goes, put Angiolina in the kitchen, but he made her his own in the eyes of God and man, after which they initiated that fruitful collaboration that produced in all twelve children, both boys and girls. Of eleven of them there is no need to speak, they were people who passed by without leaving a trace, but the eldest deserves to be remembered. He was Carlo Lorenzini, known as Collodi, who though he left no children born of his flesh, left one born of his spirit: the immortal Pinocchio.

It was not Domenico Lorenzini who acted as father to little Carlo, but the two marquises Ginori and Garzoni. They saw to it that the boy was sent to the seminary in Colle Val d'Elsa.

After three years in the seminary, Carlino returns to Florence, throws away his cowl, and gives himself over body and soul to strenuous tamburello matches in Piazza Indipendenza; in the evening he meets obliging young ladies under the portals of Via Taddei. The rebel of tomorrow was blossoming in him, as well as the Don Juan who, on the divans of the prefecture of Florence, was to make so many illustrious female representatives of the dramatic art experience the pangs and delights of love.

Since Carlino showed no interest whatsoever in theology, the two marquises sent him to the *Scolopi*,* with whom he continued to study rhetoric and philosophy. At eighteen he became a clerk in the Ajazzi bookstore, where he met the leading literary lights: D'Alberti, Ferdinando Martini, Jouaud who signed himself "Giotti." A Hellenist priest named Zipoli, with whom he lodged for a few years, supplied his mind with knowledge. But how could he listen to aorists when his country was calling? Carlo Lorenzini answers the call of the Tuscan student body, enlists in the Leonida Giovanetti Legion, and fights like a lion at Montanara.

Returning from that unfortunate but glorious campaign, Carlo Lorenzini entered the prefecture as a theatrical censor. "The environment creates the type," according to a Darwinian theory, corroborated today by prominent biologists. Lorenzini, who had never dreamed of writing plays, writes three of them in a row in the theater censorship office: *L'onore del marito*, *La coscienza dell'impiego*, and *Gli amici di casa*. Despite the enormous success that greeted them when presented on the stage, they later disappeared without leaving a trace.

As for his duties as a censor, Lorenzini performed them less on the scripts entrusted to his scrutiny than on the forms of the actresses destined to interpret them. And in his office in the Palazzo Martelli, on the oilcloth-covered divan whose vegetable-hair stuffing emerged from wide cracks, there was no beauty spot, flaw, or characteristic mark on those dramatic rotundities that, in the presence of filed reports and lists of taboo subjects, escaped the watchful eye of Lorenzini the censor.

Having fallen in love with literature, Lorenzini began contributing to *L'Opinione*, *Il Nazionale*, and *Il Fanfulla*. He was able to retire from the prefecture and found his own newspaper, *Il Lampione*, republican and Mazzinian. He suspends

---

* Teachers in the Scuole Pie, secondary schools founded in Rome in the early seventeeth century by the Spanish priest Saint José Calasanzio, for the education of the poor. (Tr.)

publication of *Il Lampione* to enlist in the Novara Cavalry, and eleven years later, in 1860, having resumed *Il Lampione*, he begins his editorial as follows: "Taking up again the thread of discourse interrupted by the cries and laments of Reaction . . ." He founded *Scaramuccia*, a theatrical journal. An excellent cook and true son of his father, he gave Lucullian dinners in his home, drank with his friends, and particularly with another famous wine bibber, Giuseppe Rigutini. The latter, along with the bookseller Paggi, urges Collodi, who believed himself cut out for journalistic polemics, to write for children. Not all friends are false.

At this point one of us asks: "And that story they tell about *Pinocchio* being written in one night to pay off a gambling debt?"

"Nonsense!" replies the cavernous voice of Frateschi. "Lorenzini started bringing out *Pinocchio* in installments in *Il Giornale dei Bambini,* which was published by Perino and edited by Ferdinando Martini."

Lorenzini was an excellent musician, and his ability to sight-read was nothing short of marvelous. No one knows where or when he learned music, but the fact is that he knew it in all its nuances and modulations.

In the small flat where Lorenzini combined the fraternal rites of Venus and Bacchus, a small black piano placed sideways was enough to fill one corner of the drawing room. The top, on which the leaves rained down from a barren asparagus plant, was crowded with photographs of primadonnas with boat-shaped hairdos, ballooning bosoms, and with the dedication written diagonally. There, as he awaits the mistress who will shortly arrive in a rustle of skirts and smelling of the wind, and like an octopus entwine her arms around his high starched collar, Pinocchio's father, his eyes rolled upward, his moustache sprayed with saliva that gushes forth with his song, abandons himself to long arpeggio improvisations that fall back on the ottomans that crouch on the carpet to smoke the narghile and on the armchairs gathered around the small table like ladies assembled for a game of quadrille. How could such a fine connoisseur fail to attend the opening of *Cavalleria rusticana* in Leghorn?

After the triumphant end of the performance, the sky opened its cataracts and Lorenzini returned to Florence amid thunder and lightning. His friends were waiting for him at the station; they hurried him into Doney's.

"Is it really the great masterpiece they say it is in Rome?"

"The stuff is there," Lorenzini replies, "but he's crazy."

"Crazy?"

"Just imagine, the tenor sings his aria in front of the curtain!"

Before '59, Lorenzini dressed like the members of Giovine Italia:* wide upturned collar, vest half-unbuttoned, French-style trousers, wide at the hips and with straps under the instep of the foot. Later he modeled his style of dress on that of the manager of the equestrian circus in which Pinocchio, changed into a donkey, was put to "work." His suits, always brown, varied only in the pattern, from broad stripes to checks.

Lorenzini spent his afternoons sitting outside the Caffé Falchetto, opposite the present Bottegone, in the "workers' corner," so called because it was where the most notorious idlers in Florence gathered. There, in the company of Pier Coccoluto Ferrigni, known as Yorick, and other carefree souls, Carlo Lorenzini sipped his absinthe and made cutting remarks about the passersby, in imitation of those cynics of ancient Athens who were called "'salts" because of their pungent comments.

In winter he wore a felt bowler, in summer one of straw. He wore it either tilted sideways, or falling over his eyes, or pushed back on his head. He had invented a kind of bowler language. The bowler was a fifth limb on his person. Not even in bed did he take it off.

Lorenzini did not go to sleep until he had first received his mother's blessing. She, for her part, did not go to sleep until

---

* Mazzini's revolutionary organization. (Tr.)

she heard her Carlino come home. But why did Carlino come home so late?

Carlino was a drinker and gambler. Card games went on until late at night at the Casino Borghese in Via Ghibellina. The church bells would be chiming three when lying anxiously in her canopied bed, her ears cocked, Angiolina Orzali Lorenzini would hear the front door creak.

"Carlino?"

"Yes, mamma!"

His legs wobbling like an accordion and his bowler askew, Carlo Lorenzini makes his way through the rooms and goes to kneel at his mother's bedside.

"Bless you, my son!"

"Urrp! . . . urrp! . . ."

The Chianti fumes form a clog in Carlino's throat, and dissolve in small explosions.

The maternal blessing was not the only obligation that Lorenzini took on himself before going to bed. A candle in his left hand and in his right the pistol he had kept from his time in the Novara cavalry, the fiery pamphleteer would make the rounds of all the rooms, look under beds and sofas, open wardrobes and the kitchen cupboard, and only when he had assured himself that no ill-intentioned person was hiding in the house did he deposit the cavalry pistol on the night table next to the flask of wine, and his cheek on his arm, like an Endymion who has sprouted moustaches, gave himself up to dreams.

When his mother died, Carlo began drinking more heavily.

November 1890 was unusually cold in Florence. Carlo Lorenzini was living at 7 Via Rondinelli, along with Paolo, his "serious" brother. Paolo's family was again in the country, but that day he had come to the city to get some blankets and woolen clothing.

In the middle of the night Paolo Lorenzini is awakened suddenly by the frantic ringing of the doorbell. He goes to the window, and in the wind that whistles through the narrow gorge of the street, he twice hears a cry: "I'm dying! . . . I'm dying! . . ."

They found Carlo Lorenzini leaning against the door jamb, "with his head turned to one side, one arm dangling, his legs crossed and knees buckled, so that it seemed a miracle that he was standing upright," and his stiffening hand on the bell, which went on ringing up there in the empty house. They carried him upstairs, lifeless as a big wooden puppet.

But this was a fiction for the family, his friends, and other people. The real Lorenzini, the one who signed his name "Collodi" and had written *Pinocchio*, which connoisseurs have called "the Bible of the heart," had meanwhile arrived at the end of Via Rondinelli, turned right into Via Cerretani, and begun his walk into immortality.

Nostradamus

I

The fields of Provence were in bloom. By focusing one's gaze and diverting one's mind from the present, it was not hard to glimpse Petrarch, dressed in his long red robe, his brow crowned with Capitoline laurel, half sighing for Laura, half stooping over the golden vestiges of Roman civilization, in an effort to decipher the words of the ancients.

We were coming from Paris and on our way to Avignon. A harmless mistral pursued the white clouds, which like fleeing nymphs tore their clothes on the sharp peaks of the Alpilles.

Honking, we entered Saint-Rémy, which lies at the bottom of the valley of Glanum, watched over by a triumphal arch and a high mausoleum. This little town can boast that Frédéric Mistral, the Félibrean poet, lived a short distance from its walls, and in one of its houses Charles Gounod, who had a head like an Easter egg and wrote a sugary melody on the prelude in C major of the *Well-Tempered Clavier*, gave the first hearing of *Mireille*. But what is the more illustrious, above all more "secret" name connected with the history of these walls, these stones, these gardens?

René Trintzius, the occult master who in our trip across France had given wings to the automobile, making me suspect that he too, in imitation of the enchanter Malagigi, commanded the spirits of the air, braked the steel beast in the Place lou Planet, and raising his gloved hand from the wheel, pointed out a large house whose face bore the wrinkles of the centuries, and on the architrave of the entrance this inscription: *Soli Deo.*

154

"Solideo," I said, "is what we in Italy call that little cap that the priest takes off only before God."

Trintzius looked at me quizzically, and in his turn said, "Nostradamus was born in that house."

After this statement, there was nothing to do but stand up and salute.

Italy, which gave Mazarin, Cardinal de Retz, and even, according to some, Louis XIV to France, as a bonus gave it Doctor Ourlady, who as a manufacturer of preserves preceded the firm of Cirio, as an artist of cosmetics preceded Elizabeth Arden, and in addition to that was able to read the future the way you, reader, are reading these lines.

The ancestors of Michel Nostradamus had journeyed from Italy to France, because people in their migrations follow the route of the sun so as not to lose its light. Provence, for its part, had the reputation of being hospitable soil for the children of Israel, and this may have been the real reason for the move.

The Jews are wanderers, and as Apollinaire said, *ils s'agitent agréablement.*

It is the earth with its fruits that halts man's anxious steps and tells him, "Here you will have your house, your homeland, your nation." But Ceres is the enemy of Israel. On the other hand, is it not significant that canned food has led to an increasing nomadism among North Americans? Two threats hang over Roosevelt's compatriots: one of being dyed the color of the children of Ham, and the other of being judaized.

The Jews are shepherds but not peasants. Celsus calls them variously "the homeless," or "those who live in carts," or "those who sleep in tents to feed their flocks." Is it their lack of rural ways that has made them disliked? Rural life is elementary and innocent. It is the exemplary life. It is the life that we all ought to lead. Why did we become separated from it? Anti-Semitism is not a result of Christianity as many believe, but is independent of it and much older. We distrust anyone who lives differently from ourselves. That person does something I don't do, he knows something I don't know; this means he is judging me. The Jews, in fact,

155

represent the *alien presence*, and in the Middle Ages they were called "the witnesses." While the peasants toiled with the plow, and the knights, melancholy and dull, set off loaded with iron toward combat and death, they, the "homeless," occupied the cities, practiced trade, surrounded themselves with the odor of spices, accumulated gold, and above all *penetrated the mysteries*. Anti-Semitism is basically the old incurable quarrel between the physical and the metaphysical. But René d'Anjou was not afraid of metaphysics. In his realm the Jews had the right to practice medicine, the arts, and even tax collection, and as for persecution, it was limited to extracting from these metaphysicians the largest possible quantity of gold sequins. One might add in passing that when one says medicine, one means at the same time Cabala and magic. The Jews rushed into Provence as to the abode of their happiness, and the banks of the Durance swarmed with Solomons and Rebeccas, in whose eyes the fever of hatred and terror gradually died, whose skin changed from yellow to rosy, and whose bones under their variegated caftans once again became visibly covered with flesh.

Out of the multitude of the circumcised emerged Jean de Saint-Rémy, astrologer, physician, and adviser to the king, who lived for many years at René's court and enjoyed the friendship and esteem of that good prince.

In homage to his royal protector, the astrologer named his favorite daughter Renée, and she, upon arriving at marriage-able age, took as her husband a notary named Jacques or Jaume, whose surname, because he lived in the quarter of Our Lady, was de Nostredame, which he later latinized as *Nostradamus*, in accordance with the custom of the time.

The product of the Talmudically legal loves of Maître Jacques and Renée, born at high noon on Thursday, 14 December 1503, was Michel de Nostradamus, who lived in the sixteenth century and saw everything worth seeing in his century, and furthermore saw everything worth seeing in ours, and not only that but saw what our children will see in the year 2000.

Michel was not circumcised but baptized.

With the death of René the Good, Provence passed by testament to the French crown, which at that time encircled the head of Louis XII. This king, who nourished sentiments much less liberal toward the children of Israel, required them by the edict of 26 September 1501 either to be baptized or leave Provence at once. Loud lamentations went up along those same banks of the Durance that shortly before had buzzed with joyful whispers, the fever was rekindled in the eyes, the rosy skin returned to yellow, the flesh shriveled on the bones. The old people as a sign of mourning torn their clothing sideways, and the diaspora began again.

Or rather the diaspora began again for those who did not own land. And when the columns of the afflicted had departed, clothed in rags and followed by starving dogs, some toward Spain, others toward the lands of the East, the well-to-do lined up in front of the baptismal fonts and one by one immersed themselves, after which by virtue of their newly acquired rights they purchased estates, castles, and titles of nobility, and founded the La Tour, Puy-Michel, Cadenat, and Arlatan-Lauris dynasties, which today constitute the cream of Provençal society.

Among those rushing to the baptisteries was Jacques de Nostredame, even though he descended in a direct line from the illustrious tribe of Issachar, of whom the First Book of Chronicles says: "And of the children of Issachar, which were men that had understanding of the times, to know what Israel ought to do; the heads of them were two hundred; and all their brethren were at their commandment."

"To have understanding of the times" in plain language means to have the gift of prophecy. Michel had descended "through the branches."*

Although Ramazzini in the early eighteenth century had provided an idea of psychology as applied to profession, and Campanella alludes to it in *La Città del Sole,* psychological

---

* *"Rade volte risurge per li rami/l'umana probitate . . ."* (Rarely does human integrity rise through the branches . . .). Dante, *Purgatorio,* VII, 121–22. (Tr.)

technique is an art still in its infancy and its first cries echo on the threshold of our own century. In the sixteenth century the search for individuality was a problem about which no one felt much urgency, and since the principle of heredity was not limited to royal families alone but extended to all families, the result was the formation of long generations of painters, herbalists, and butchers.

In the Nostredame family, medicine was traditional. Jacque's father, Pierre de Nostredame, had been a doctor in Arles. He treated his patients with remedies of his own composition, whereupon the cheated druggists denounced him as a falsifier to the city authorities. Stripped of his medical position, Pierre de Nostredame first entered the service of the Duke of Calabria, then that of King René, who employed him as his principal physician. The king enjoyed secluding himself at night with the old sage, and listening to his talk of celestial matters under the far-flung firmament. So as not to break the tradition, it was decided that Michel would study.

II

On a sun-drenched noon, Michel de Nostredame made his entrance into the Land of Boobies. He wore a flowered doublet, and two enormous black pupils were rotating in his awestruck eyes.

To identify Avignon with the extraordinary place where Candlewick and Pinocchio were turned into donkeys is less arbitrary than it seems. A century and a half earlier, Gregory XI had placed the triple crown on his head and moved the Holy See from the banks of the Rhone back to the banks of the Tiber. A wind of madness was blowing on Avignon, where, attracted by the liberality of the papal legate, all the malefactors and paupers of France, assassins, brigands, receivers of stolen goods, pickpockets, and highwaymen found a prompt and festive welcome. Speaking of identification, we might add that Michel himself was a faithful prefiguration of Pinocchio, because young men, when they are truly absorbed in their studies, have the seriousness and stiff walk of puppets.

The city was excited and noisy. A dense chiming of bells rose from the towers like smoke, and men and women below, in order to communicate the simplest thoughts, had to shout themselves hoarse as in the middle of a storm.

People knelt in the fetid alleyways as the penitents went by. The black throng was luminously interspersed, like doves amid crows, by the "palace waiting maids," who according to the testimony of Garganello, "give the sweetest kisses in the world."

Nostradamus went by and did not see. He did not see the Avignon beauties who in Pantagruel's words *"jouent volontiers du serrecroupière";* he did not see the papal soldiers who sported variegated tunics, nor the officiants on mules tinkling with bells, nor the prelates being carried past like fragile treasures suspended in litters that dripped with golden tassels. Nor did he even see the miracles of which this city of bells and madness is full. He did not see Saint Agricola at the crossing of two streets, dressed as a statue but free in his movements, summoning the storks from Alsace with one hand and with the other dispatching them to Africa. He did not see the miraculous Virgin in the Rue des Fourbisseurs, her cheek still tinged with blood from the slap she had received two years before from a disappointed gambler. He did not hear the howling that arose from the sewer in Rue Bonneterie of the servant woman transformed into a bitch because one day she had thrown the bread of the poor to the dogs. He did not see the stone rooster in Rue Saint-Didier, erect on its spurs and its wattles quivering, ready to announce the end of the world with its fatal cock-a-doodle-doo.

He saw nothing, either then or later, this young metaphysician who only had eyes for the "secrets of life." His companions divided the day between the study of the liberal arts, namely grammar, rhetoric, and philosophy, and certain still more liberal studies that were conducted in the "Street of the Recumbent Magdalen."

In this street, so aptly named, Michel de Nostradamus never set foot. If they asked him why, he answered that he preferred to rest his eyes on *some beautiful natural phenomenon* . . . As though woman were not a beautiful natural phenomenon!

Like all predestined souls, Nostradamus was a misogynist and chaste. His memory was so prodigious—*memoria pene divina proeditus erat*—that he has no equal except in Arturo Toscanini, who one day in our presence took a page ruled with thirty-two musical staffs and dotted with little black notes like a piece of flypaper, placed it horizontally in front of his nose, "swept" it with a casual glance, and in a twinkling committed it to memory.

At dusk, when his companions, filled with contrition, emerged from the Street of the Recumbent Magdalen, Nostradamus lined them up in twos and took them outside the walls, under the astrological and vertiginous sky.

The crepuscular light was traversed by those fires that philosophers call "wandering stars," and which Nostradamus's companions thought were stars detached from the sky. Nostradamus undeceived them, and taught them that such fires are sulphurous exhalations ignited by the wind the same way it ignites charcoal.

He also taught that the clouds do not derive from the sea, but are composed of the vapors that can be seen to rise from the earth when the atmosphere is foggy. He taught that the earth is round and that the sun at the horizon is illuminating the other hemisphere. He taught the movements of the planets and the annual rotations of the earth around the sun. He talked so agreeably about meteors and stars that his companions dubbed him the "young astrologer."

How far would Nostradamus's science have gone? It's easy to guess: it would have caught up with Galileo, Kepler, Newton, Schiaparelli, and Einstein, and passed them all by had not his notary of a father, thinking that the discovery of celestial truths often puts man at the risk of being turned into a beefsteak, stopped him, so to speak, at the edge of the grill.

And from that day on, whenever anyone asked him what the earth was or what the sun, Nostradamus replied that the earth was a flat surface enlivened by gentle little hills and little green trees, and the sun a fiery disk revolving around it by the will of God.

For greater prudence, Nostradamus went to study medicine in Montpellier.

There the young astrologer happened on another Land of Boobies. Having crossed the threshold of the School, the neophyte or *"bec jaune"* was taken in hand by an older student, and initiated into the mysteries of the "city of schoolboys."

Aspiring doctors in Montpellier enjoyed privileges and impunity. They contracted debts but not the obligation to pay them; they had the right to have noisy neighbors evicted, such as blacksmiths, carpenters, and others who distracted them from their studies; they were exempt from taxes, and there was no crime for which they had to appear before ordinary judges. And yet in that city the judges could seize you as a foreigner and hurl you into the darkest and dampest cell if any citizen lodged a complaint that you had damaged his interests. Who dares deny the majesty of Science?

A bell rang the hour of the lecture, and the two students, supplied with quill pen and writing board, started off toward the hall. At that moment a tumult broke out in the passageway, and a strident old man's voice shouted: "Give me back my corpse! Give me back my corpse!"

Nostradamus ducked just in time. A greenish hand dripping blood described a sinister arc, struck the wall where its imprint remained like the sign of a curse, and fell on the floor with a horrible "plop."

Two old men, both in red robes and black caps with crimson tassles, came out of a doorway shoving each other, and lugging, one by the arms, the other by the feet, a headless corpse in a state of advanced putrefaction, while a third old man, he too in doctoral costume and holding a scalpel, amid his own sharp cries and those of his colleagues, was dissecting the dead man.

With all the pushing and pulling, the sinister cortege went on its way, surrounded by a clamoring swarm of students and scattering blood and pieces of cadaver behind it. A dull light came through the window panes and swept the black traces of dreams from the walls. And since classes began at daybreak, the cries of the old corpse-killers were joined by those of roosters announcing the sunrise.

"What's happening?" asked Nostradamus, with a rasp in his throat.

"Our School," replied the other student with obvious satisfaction, "is more advanced than the others and has practiced dissection since 1376, when the Duke of Anjou gave us permission to request the body of an executed criminal every year. But what good is only one corpse a year? That's why this annual dead body is awaited so impatiently and once it gets here is fought over like pirates over a treasure."

"What about the lecture?"

"Since the dead man is reduced to mincemeat before he can reveal his secret, the lecture gets postponed from one year to the next."

In the evening the older students took the *bec jaune* for a tour of the city. There was no sound except for shutters being closed, doors bolted. At the students' approach, the burghers locked themselves in their houses, as though the lansquenets were coming.

"You who have *pulchras uxores*," shouted Nostradamus's mentor, "open in the name of Science! A new scholar has arrived!"

The chaste Nostradamus would have liked to sink into the ground, and the night hid his blushes. In the sepulchral silence, from the top dormer window of a tall house, a voice replied:

"Go away, you frothing swine, impudent bull calves who infect the air with your billy-goat stink!"

"Don't be fooled," admonished the other student. "These burghers may be timorous and mild in appearance, but all of a sudden they turn out to be wild beasts, like the day they attacked the Duke of Anjou's commissaries, tore them to pieces, and made a meal of their baptized flesh."

"And you," he presently asked the new student, "are you baptized?"

"In the name of the Father, the Son, and the Holy Ghost," murmured the son of Jacques de Nostredame, bowing his head and with his hand embroidering crosses on his chest.

The moon shone over the blind and barricaded city, and the students went away holding onto each other in a human chain, skating over the filth that formed a slippery skating rink on the ground.

After three years of study and concentration, Nostradamus was subjected, like the worst of criminals, to the strictest and most subtle questioning in the chapel of Saint-Michel in the church of Nôtre-Dame-des-Tables.

This was the required technique of examinations.

In the end they put the square cap with the crimson tassle on his head, the gold ring on his finger, tied the sash around his waist, solemnly handed him the book of Hippocrates, made him sit on the dais, kissed him, blessed him, and shouted at him in unison: *"Vade et occide Caim!"*

No one has ever understood what this formula was supposed to mean, but it was necessary if one was to go from being a student to being a "doctor."

III

Nostradamus rode away on muleback and by short stages, botanizing and classifying simples.

The cicada sings all summer long in the olive trees of Provence. In addition to its leafy garnish, the tree has an auditory garnish all its own. Then in the autumn the tree falls silent. The cicada leaves its transparent carcass on the trunk, like a raincoat that it will find again the following summer, and its melodious soul exiles itself to the paradise of the troubadours, where between Raimbaut d'Aurenga and Bernart de Ventadorn it goes on singing *"qui plor e va cantán."*

163

Like his friend Rabelais, Nostradamus stopped to converse with spice dealers about the best way to prepare jellies and jams. Each person has his own overriding thoughts. Those of the "daytime" Nostradamus revolved around medicines and marmalades. To Nostradamus jam making was a science, and in Avignon in 1526 he prepared a quince jelly of such "sovereign exquisiteness and excellence" that a gift of it was made to Monseigneur the Grand Master of Rhodes. Nostradamus solemnly ascended the steps of the papal palace to offer a taste of jelly to the cardinal legate of Clermont. François I, who tasted it later, also found it excellent.

From Avignon Nostradamus went on to visit the cities of the Garonne.

For Saint Jerome, Toulouse was the "Rome of the Garonne" and its city magistrates proudly called themselves "barons of the Capitol." For three centuries the Inquisition had reigned there supreme, and according to Michael Servetus not even Saragossa hummed with so many masses, thundered with so many bells, or shone with so many altars.

For his part, Sidonius Apollinaris called Toulouse "the city of Athena," and who knows?—if the wisest of goddesses had not been deposed, that iron cage, in which blasphemers were locked and submerged in the river until they drowned, would not now be hanging under the arch of the Pont Saint-Michel.

In Bordeaux the wandering herbalist found no business going on, except for stevedores playing cards on the river banks. The university was slumbering and the ratio of professors and students was two to one. There was no lack of good spice dealers, who might have furnished Nostradamus with new recipes for jam, but the garbage lay in such mountains in the streets that it obstructed the doors of the shops. The clamor of fishwives filled the city, and to quiet the women selling tripe in the Rue Malbec, the police magistrate would take them by the feet and plunge them three times in the waters of the Garonne.

Two men coexisted in Nostradamus: the daytime one and the nocturnal one. On the nocturnal one weighed grave suspicions of witchcraft and of commerce with the spirits; the daytime one was an upright citizen, who when he was not kneeling in church or standing at the bedside of his patients, was intent on the fruits that the peasants brought him from the countryside, scrutinizing them with a knowing eye, feeling them with hands accustomed to squeezing tumors and drumming on stomachs, sniffing them, putting them to his ear to listen to their water content, and measuring their weight on scales.

The skin of woman, that silken covering of the female body, that envelope joyous to the eye and sweet to the touch, is the constant preoccupation of the "daytime" Nostradamus. It is with him that those "beauty products" originate that will later achieve such a glorious development and so high a destiny: creams, lotions, unguents. The iridescent spectrum of makeup arises out of his hands, like a rainbow caught and placed at the service of cosmetics. His skull is the cradle of the beauty parlor. What would Elizabeth Arden, Helen Rubinstein, even the great Antoine, be without the teachings of Michel Nostradamus?

I ask my female reader to incline her head with mine over the venerable *Traicté des fardemens;* let us read in two voices, like a duet, the magician's words:

"Every woman, often even as a girl, declines every year by five per cent, like the cassia fistula, for whatever time she may have. She naturally desires, if she cannot increase her beauty, at least to preserve it, starting when she is eighteen to twenty years old. This she will undoubtedly do until the age of sixty, if she makes due and proper use of the sublimate compound herein contained and placed at the beginning of the first chapter. For if the said sublimate is prepared just as is written, the face will undoubtedly be preserved in beauty for a long time and make Hecuba become Helen."

What medal does not have its reverse? Fooled by the extraordinary transformative virtues of the "sublimate," one could cite cases of men who thought they had met Helen and instead found themselves with Hecuba in their arms.

To preserve the secret of the precious *fard,* the ladies of

Spain and Italy did not transmit it to their daughters in writing, but by word of mouth.

Rome, otherwise known as Amor and Flora, had a fourth name as well, the most mysterious of all, and the secret of this name was so well guarded that now no one can remember it. The same thing happened with Nostradamus's "sublimate."

We know, however, that the principal feature of this *fard* consisted in carefully dissolving six ounces of sublimate by mixing it with the saliva of a person who had gone three days without eating garlic or onions.

The custom of mixing cosmetics with saliva, and particularly the saliva of a fasting woman, is very ancient and prescribed by Pliny himself in the thirty-eighth chapter of his book. In order to perfume rouge, a slave woman known as the *cosmeta* would chew aromatic pastilles, and before spitting breathe on a metallic mirror that would then be handed to the mistress so that she could determine whether the saliva was healthy and perfumed to her taste.

An American traveler some years ago made an expedition to the Amazon region, to study the life of vampire bats and discover the secret of the "headhunters," the method they used to reduce the head of a slain enemy to the size of a fist. Before venturing into the monstrous jungle, the traveler stopped in Quito, the capital of Ecuador, where at the close of a meal consumed in the best local hotel, he was offered a liqueur made from a fruit similar to bitter cherries, which the old Indian women masticated with their toothless gums to extract its essence.

The traveler refused this overly human liqueur, but a few days later, as a guest on a plantation a few kilometers from Quito, he was offered the same liqueur by his host, who, with keen solicitude, informed him that the fruit had been personally chewed *por su señora*.

"What an honor!" murmured the unfortunate explorer, and he had no choice but to drain the glass to the dregs, under the gaze of the old *señora* of obvious Indian origin, and who from under eyebrows resembling cockroaches was staring at him with two jets of acetylene flame.

166

In another chapter of the Treatise, Nostradamus gives recipes for various jams, including one made from pumpkin pulp, a very tasty and cooling concoction, and tells how to prepare nuts, oranges, candied lettuce, and bitter cherries, which "when eaten by a sick person, seem to him like a balm or *restaurant*."

In Nostradamus's time, *restaurant* did not mean a place to eat, but merely indicated an especially "restorative" broth that was given to convalescents and women in childbirth. In 1765, a certain Boulanger opened an inn with the name "Restaurant," and with this alluring inscription: *"Venite ad me omnes qui stomacho laboratis, et ego restaurabo vos."* The word prospered.

Nostradamus did not forget love. A certain oil in chapter XVII makes the sterile woman fruitful, and "gives matchless vigor to the old and impotent man." In chapter XVIII, Nostradamus shows the "true way to prepare the *poculum amatorium ad evenerem* used by the ancients," and follows the recipe with this dire warning: "Whoever takes the specific in his mouth and does not at once clasp the object of his ardor in his arms, will die in frenzy amid horrible contortions."

It was in Montpellier.

One day the sky darkened to the east, and a horrible monster appeared on the horizon. It was a giant black skeleton, on whose shoulders beat two huge creaking bat wings, and who carried in its right hand a torch that gave off rings of yellow smoke. Its hooved feet trampled the air, in which the monster swam rather than walked, and a sinewy kangaroo tail hung down behind it and swept the earth like an enormous snake.

A sentry on the watchtower cried, "The Plague!"

Immediately the cannoneers hoisted the heaviest bombards in their arsenal onto the bastions, and opened hellish fire on the monster, which kept advancing with long strides and paid as little attention to the bombardment as though it were a discharge of fresh peas.

The astrologers for their part rushed to their paper cannons.

Alas! Conditions in the sky did not hold out much hope: strange haloes encircled the sun, globes of fire revolved in the clouds, and comets, their tails turned eastward, trailed behind them an abundance of rays resembling flaming swords.

It was the plague: what Galen calls a "wild beast," and whose origin Guy de Chauliac, physician to Clement VI, discovered in the conjunction of Saturn with Jupiter and Mars.

In the Middle Ages and the Renaissance, Europe was devastated by the plague. The sixth-century epidemic piled up so many corpses that, as Gregory of Tours writes, it was impossible to determine their number. Between the year 1000 and 1400 the "wild beast" launched thirty-two assaults on Europe, including the famous Black Death, which lasted for sixteen years, from 1334 to 1350, and destroyed 25 million Europeans out of the 105 million that at that time constituted the population of our continent.

In the next centuries the scourge continues to rage, but never again reaches that frightful record. Little by little it abandons Europe, diminishes in Asia, and does not go beyond the Middle East. Europe today is free of plague.

For what particular reason?

The plague is a pathological drama involving rats, fleas, and man. Transmission between humans is very rare, less so in the forms of pneumonia and septicemia. The rat, on the other hand, cannot be blamed for the great epidemics of antiquity and the early Middle Ages, if this rodent did not arrive in Europe until the aftermath of the Crusades. The microbe, for its part, has lost none of its virulence. And so?

Given such doubts, we too, like our ancestors, believe in a "genius of the plague," which capriciously approaches and kills or else withdraws and allows life to go on.

IV

With the announcement of the plague, churches were suddenly filled. Part of the population went to Arles, to prostrate itself before a tibia of Saint Roch. Many prayers were directed to Saint Carlo Borromeo, who on the occasion of the plague in Milan had proved to be an effective protector.* The most judicious advised doing what had been done in 1397, when by order of the consuls a line of church candles was fashioned long enough to surround the whole city, bastions and all.

The imminent danger did not make people forget administrative matters. Notaries, not knowing which way to look, gathered in the middle of the street with their tablets and drew up hasty testaments, while candidates for the black death shouted their last wishes from the windows and balconies.

Students closed their books and took off without paying the rent. This form of departure is called *à la cloche de bois*, and the students practiced it whenever the occasion arose.

Variations on departure "by the wooden bell" have come down to our own day. In 1897, on the fields of Thessaly, the Greek army commanded by the diadochos Constantine clashed with a Turkish army commanded by Etem Pasha, and got the worst of it. For many years in the cafés of Athens, which especially in summer are extremely crowded, all someone had to do was to shout "Etem is coming!" for everybody to sneak away as one man, without paying for his drinks.

The few inhabitants left in Montpellier crossed the streets in a great hurry, greeting the sky with the Communist salute and wearying their jaws by chewing cloves of garlic.

The plague is not of a sedentary temperament. It follows the course of rivers and moves from city to city.

Faithful as a lover, Nostradamus followed in the footsteps of the being that inspires universal terror and repugnance, but which for him was a divinity to be worshipped.

What magic surrounds this man?

---

* Cardinal Borromeo (1538–1584), thirty-five years younger than Nostradamus, distinguished himself during the 1576 plague in Milan, i.e., ten years after Nostradamus's death and when the cardinal himself had obviously not yet arrived at sainthood. (Tr.)

* * *

The plague is fantastic and bizarre. It takes some cities by the throat, shakes them like salad baskets, and makes them scream like pigs in the slaughterhouse; others it empties, extinguishes, and silences; in others, along with death, it spreads a strange erotic frenzy.

One of these was Marseilles. The ancient city of the Phocaeans was in the grip of love and death. Howls of agony and howls of pleasure rose from its hovels, spread outward through the leaden countryside, and were carried by the wind over the venerable sea. To arrive at the pallets of his patients, Nostradamus had to climb over bodies entwined like serpents in winter hibernation.

Their mouths full of garlic, their nostrils stopped with sponges, and their eyes protected by thick lenses, the doctors wore the "diving suit of the plague," airproof overalls of Moroccan leather, and next to their skins they wore a shirt soaked with juices, oils, and seven different powders.

Like divers circulating among undersea horrors, the "health divers" circulated in the hospitals, among the beds that collapsed under the weight of the sick. Into each bed, made for two persons, six had been jammed side by side, three with their heads one way and three the other, with no distinction of age or sex.

Only Nostradamus went about without a diving suit, without garlic in his mouth, sponges in his nose, or lens to cover his eyes. What occult means did this man have at his disposal that made it possible for him to confront the scourge with impunity? Of what remedies was he the author, remedies that in his passage spread the miracle of health?

"Take an ounce of cypress wood sawdust," he writes in his *Excellent et moult utile Opuscule à touts necessaire qui desirent auoir cognoissance de plusieurs exquises Receptes,* "six ounces of Provence iris, three of gillyflower, three grams of sweet flag, six of aloeswood. Take three or four hundred red roses well trimmed and fresh and cut before the dew, and having crushed them, put them in the powder. When everything is well mixed, make many pellets and put them to dry in the shade. Aside from the goodness and perfume that this composition gives to things, if you put it in your mouth it will smell sweet for the whole day; whether the mouth is stinking from decayed teeth or from bad odors arising from the stomach, or if anyone has a fetid ulcer on his body or some other strange condition, let him keep a little in the mouth and in time of plague make frequent use of it, so that there be no odor and the corrupt and pestiferous air be quickly dispelled."

Under the personal supervision of Nostradamus, this specific was prepared by the "pure and sincere" Joseph Turiello Mercurino, a druggist in Marseilles: all those who used it were protected from plague; anyone who did not use it unfailingly died.

In Aix Nostradamus found the city as though it were encased in gelatine. The houses were as empty as skulls. In the deserted shops, the worms with infinite patience were digging their labyrinths in the abandoned merchandise. The skeletons of horses, saddles still on their backs, were attached by their bridles to the hitching rings on the portals. Every window had its cage, and every cage its tiny canary carcass inside, lying on its back, its little claws as stiff as dried flowers. Dead plants hung from their vases like puppets abandoned on the stage of a toy theater.

Nostradamus walked on tiptoe so as not to awaken the dead, who from the houses, shops, balconies, and street gazed at him with wide-open eyes. He heard someone calling him.

So they could speak too, as well as gaze?

A face had appeared at a window. Nostradamus climbed the stairs. In the middle of the room, a woman, black with plague, had just finished sewing the shroud that covered her.

Later Aix rose in fame because of the glory brought to it by Cézanne. But at that time its one claim to fame was the modesty of its women. Until the moment of death, they were governed by a constant concern not to let themselves be seen naked.

What better proof?

171

When Nostradamus bent over to offer the modest lady his miraculous pills, she, black as a mummy, gazed at him with eyes of glass.

Wherever Nostradamus went, the miracle of healing was renewed. People threw themselves at his feet, kissed his hands, and called him "savior."

The plague was finally tamed. The "wild beast" slunk away toward the east, the torch spent in its hand and its bat wings drooping like sails without wind.

All of Provence wanted to honor Nostradamus. Marseilles voted public thanks and a generous income for life. The notables loaded him with gifts, and artists painted his portrait.

Nostradamus summoned widows and orphans, and distributed his gifts, gold, and wealth to them.

Everything about him is mysterious. Even the money with which he is inexhaustibly supplied, no one knows where it comes from.

So is he a counterfeiter? Has he discovered the philosopher's stone? Or perhaps, as in the case of Isaac Laquedem, did five sous perpetually renew themselves in his purse?

It is a bucolic apotheosis. Beautiful young girls, waving garlands of flowers and shouting "hosanna," form a procession behind the savior's mule.

The "doctor," in his long robe and astride a mule, certainly does not present the fine appearance of a warrior decked out in armor and sitting upright on a fiery charger. What does it matter? Nostradamus, in his way, is not lacking in appeal. Indeed his virtues are deeper and more lasting than those of a sword wielder. First of all, his great seriousness of mind: that seriousness that women like and which above all inspires trust.

Love in woman has a domiciliary character. The woman who loves places herself, so to speak, in the mind of the man she loves and lives by him. Before, however, deciding to move in, she wants to assure herself of the seriousness of the domicile, just as one who takes a house wants to be assured that the walls are strong, the frames solid, and the roof impervious to rain.

What is happening in the mind of the "doctor"? He, who has confronted the Black Death without batting an eyelash, all of a sudden feels an overpowering fear that tightens his stomach and makes his knees wobble. Something obscure is awakening in his depths, which can only become clear to him through the meaning of a proverb: *"La joie fait peur."* Nostradamus digs his heels into the mule's flanks, and launches the poor beast into a jolting gallop devoid of elegance.

What has Nostradamus seen? Is it true then that felicity is a danger?

The mule gallops. But the gallop of mules—those plebeians of equinity, in which donkeys play the part of respectable folk—is in any case a bastard and promiscuous contest of speed, to which victory is denied, like everything that lacks style.

Nostradamus feels behind him the breath of those extolling him. But above all he is gnawed by curiosity, to look face to face at that ineffable figure that he has only been able to glimpse.

A desperate resolution blocks his path. The mule turns back on itself. Like a platoon still in the heat of battle, there in front of the stalled Nostradamus are the inflamed cheeks of the girls, their shining eyes, their chests heaving like jellyfish on a turbulent sea. And among them, a taller, more shapely, more beautiful woman, whom he alone sees. She detaches herself from the group and comes forward, her hand extended.

"Nostradamus," she says, "your hour has come. I am Felicity. Give me your hand and let us try to keep each other company."

And since a minute goes by and Nostradamus has not yet decided to respond, the woman adds with a certain irritation in her voice:

"Anyway, there's not much choice. When Felicity offers herself, no man can say no."

"How much better it would have been if I'd kept going!" Nostradamus thinks to himself, inspired in spite of himself by that gift of prophecy that ever more clearly has been manifesting itself in him.

V

The bold and peremptory hand of Felicity does not release Nostradamus's arm, but closes around his wrist like a ring that anticipates the unbreakable nature of handcuffs.

"This will be your wife," says the robust woman in a tone admitting no appeal, and when Nostradamus raises his eyes, veiled by myopia, to look in the face the toad he is being forced to swallow, he realizes that obeying the suggestions of this overbearing woman is not the great calamity he had feared.

Before him stands a maiden shining with grace and blushing with modesty, and who looks all the more indistinct to the candidate bridegroom since his nearsightedness blurs her outlines and embellishes her nature.

"Furthermore," adds Felicity in the tone of a gendarme, "she is a woman of high lineage and much better than you deserve. Consider yourself content."

Not only was he content, but love had struck Nostradamus's heart with its sharpest arrows. Nostradamus's compatriots call this kind of love at first sight *coup de foudre*, which counts chiefly as an artistic representation, since it conjures up the lover with a lightning bolt zigzagging on his chest, a gold one for the well-to-do classes, nickel silver for more modest pocketbooks.

Nostradamus was prepared for this "lightning bolt," one might say, through sympathy and imitation. During the plague epidemic, the young doctor had had the honor to make the acquaintance of one of the outstanding scholars of the century. He was called "Julius" because this name had been given him at the baptismal font, "Caesar" in homage to ancient Rome, and "Scaligero" because he could boast of belonging to the Della Scala family of Verona.

Jules-César Scaliger was a big, muscular, broad-shouldered man. His shaved blond head, large and round as a cannon ball, was internally furnished with humanity. His large blue eyes were phosphorescent, like the dials of certain wristwatches, and at night, provided the letters were not too small, he could read without the benefit of light.

*   *   *

This giant with luminous eyes was born in Riva in 1484, and Antonio della Rovere, bishop of Agen, who had met him in Verona in 1525, hired him as his personal physician and took him back to his diocese.

The hand of Jules-César, which now wrote Latin elegies with the greatest elegance, had brandished the sword at the battle of Ravenna and in other memorable combats. Hence the taste for polemics had remained in Scaliger, and his pen "slew his adversary" no less than his sword. True, as in the cases of Erasmus of Rotterdam and Jerome Cardan, Scaliger chose his adversaries when they were very old and with one foot in the grave. One touch and they fell to pieces.

A Platonist and humanist, Scaliger conceived love only in its ineffable form of a communion of souls, and he placed his own soul in communion with that of Andiette de la Roque-Loubéjac, a flower barely formed by thirteen spring-times. Was it a mistake or the perfection of platonic love? The forty-five-year-old Giulio Cesare della Scala dei Bordoni (such was his original name) and the beautiful Andiette produced one after another fifteen children, both boys and girls, after which, burdened with years and glory, he curled himself up in bed and went to join his ancestors.

To pay a visit to Scaliger on his small estate at the bottom of the shady Escalle valley; to savor in such company the noble joys of erudition; to re-evoke the lyricism of poets, the eloquence of orators, the thought of philosophers; and at the same time to witness what he himself lacked, the conjugal happiness of Jules-César, had been a cruel trial for poor Nostradamus. And it may have been so that this friendship would not be transformed into torture that Felicity took care to give Nostradamus as well that portion of earthly well-being to which every man, as Stendhal was to say three centuries later, has the right.

The portion of earthly well-being that fell to Nostradamus offered itself in the guise of an appetizing maiden whose cheeks were tinged by modest blushes. Henceforth with no fear of competition, the friendship between the two doctors and humanists, so different in age but similar in mental disposition, was consolidated. If any spot ever tarnished the brightness of that friendship, it was one of religious passion. Scaliger sympathized with the Protestants, while Nostradamus was a fervent Catholic. And it was fun to see this scrutinizer of the occult, this hunter of mysteries, this hook-nosed astrologer with his drooping, drooling lip and clouded, bulging eyes, fly into such a rage because a few sheep were being led astray by a false shepherd.

The broad-shouldered humanist's house was also frequented by Matteo Bandello, the erudite Dominican who fled to France following the battle of Pavia, the first to tell the story of Romeo and Juliet, author of tales that are sometimes salacious, sometimes moving, that sometimes excited our grandfathers and sometimes drowned them in a dark sea of melancholy, and which nobody reads any more.

Now Nostradamus too has a house, a woman, children. Felicity has loosened her grasp around his wrist, and leaves him free to enjoy his talent, just as a mother leaves her child to pursue his games. This knot of affections, this burden of human flesh, these warm ties with life were more necessary to him than to anyone else: to him, an alien and intruder in this world, whom a malignant fate would like to see *glide* over the "things" of existence like water over stone, and who in the midst of weighty men attached to the earth is like a cloud driven by the wind.

The house he has built is a "tower of happiness." Custodian, guardian, and protector, amid the things he watches over in the uppermost chamber are the magical instruments of his mission as a birdcatcher of mysteries. This secret laboratory, this dangerous workshop, which—as Nostradamus knows—is a door open to the adversary, is here supported and "disinfected" by a foundation of innocence and good. Through the planks of the floor, the comforting noises of the lively and well-ordered house rise up to Nostradamus: the chattering voices of the children; the singing of the maidservants, long and undulating like funeral lamentations; and like the sounds to the ears, so to the nostrils of the tempter of God rise the pleasant odors from the kitchen.

Many times Nostradamus has tried to smother the voracious temptation that burns his soul. He has made vows, drawn up pacts with himself, uttered oaths. All in vain! How to free himself from this vice? How to slake this thirst, appease this desire, which, with the aid of all the senses vibrating like tongues of fire, cries out its demands from the depths of his brain?

Now, and for an unexpected reason, the alliance contracted with the legitimate forms of life, instead of having an opposing effect on Nostradamus's secret operations, stimulates and encourages them. This feeling of playing a double game, protected by a consecrated love and by the sacred love of his children, this sweet human ballast that gives equilibrium to the ship of his destiny, embolden Nostradamus not to restrain his secret temptations, and to venture defiantly into that obscure and perhaps cursed world, which more than ever he feels to be the only one that truly belongs to him.

Like Cavour much later, he sleeps only four hours a night.

Noche tinta, blanco el día. At night, at the top of the house, in the pride of his secret life, the thought of that innocent flesh sleeping safely and tranquilly on the floor below vexes him like a useless and shameful burden. Such is his scorn for that too human life! But by day Nostradamus's "white" life continues more orderly and honored than ever. Every morning, on the patient back of his mule, he makes his rounds through the towns and fields, all the more anxious to bring health and comfort to those who are denied these gifts, while knowing, by the magical balance of assets and liabilities, that by this work as a healer he is paying off a large IOU of happiness.

His work as a doctor is all the more appreciated, its results all the more certain, in that Nostradamus practices a direct and proven medicine, not a theoretical and bookish kind like his colleagues. They study Aristotle and Galen, Pliny and Theophrastus, but they do not even look at the patient. Erasmus, on a visit to Ferrara, asked Nicola Leoniceni "why he didn't visit the sick." "So as not to waste time that could be devoted to learning from books," Leoniceni replied.

Furthermore—and here too he differs from his colleagues, who so as not to degrade the dignity of the physician take care not to pick up a scalpel—Nostradamus performs punctures and incisions himself, as well as all those manual operations that are the province of the barber-surgeon.

Happy when the mule in the early morning carries him around on his visits, he is happier still when it carries him home at noon. Four pristine little children's arms entwine around his neck as he stoops to kiss his little son, his baby girl.

His wife awaits him on the threshold, tall in her red clogs, taller still because of the ornamental comb radiating from her twisted headdress of raven-black hair. Michel embraces her. Through the odor of her freshly laundered chemise comes the soft perfume of the living, breathing skin, something between that of warm hay and of a garden under the rain.

Which is the more agreeable of the two aromas, this one of his woman, or the one that steams from the tall copper cauldrons, glowing as red-hot metal, in which boil his jams, which a servant girl is skimming with a wooden paddle, as though slowly scraping away the impurities in those fruits that are being transformed and purified?

The cultivation of the human vegetable has always been his chief concern, and now all the more so since it is a question of his own garden. What would Nostradamus not do to give nourishment and luxuriant growth to these dear vegetables of his, these adored fruits? He would even transform himself into fertilizer.

But such a sacrifice would be pointless: Nostradamus is capable of something greater and better. Now finally the usefulness of his long studies stands revealed, of his patient botanizing under the sun of Provence, of his testing the virtues and properties of simples, of his analyzing and measuring the essences of plants and fruits.

Only the ignorant see in his jams and jellies nothing but "things" to eat; in truth they are filters, means, and moreover highly pleasant ones, for introducing the most secret, most nourishing juices of nature into the human organism. The same goes for his "virginal milk," all the creams, lotions, pomades, and cosmetics created by him after such patient research, and which now give brightness, rosiness, and purity of skin to the creatures of his blood.

VI

That day Nostradamus came home at noon as usual, but since it was May and the sun had wilted his brain, he went upstairs before lunch for a short rest in the chamber where he led his secret life.

As he returned to the city, lulled by the clip-clop of the mule, strange visions had crossed his sight, similar to the phosphenes that deceive the watchful eyes of pilots. But he put them down to the heat and his tiredness.

The fields were green and in bloom, but the foliage on the trees was beginning to wither and droop, leaving the naked skeleton of trunk and branches. The sky darkened, densely criss-crossed by veins of silver, like motionless and intersecting arrows. The earth sucked in its grass and flowers, and displayed a skin as dry and wrinkled as the hand of an ape. Then, as the first houses came into view, the natural look of things was restored.

Now Nostradamus sits motionless in his tall armchair. All around him stand magical apparatuses, familiar instruments, with the timid and diminished appearance that nocturnal things take on in the light of day. And yet the light that enters the chamber of the secret life is not naked. The Renaissance, which is the eye of the awakened man, has only partially overcome the Middle Ages, the eye of the man who dreams. And in addition to man and woman, the Middle Ages have also clothed the light, which does not enter people's houses except as it still does today the houses of God, dressed in the dark colors of stained glass.

There are two human heads in the chamber of the secret life: the living one of Nostradamus, leaning against the back of the chair, and that of the "dead brother," placed as a sign of humility on the desk, the eyesockets hollow and the magnificent teeth bared, like a neighing horse. *Palma Christi,* which drives away harmful phantasms, burns in the censer. Hebraic formulas and geodic circles are traced on the walls. Next to the armillary sphere and the astrolabe, shines the cold glitter of the magic mirror.

Nostradamus looks at the walls, but he sees neither the Hebraic formulas nor the geodic circles. His eye is opaque and staring like that of a boiled fish. And now the wall darkens and throws forth a dense flowering of stonecrop. Then it swells and opens in long cracks, while the plaster falls in a silence of cotton wool. Finally a very silent fire devours the walls, the instruments of the secret life, the floor, the roof; and Nostradamus finds himself suspended in the void, while below him, in the streets of Salon, men and women, the same and yet "different," circulate with unusual speed, dressed in strange fashions.

The manifestations of the mysterious disease from which Nostradamus has suffered since childhood, but in which only recently has he diagnosed the *morbus propheticus,* are accentuated and increasingly multiply.

The precursory symptom is an extended tingling, in which the blood seems to be converted into mercury. Nostradamus purifies himself of the present. Nothing better defines the state of acute visual sensation with which the preliminary phase concludes than the approximation of this visual sensation to the extraordinary mental lucidity preceding an epileptic fit.

Simultaneously the appearance of the life around him changes to the eye, whether more or less depending on the intensity of the prophetic attack. The decay of bodies, the mask of old age are completed with the motion of a candle being extinguished. At times Nostradamus sees men standing there in front of him, moving and speaking, go pale from head to foot and dissolve in the light.

He felt the attack of clairvoyance arrive the way a consumptive feels a hemorrhage. Not always, however. Sometimes "lucidity" arrived unannounced.

Seated in the shade of his house, his eyes closed as though he were sleeping, Nostradamus is enjoying the cool air. It is spring, and the blood is stirring under the skin of the womenfolk.

A neighbor comes out of her house, clattering hurriedly along in her clogs, and passing in front of the stargazer, cries, "Good morning, M'sieur de Nostredame!"

"Good morning, child," Nostradamus replies, without unlocking his eyes, which he keeps closed for another two hours, until the neighbor returns, clattering with less haste.

"Good afternoon, M'sieur de Nostredame!"

"Good afternoon, woman," replies Nostradamus, his eyes still shut: between good morning and good afternoon the neighbor has had a "conclusive" rendezvous with her sweetheart.

To the windows that opened on what was yet to happen, Nostradamus was unable to become accustomed. The possibility of "seeing" the future frightened him. He feared lest that terrible faculty be exercised on his children, on his wife. When he is in their company, he shrinks in dread of the precursory tingling, like someone in hiding who fears the cough that will reveal his presence.

Once the fear turned into a wish. It was a sunlit morning. They were seated, he and his wife, in the garden under the orange trees, which surrounded their heads with haloes of golden fruit. Yielding to a "masochistic" curiosity (there is nothing unusual about a prophet in 1540 knowing the words that 350 years later will emerge from the name of Sacher-Masoch), Nostradamus made a concentrated effort, and when he felt that his eye was sufficiently sharp, he directed it at the face of his beloved with the agonizing and at the same time sweet hope of seeing that face shrivel with wrinkles, strip itself of flesh, become filled with worms. But the white and rosy skin did not change, nor was the light in the eyes veiled. So had divination no effect on that beautiful and adored face? Nostradamus felt a grave disappointment.

Meanwhile the practical consequences of this extraordinary faculty were neither ignored nor despised by Nostradamus, and the editing, publication, and sale of his almanacs became a flourishing industry for the descendant of the tribe of Issachar.

One day when Nostradamus was crossing the public square of Salon on his way to visit his patients, he suddenly got off his mule and knelt down before a young Franciscan friar who was passing by.

"The Sieur de Nostredame is going crazy!" shouted Girard the sword maker from the back of his forge, and at that cry the cobbler, the blacksmith, and the miller came to the doors of their shops, while at every window appeared a white bonnet, with two staring eyes underneath and a mouth gaping with astonishment.

"What are you doing, doctor?" asked the druggist Craponne, who was in Nostradamus's confidence.

"I am bending my knee before the Pontiff!" Nostradamus replies with solemnity, and in so saying he pointed to the poor little monk who, timid and embarrassed, was making himself as small as he could inside his brown cowl, but who forty years later, relinquishing the name Felice Peretti for the much more glorious one of Sixtus V, ascended by acclamation of the conclave to the throne of Saint Peter.

Disappointed sweethearts, betrayed lovers, suspicious husbands, and treasure hunters came to the soothsayer from all parts of France and abroad.

Since there was not enough time to receive them all, Nostradamus began publishing those prophetic annals known as "'centuries," each containing one hundred divinations in the form of quatrains.

During the day, between consultations and the compilation of horoscopes, Nostradamus had so to speak domesticated the future. The art of divination was reduced to a matter of ordinary administration. Reading the future was no longer frightening. It was a game now scarcely mysterious. But at night terrible temptations reawakened in Nostradamus.

One of the lord of Beauveau's pages, having lost a fine greyhound that had been entrusted to him and fearing the consequences of his carelessness, came one evening to knock on the soothsayer's door, shouting that he came from the king. While the maid blocked his entrance, he heard from the rear of the house the voice of Nostradamus:

"Why all this uproar, king's page? Go to the Orléans road and there you'll find your greyhound being led on a leash by a footman."

And so it was.

Next day François Rabelais, who signed himself Alcofribas Nasier, came to visit Nostradamus in his house, and while they were discussing the best way to cure whooping cough, Nostradamus saw his colleague change from a physician into a parish priest, seize an omelet that was on the table, fling it out the window at the violent thunderstorm that was erupting, and shout: "That this should ever happen! So much fuss over an omelet!"

"Why did you throw the omelet out the window?" asked Nostradamus.

"Omelet out the window?" Rabelais repeated, staring wide-eyed at his colleague.

Many years later, in a serious infraction of the law, especially since in the meantime he had become parish priest of Meudon, François Rabelais wanted to eat an omelet on Good Friday, but had to throw it out the window to placate the violent thunderstorm that broke out at his first mouthfuls.

At night Nostradamus climbed up to the chamber of his secret life. While sleep and silence surrounded him, in his mind the most fearful secrets, the most frightening revelations, were voraciously kindled. The game with Death had begun.

Sometimes the game took a while to complete.

As on this night. There is a long wait. Shortly before, Nostradamus had been seated at the desk, and in order to solicit the arrival of that terrible grace, he composed the two quatrains that are now written out on large sheets of parchment in twisted, spiny letters:

Seated by night in secret study,
Resting alone on the bronze stool,
A slender flame out of solitude
Makes prosper what it is not vain to believe.

Rod in hand, set amid the Branches,
In the wave he bathes both limb and foot:
Fear and trembling voices through his sleeves:
Divine splendor. Divinity seats itself beside him.

But "divinity" is deaf to the invitation. The instruments of magic are spent and inoperative. The water in the bronze basin, over which Nostradamus has repeatedly bent his ear, has given no sound, and has not been blurred by the slightest ripple.

Nostradamus goes back to sitting in the armchair, his gaze fixed on the magic mirror.

And there on the shining glass three figures, like fishes rising from the deep, emerge little by little: a woman and two children, motionless, composed, horizontal; their eyes closed, their arms folded on their chests, each guarded by four lighted candles; and still glowing, swollen with that beauty, that health that Nostradamus has infused in them with his magical jellies, his miraculous creams, his boundless love.

Nostradamus can hardly believe his eyes, hardly understand. All of a sudden a sharp cry, like that of a strangled hoopoe, pierces the night:

"I'm no prophet!"

The cry is repeated, again and again: "I'm no prophet! I'm no prophet!" It emerges from all the floors, all the windows, all the doors, all the cracks in Nostradamus's house: "I'm no prophet! I'm no prophet! I'm no prophet!"

The windows of the neighboring houses are flung open. Men lean out in their nightshirts, nightcaps on their heads and harquebuses in their hands. The street is lined with lights. A dance of large crazed fireflies breaks out around the seer's house. And the cry continues: "I'm no prophet!"

No one ever knew what it was that Nostradamus's wife and two children died of all of a sudden, nor was he himself able to find out. And they said that Nostradamus could raise the dead! They said he had brought dead infants back to life before baptism, for that brief moment that was needed to receive the consecrated oil!

Hearing those cries, some of the townspeople, having awakened with a start, believed it was the sudden return of the plague, and alarm coursed through the city.

Then the huge roars of bombards thundered in the night, fired at the "wild beast."

Was it for this fine result, O Felicity, that you insisted so much on offering him your favors?

VII

Nostradamus disappeared. There were rumors that he too had died suddenly of unknown causes, but where was the corpse? Some said Nostradamus had committed suicide, others that he had turned into a dog, still others that he was going around invisible, and this rumor was credited more than the others. From a man like Nostradamus anything was to be expected.

One day, some peasants in the Vaucluse recognized the stargazer in a kind of self-propelled scarecrow that having broken free from its moorings to the pole, was wandering around the fields under the sun of Provence and being blown about by the mistral. A black tribe of low-flying crows accompanied it, as sharks escort a ship in expectation of food. The rich doctor of Salon and soothsayer of universal fame was reduced to the state of a ghost that has not succeeded in separating itself from its mortal remains, and drags them along like the highlander his swollen bagpipe, or as Saint Bartholomew carried his own skin folded on his arm, like a spring topcoat.

The peasants began following the ghostly prophet. Others joined them along the road. As they passed through villages and cities, new people were slowly added to the procession. People came from abroad, odd characters, important figures, emissaries of the king. The fame of the man who had not only divined the fate of others, but had foreseen the death of his own wife and children, grew immeasurably. What better proof that Nostradamus was "'serious"? Like a huge black and rampant cloud, those thirsting for divination walked through fields, forded rivers, and crossed mountains in the wake of the advancing ghost.

"Speak, Nostradamus! What will become of us? Tell us about tomorrow!"

Nostradamus made no reply. Forward he went like a limping nag, looking straight ahead, his eyes two wounds.

From time to time the prophet threw himself on the ground, less to rest than in the hope of never getting up again. His persecutors surrounded him, like ants around a dead worm.

"Speak, Nostradamus! Tell us what you see, what will become of us!"

Urged to reveal the future, Nostradamus was convulsed by a long tremor. Be that as it may, he set out walking again with the desperation of a man trying to flee, even on all fours, clutching at bushes and dragging himself along the ground.

One night Nostradamus disappeared. Once again rumors of his death spread. Some people suggested that the seer was hiding underground, like a mole. He had been reduced to a state too wretched to justify his ascension to heaven.

Disappointed, the human cloud gradually dissolved.

Nostradamus's disappearance coincided with the addition of a new friar to the abbey of Orval, near Montmédy. Whoever knocked at the door of that famous abbey of the Cistercian order was considered to have been sent by God. The doorkeeper gave the *Deo gratias* to the weary man standing on the threshold and took him to the father prior; the latter welcomed him as a son, and taking him by the elbow escorted him to a small cell, assisted him to lie down on the bare cot, and brought him food and water.

The weary man asked to enter the order. He spent his days in the cell, staring at the whitewashed wall, while long tears trickled from his eyes and disappeared into his beard like brooks under foliage. Severe as it was, the regime suited him; only the allotted supply of votive candles was never enough, and he kept asking for more.

Little by little the tingling recommenced, as did the rarefactions of the fabric of time, the apparitions of things that had not yet occurred. In vain the weary man tried to smother in prayer the attacks of the prophetic disease. His nights were consumed in useless struggle.

The bell of the abbey rang twice. Someone entered the cell without opening the door. The weary man thought it was the father prior, but raising his eyes did not recognize him, and noticed that through the body of the Stranger, so tall that he had to stoop under the beams of the ceiling, he was able to see the black crucifix on the wall.

"I appreciate your effort," the Stranger said, "to make yourself worthy of this place of peace. But no one can escape his destiny. Your motto, *'Felix ovium prior aetes,'* shows your incurably pagan soul. Your curiosity is great, your temptations ardent. This is no place for you, where the sole acknowledged virtues are patience and the sincere, convinced, heroic renunciation of any form of knowledge. Go, the century awaits you!"

The weary man rose from the cot on which he had been seated in a slump, opened the door of the cell, and went out in the corridor.

"One moment!" exclaimed the Stranger, pointing with his extraordinarily long and white forefinger at the empty shadow between the edge of the cot and the brick floor. "You are forgetting something."

The weary man became distressed and tried to deny it.

"No use!" the Stranger interrupted him. "We know everything." The weary man stooped and drew a roll of paper out from under the bed.

"Think how unfortunate it would be," said the Stranger as they crossed the gallery, "how unfortunate if these papers, in which you predict the tragic destiny of the world, should fall into the hands of these poor creatures, who shut their eyes and plug their ears to shelter themselves from reality!"

The doorkeeper was snoring with his cowl pulled over his eyes. The Stranger noiselessly opened the door. Nostradamus, with the *Prophecies of Orval* rolled up under his arm, set off down the road with a much more vigorous step than the one that three months earlier had brought him to the monastery. The moon shone in the sky. A silvery foam swelled around the twisted tree trunks.

Nostradamus's prophetic life resumed its interrupted course, since no one, as the Stranger had said, can escape his destiny, but now his body had been cut in half: one hand, one foot, half a mouth, and his soul—if soul is feeling, passion, communion with human beings, things, and life—no longer existed.

This miserable residue of life is concealed by Nostradamus behind the appearance of a complete life. He pushes the fiction to the point of seeking a second wife, and on 11 November 1547 marries Anne Ponsart Gemelle, widow of Jean Beaulme, and the fiction of happiness is added to the others. His glory extends far and wide. His house, in the Ferreiroux quarter, in the shadow of the castle of Salon bristling with large and small towers, is the goal of continual pilgrimages and the new temple of Osiris.

Salon betrays its name: it is not a salon, but a fetid place where man is blinded and suffocated by the clouds of dust stirred up in blasts and eddies by the mistral. As for the people of Salon—we were about to say "saloon"—they are, according to the testimony of their illustrious fellow townsman, "brute beasts and barbarous people, mortal enemies of literature and memorable erudition." This notwithstanding, and since the sorcerer has again chosen it as his headquarters, Salon becomes a tourist center and the National Tourist Office of the time multiplies the number of inns and taverns.

Nostradamus begins again to construct the circle of *"Floram patere"* and the sepulcher of the *Grand Romain,* i.e., to prophesy. "I do not receive divine illumination by lymphatic movement nor by bacchic furor," declares the prophet, "but directly from God, who operates in me while I observe astronomical assertions." And in line with those who uphold content over form, he adds: "I compose by natural instinct accompanied by poetic furor, rather than by the rules of poetry."

Nostradamus inherited his method, so very different from current astrology, from documents that came from Egypt and from the Persia of the Magi.

Before setting out on the Exodus, the Jews plundered the documents in the initiation crypts of the Egyptian temples, and they were to make use of these algebraic and geometric formulas in their turn for the Torah and the Temple of Solomon. But one day Titus destroyed the Temple of Solomon ("Titz hora!" the Jews of Galicia still say today, cursing in the name of that emperor, whose clemency on the other hand was sung by the "divine" Mozart) and the diaspora began. But before the temple collapsed the documents disappeared, and when the soldiers entered the Holy of Holies they found it empty. Who had made off with the documents? Those of the tribe of Issachar, who had always lived close to the temple and kings of Jerusalem.

Let us not forget that the Companions of Duty have derived their traditions from Provence, where the builders of the Temple had taken refuge (not for nothing are the members of the French Radical Party, the Daladiers and Sarrauts, so tenaciously attached to Freemasonry, among whose initial goals is the rebuilding of Solomon's temple), and these priceless documents, handed down from father to son, ended up in the hands of Nostradamus, who burned them before his death.

"An unusual brightness illuminated the air," the seer wrote to his son César, "clearer than natural flames, similar to lightning."

Thus if the prophetic spirit has come to be missing from the world, if nothing else we now know the reason.

VIII

The "regal" prophecies of Nostradamus resounded over Christendom. In the thirty-fifth quatrain of the First Century, he had written:

> *The young lion will overcome the old one,*
> *In single combat on the field of battle,*
> *He will strike the eyes in a golden cage,*
> *Two wounds one, to die a cruel death.*

Apprehensive, Henri II wrote to Claude of Savoy, count of Tenda and governor of Provence, asking him to persuade the prophet to come to court. And on 14 July 1556, which was not yet the French national holiday, Nostradamus arrived in Paris—a Paris resounding with bird song, in which only three carriages circulated: the queen's, that of Diane de Poitiers, and that of Raymond de Laval, a rich and obese gentleman.

Nostradamus traversed the Louvre, to where curtains parted and the king appeared, looking flabby on the long legs of a wading bird, his pale face resting on a starched ruff, like the head of the Baptist on the silver platter.

"You foresee my death?"

"Not I, sire, but the stars."

Three years later, on 1 July 1559, in a joust near the Bastille Saint-Antoine, the count of Montgomery (young lion) stuck his lance in the right eye of Henri II (old lion), who was wearing a gold helmet (cage, as the quatrain called it).

Years go by.

At the queen mother's invitation, Nostradamus becomes astrologer to Catherine de Médicis. In the castle of Chaumont on the Loire, where *"l'Italienne"* had set up and equipped a cabinet of occultism, they both bent over to peer in the steel mirror, he already old, she pyramidal, covered with brocade and looking like an enormous sofa.

Years go by, and Nostradamus's prophecies come true with inexorable punctuality: the Amboise plot, the Lyons conspiracy, the death of François II.

On 17 November 1560, François II faints during a religious ceremony in Orléans. "To the courtiers present," the Venetian ambassador Michieli reports to the doge, "the 39th quatrain of the Tenth Century comes to mind, and they remark on it in low voices." A dispatch from Tornabuoni, the Tuscan ambassador, to the duke of Florence, sent on 3 December 1560, reads: "The king's fate is highly uncertain: Nostradamus in his prophecies for this month predicts the unexpected death of two young members of the royal family." François II dies on 5 December, followed a month later by the Marquis de Beaupréau, son of the prince of La Roche-sur-Yon.

But not all of Nostradamus's prophecies are of a fatal kind. In 1561, the duke of Savoy asks Nostradamus for the horoscope of the child with which his wife is pregnant, and the seer foretells "a prince who will be named Charles Emmanuel and be the greatest captain of his century."

Years go by, and Nostradamus no longer moves from Salon. If kings or princes want to ask him something, they must bestir themselves and make the journey to Provence.

On 17 October 1564 the royal cortege arrives at the Porte Saint-Lazare, and to the consuls, assessors, treasurers, and captains who come out in great pomp to greet him, Charles IX, young and bold on his white charger, says, "I have come to see Nostradamus."

Years go by, and the boredom is ever more voracious. His legs are swollen with dropsy. Large bags of yellow chicken fat hang under his eyes. In order to write—because write he must, he himself has said so:

> *After my earthly departure*
> *My writing will do more than ever living word.*

—he has them tie the quill to his hand, just as three and a half centuries later Renoir, he too with hands stiff as a chicken hanging from a nail, has them tie his paintbrush.

What do the prophet's eyes discover, while his bloated paunch rests on a supporting stool, and his soft legs dangle like colossal sausages? Nostradamus keeps looking farther and farther into the future. His gaze traverses the years, the centuries, the millennia, making a broad sweep of the future . . . In vain! The same boredom, always, everywhere, endless.

And in the middle of that frightening desert, a minuscule personal event.

Nostradamus had written:

> *Family, friends, blood brothers,*
> *Will find me dead, near the bed, on the bench.*

The morning of 1 July 1566 (summer is fatal for the most precious lives) Nostradamus was on the bench, near the bed. Someone, friend or blood brother, put a hand on his shoulder. Nostradamus leaned forward as though trying to look at something on the floor, then slowly collapsed with a fat "plop."

Between toads and prophets there is an affinity of sound.

When Trintzius had stopped speaking, we realized that in re-evoking Nostradamus's extraordinary faculty, a faculty no less extraordinary, but the opposite of his, had been revealed in ourselves: hindsight.

That same evening we arrived in Monte Carlo.

Like Atlantis under a thousand meters of water and pheasant breasts under a layer of jellied consommé, Monte Carlo slumbers in its gelatinous atmosphere, and perpetuates in transparency the curling charms of Art Nouveau. A few families from La Turbie were walking calmly along the blue conglomerated sea: from time to time the father dipped his finger in the dense substance to see if it was still salty.

We parked at the hotel.

In this demodé city, even the most expensive hotels have the shabby look of family pensions. Yellowed lace curtains fell like rain over the windows of the dining room, while innocent and timeless liqueurs stood lined up in their parrot colors on the shelves of the sideboard. The Englishwomen, eating at separate little tables, were dressed like sofas in flowers; under the pouf that served as a hat, they displayed the sad and at the same time comical faces of circus dwarfs, and a rigid lunar hilarity. Shortly before, in the W.C., which opened on steep, muscular mountains, I had deciphered this enigmatic bilingual notice: *"Please do not throw down flowers in w.c. . . . Prière de ne pas jeter des fleurs dans le cabinet."* To what floral idylls, what anthological loves do these seventy-year-old virgins devote themselves?

"Nostradamus," Trintzius went on, when our tea had been served, "predicted the French Revolution and the arrest of Louis XVI at Varennes:

> *By night will come through the forest of Reines*
> *Two couples by a roundabout way Queen white stone*
> *Black monk in gray into Varennes:*
> *Chosen Capet to bring about tempest, fire, blood, slice."*

At a nearby table a corpulent and bearded gentleman was drinking mineral water and reading *La Croix*, the organ of French Catholics.

"He predicted Napoleon:

> *An Emperor will be born near Italy*
> *Who will cost the Empire dearly.*
> *They will say that with such people surrounding him*
> *They deem him less a prince than a butcher.*

He has predicted a war in the Mediterranean for 1968. He has predicted the destruction of Paris for 1999, through the actions of an airborne armada coming from the Far East. He has predicted the expulsion of the 'barbaric sect' from Italy and Germany, then from Spain and France. He predicted *Hidger, who will bring order to Germany.* And he's not through predicting."

Trintzius brought his chair close to mine, and lowered his voice:

"Because Nostradamus is not dead. He had himself placed standing up in the wall of the church of the Friars Minor, with light, paper, pen, and inkwell. No one was supposed to open that tomb, but in 1791 it was violated by the sans-culottes, and now Nostradamus is probably wandering around the world."

What bad news was our neighbor reading in *La Croix?* He crumpled the newspaper with rage, pushed the table with his fists, and with difficulty got to his feet.

"How can we be sure that's not Nostradamus?" whispered Trintzius.

Clutching at the furniture for support, the irascible sufferer from gout crossed the dining room on soft rubbery legs, and disappeared into the dark corridor.

"How can we be sure?" repeated Trintzius.

The shadows deepened. Through the faded lace curtains, Hesperus shone.

Every star has its particular function. That of Hesperus, according to Sappho, is to bring each thing back to its place: the wine to the lip, the ewe to the sheepfold, the boy to his mother.

"And me?" I asked, looking at the star intensely.

"To . . ." the voice of an invisible presence replied from the shadows.

There followed a strange word, which I was hearing for the first time, and anyway have forgotten.

Isadora Duncan

I

It is a great privilege to be born in the shadow of the Parthenon—that marble skeleton that casts no shadow. One becomes heir to a source of inner light and a pair of transforming eyes. This was the privilege that befell Nivasio Dolcemare. And what of the million human beings who inhabit present-day Athens? No. The native has no right to these gifts, his nose is unresponsive to the aroma of the gods; only the lonely, isolated individual, one who, though born in Greece, is not Greek. Like Nivasio Dolcemare, who came into the world in Athens, from the union of a Ligurian tritoness and a Tuscan centaur. One recognizes in this the hand of Destiny, its will to choose. Destiny says to the privileged one: "Take this light that pierces the hardest metals and store it in secret behind your eyes; inhale this mixed aroma of musk and sweat, which is the genuine *odor dei*, and conceal it in the hollows of your nostrils. He who has recourse to these infallible means of comparison is condemned to a priceless unhappiness. Go and bear your pain. Adieu!"

When, in the sixteenth year of the reign of Antoninus the philosopher, Pausanias visited Greece, the gods had long been dead. There were no voices to be heard but those of the sea and wind. The temples offered to the sky their illustrious and gaping holes. The drums of columns lay on the ground, beads from colossal broken necklaces. Wild horses wandered on the deserted beaches, stopped to listen, looked back with

195

mad and bloodshot eyes, then fled at a gallop, frightened by the immense void.

Later came the pashas with their little gold boleros and silver scimitars. The whole range of noble metals and precious stones was represented on these soft human spheres, who rocked on their gondola-shaped slippers like tilting dolls. Slender minarets had taken the place of Doric columns as nesting places for the storks and their young. Time passed cheerfully, between cutting off heads as though they were coconuts and sipping coffee as thick as syrup in tiny cups like thimbles.

Still later came that flourishing time in which Europe was a mother to everyone. From among the Wittelsbachs she chose a big handsome prince of pure Bavarian blood, and gave him to the resurrected Hellas to be its king. But Otho and Amalia were not loved by their subjects, though they even went to bed in the national costume, she with necklaces of gold coins on her forehead, he in Albanian shirts and pointed slippers embellished with red tassels. South of Athens, at Ano Patissia, the ruined ogives and decapitated turrets of what was to have been the summer residence of King Otho and Queen Amalia lay in the tall grass and nettles. Before it could be finished, this oversized Gothic palace passed to a state of ruin without history or nobility.

We come to 1900 and the triumph of Art Nouveau, swan song of Arabo-Gothic civilization. Athens is one big suburb, the suburb of a city that does not exist. For many hours of the day the inhabitants stay holed up in their white houses, flat on their backs on the tiled floor, naked and with newspapers over their faces. The mice come out and sniff them suspiciously. A cockroach crawls slowly up the whitewashed wall. Athens resembles those ghost towns that the Turks razed to the ground before leaving Albania. The chirping of the cicadas is so insistent that it seems on the point of uprooting the white city like a round of sheep's cheese and lifting it into the incandescent sky. As the afternoon declines, with the sun losing its bite and the Acropolis extending its longest shadow over the city, a victoria passes at a gallop along Kefissia

Avenue, followed by a cloud of dust like the wake of a ship. In the box is an evzone, proud as a peacock in his little skirt. In the carriage sits the royal couple. Olga wears dark glasses, and in her black clothes looks like a monk of the Misericordia. George I winks to right and left with his myopic eyes, and alongside his funereal consort seems to be flirting gallantly with the wives of all his subjects.

Peace reigned, together with mediocrity. There was little circulation of money, and even less of ideas. To pay five drachmas, you tore a ten-drachma bill in two and handed over half. For ideas, not even this operation worked. The rich sat in the cafés, black-haired and dressed in white, and ordered glasses of water. Socialism was tormenting faraway industrial countries, but amid the olive trees of Attica there was no word to express the concept. Protest meetings were not unknown to the Athenians, the streets barricaded by soldiers with guns at the ready, the three whistle blasts that make you turn around and take to your heels; but these were gatherings of students and seminarians against the archimandrite, who had taken it into his head to translate the Gospels into *maliará*, the "hairy" language of the people. It is in this tranquil atmosphere that an unheard-of event takes place, unhinging the life of the Athenians and unleashing a wind of madness on the city of Athena's owl.

It must have been around four o'clock. The city was still in the grip of that fiery stasis that descended on it at the stroke of its terrible noon and did not let up until sunset. The precincts of the Astinomia[1] lay submerged in the silence of the tomb. In the guardroom the policeman Pelopidas sprawled like a corpse on the plank bed. On the floor the shoes of the custodian of law and order, flaring like Turkish barges, emitted residual fumes. Flies flew in spirals around the sleeper, alighting in turns on his curling lip surmounted by a bayonet mustache, on the heavy eyelid through a slender crack of which the white of the eyeball shone as in the

---

1. Police headquarters.

dead, on the chest tattooed with the image of the god of love, on the naked feet the color of eggplants.

"Halt or I'll shoot!" cried Pelopidas, jumping up out of his sleep with the impetus of someone battering down a door and pointing at the enemy a soft-drink bottle that he had found beside him on the plank bed. But instead of the impossible detonation of that glass weapon, all that could be heard was the soft "plop" of the policeman's feet making contact with the floor. The flies dived in a whirl, then rose all together to the ceiling. As for the "enemy," held at bay by the soft-drink weapon, and who had rushed into the guardroom accompanied by a horrid stink of old and recent sweat, he was trembling under the rags that scarcely covered his body and was unable to utter a word.

The "enemy" was named Gargaras, and he had much in common with sylvan creatures. Athens was not one of those sprawling cities that close their gates to the countryside and spread within themselves the disease of their centrifugal dynamism, burning the grass, cutting down the trees, and infecting the air. The city life of Athens was still "watered" by country graces. Grass bordered the streets, magpies came to feed at the doors of butcher shops, goats grazed under the peristyle of the Court of Assizes, while legal documents blown by the wind added a little variety to their diet. Gargaras too was one of the "contributions of the countryside." He passed for an innocent, but no one had yet ascertained whether his innocence was a natural state or a pose. Besides, among Mediterranean peoples, pure innocence cannot be said to thrive. Gargaras lived on the slopes of Mount Aegaleos, among pale olive trees contemporary with the divine Plato. He turned up in the city in the hours when it was most deserted, and would sit down at street corners and on a *floghera*[2] play an endless, wavering dirge from far-off times, fragile as a spider web. And since the essence of midday is an unfathomable sadness, certain old Athenians rich in experience justifiably reasoned that

---

2. Rustic copper flute.

Gargaras's dirge was the plebeian successor to the noonday song of Pan.

"What do you want?" the policeman Pelopidas repeated for the third time, and realizing that the pistol he held in his fist bore a strange resemblance to a soft-drink bottle, he threw it away in a gesture of profound disgust.

"*As-ti-nó-mos*,"[3] Gargaras finally managed to blurt out, with the voice of a talking dog.

"What do you want from the *astinomos*?"

"My eyes have seen a miracle! Great danger for the city!"

"The *astinomos* sees no one. Tell me what you want to say."

"No . . . no," Gargaras repeated, shaking all over, from his louse-ridden head to his muddy feet, to emphasize his refusal. "*Astinomos* will hear Gargaras, and when *astinomos* hears Gargaras, *astinomos* will bless Gargaras."

Driven by his faith like a balloon by the wind, Gargaras ran from the guardroom toward the door at the end of the corridor, where the word "*astinomos*" stood out in black letters on a white background. But the exercise of authority makes a man arrogant and violent, especially one so lacking as Pelopidas in the divine gift of thought.

"Come back!" roared the policeman, who widely as he had read had never got as far as the Manual of Epictetus. And after brutally striking the sylvan creature at the end of the corridor, he added in a tone that offered no possibility of appeal: "The *astinomos* is busy right now."

The two men, one authoritarian, the other submissive, stood motionless and silent in the corridor. Then, through the door, came a long snore, deep, mellow, and hearty, followed by a short descending bray.

"Captain!" begged the innocent, his greasy face streaked with tears, "there's an awful creature in the city, if we don't tell the *astinomos* right away, we'll all die a terrible death!"

The policeman Pelopidas touched his moustache in perplexity, and Phobos, Fear, furrowed his dull brow. For the first time since he had taken up the tasks of a municipal

---

3. Police chief.

guardian of law and order, doubt, terrible doubt, shook that mind of stone.

He listened, opened the door, and tiptoed into the little private paradise of his superior. The faint light was fresh and strewn with mirages. An earthenware jug leaned its sweating paunch against the half-drawn blinds, its neck covered by one of those bitter oranges known as *neranzakia*. The window was half covered by a painted shade, on which transparently shone the shady woods and roaring brooks of Attica as described in the *Critias*, or before disaster denuded it and reduced it to its present state of wretchedness. The *astinomos* was sleeping like Holofernes on an oilcloth sofa, which exuded its stuffing of vegetable fiber from a gaping wound in the back. His feet rested on a stack of blank arrest warrants. His hand hung to the floor, where, like a revolver next to the hand of a suicide, lay a little propeller fan. His moustache net gave the police chief's face the ferocity of a cat spitting with rage. When removed from their forced position, the ends drooped on his neck, like seaweed from the head of a marine god.

It was all they could do to arouse the *astinomos* to a sense of reality. Finally: "What has this man seen?" he asked with the scowl of authority, using indirect interrogation to reinforce his own prestige.

"He says he's seen a god, sir," answered the policeman Pelopidas, bringing his naked heels together in the position of attention.

"A god?" the *astinomos* repeated doubtfully, and he laughed twice: "Ha! ha!" He went to take a riding crop from the wall, then lashing his pigskin leggings, came back and planted himself in front of the beggar. "Have you looked at yourself in the mirror?"

"No, sir."

"Take a look. The gods don't show themselves to ugly mugs like yours."

"It was a god," Gargaras insisted sweetly, "a ghost."

"God or ghost?" yelled the *astinomos*, accelerating the

lashing of his leggings, as though he were practicing before going on to the face of someone who "had seen a god."

"God and ghost, sir. One of our fathers."

The face of the *astinomos* went bright red, like a fighting cock's. And since the fault of not understanding could not be attributed to his own underdeveloped intelligence, he became furious at Gargaras and called him a "beast."

"Not a beast," the innocent replied more sweetly than ever, altering the direction of the epithet, "but an *ancient.*"

"An ancient?" repeated the *astinomos*, opening his eyes wide. And in order to swallow so astounding a piece of news more easily, he went to the window, removed the *neranzaki* from the neck of the coolly sweating jug, and took a long drink.

Finally, and after a "meticulous cross-examination," the *astinomos* succeeded in finding out what Gargaras had seen, and he would have succeeded in finding out much sooner if he hadn't raised the obstacle of his authority to what had been offered as the most spontaneous of confessions.

Gargaras had seen *an ancient Greek.* He explained that as he was walking by the gate of Parliament Square, the unexpected visitant had crossed the deserted square and disappeared behind the Chamber of Deputies.

"Anything else?"

The innocent knitted his brows with all the concentration of a counting horse.

"Yes. When he got to the front steps of the Chamber, he stopped, bent his knee, and raised his arm."

"Just what I said!" exclaimed the *astinomos*, giving a tremendous lash to his leggings. "No doubt about it, it's an ancient Greek. He mistook the Chamber of Deputies for a temple of Apollo. That's the trouble with neoclassical architecture."

The *astinomos* asked for further details, and Gargaras replied that the ancient Greek had walked fast and "in profile."

"In profile?"

Suiting his actions to the word, Gargaras spread his legs,

lifted his arms like a candelabrum, and assumed the likeness of Boreas the wind as painted on clay pots.

"Pelopidas!" cried the *astinomos*, rediscovering after a moment's bewilderment a freethinker's strength and lucidity. "Take ten men, search the city, and bring me this ancient Greek dead or alive. Have you got your handcuffs?"

"Yessir," replied the policeman, and as he spoke he took from his trouser pocket two greasy knotted cords. For beautiful shining handcuffs, the glory of the American cinema, were at the time still unknown in the Greece of George I.

Bewilderment paralyzed the city, then tossed it around like a salad. At first Gargaras's revelation was called a "vision." Above all no one cared to believe the words of a paranoiac. But the testimony of the man of the woods came to be corroborated by serious citizens, highly placed persons and authorities, such as General Vournasos, the magistrate Sclep, Monsieur Jean Bidet, second secretary of the French legation, and the flute teacher Wassenhoven at the Conservatory. Who was this ancient Greek? And was it a true ancient Greek or a false one?

To tell the truth, this second hypothesis never even crossed the minds of the Athenians. False ancient Greeks circulated freely in Montmartre, in Hyde Park, in Schwabing in Munich; they formed part of those shockingly mixed populations, along with false Christs with sandals, flowing hair, and eyeglasses. But Athens was not only immune, it was very remote from such contaminating influences. Modern Greece was the only country at the time in which ancient Greece was neither re-evoked nor paraphrased in some intellectual way. (Later it too let itself be contaminated.) Can one perhaps re-evoke one's own father in disguised, masked, cosmetic form? And yet the appearance in modern Athens of that ancient Greek aroused neither mental excitement nor intellectual curiosity, but only sacred horror and portentous fear, as a son might feel upon the terrible reappearance of his father who had died thirty-four years before. As for the suspicion that it was a god—an idea worthy of a Heinrich Heine, of an intellectual, of a *pasticheur*—this did not even arise in those straightforward and uncomplicated minds, and there were other reasons besides that acted to prevent such a hypothesis. Greek Christianity was still so harsh and distrustful as to exclude more than in any Catholic or Protestant country even the slightest or most innocent pagan survival. Also the gods, conceivable as long as they remain concealed, become inconceivable and absurd once they let themselves be seen.

A few days later, the "ancient Greek" proliferated. Other ancient Greeks were seen walking rapidly across Athens: fleeting and colorful forms, parrots among a tribe of crows. Some women too, even a child, a *pais*. Had they been exhumed? Resurrected? Flowers of a living archaeology? None of the hundred thousand Athenians of the time, all of them people who thought with only part of their minds or did not think at all, was capable of clearing up the mystery. Nor were the "Europeans" living in Athens, namely, the members of the diplomatic and consular corps, a few professionals, some colonial drug merchants, who represented little but the most inferior and philistine aspect of Western culture, and whose Europeanism was limited to playing *maus*, or for those of Anglo-Saxon origin, tennis. Only Schliemann would have been up to it. What a joy it would have been for him, what a consolation to find those of whom he had spent his life thinking alive again! But Heinrich Schliemann had died a few years earlier in Naples, near the mysterious city of Hercules that night and day, in a voice of stone and with smothered accents, called to him from under its layers of solidified mud. He had left a son in his house in Athens, a house known as *Iliou Melathron*, but in intelligence the son resembled Gargaras, without the sudden flashes, the mysterious reflections that from time to time illuminated the mental darkness of that innocent soul.

As in countless previous circumstances, the zeal of the *astinomos*, his anger and threats, turned out to be ineffectual and vain. The greasy, knotted cords of the policeman Pelopidas did not touch the wrists of anyone who might have been related to Poseidon. Once the period of fear was over, followed by that of astonishment, the population gradually became familiar with these representatives of a remote and illustrious age, all the more since they proved not only harmless but indifferent, absent in spirit, as though far from human eyes. No one as yet had ventured to communicate with them, besides which an ancient Greek obviously speaks ancient Greek, and not one of those Athenians was capable of formulating a single idea in that tongue. But they were followed ever more closely by ever larger groups, examined with growing curiosity, studied, remarked on, even scoffed at. That highly dangerous moment for superhuman creatures, when the devil turns out to be merely an old billy goat, was approaching.

One day the first "ancient" encountered by Gargaras was seen crossing Concord Square with a goat on a leash. The teats of the patient beast, generatrix of feta cheese, were enclosed in a cloth sack. A procession formed behind the mysterious personage and his bearded companion. Slowly collecting new adherents as it went, it followed Stadium Street, crossed Constitution Square, then took Queen Amalia Boulevard under its dense canopy of pepper trees, which induce sneezing. It ascended the steps of the Zappeion, passed in front of the marble Byron expiring in the arms of a Hellas in a dressing gown, crossed the Ilissus, climbed the hill of the Cemetery where the Athenian dead lay under the cypress trees, and when it arrived in the locality of Kopanos, as bare and stony as a land flayed by a furious god, thousands of men, women, and children surrounded the encampment of the strange clan. And they, as though in the middle of a desert, continued to busy themselves with their own affairs, churning butter, poking the fire under the pot, and mending the holes in chlamyses and peploses.

It looked like a pioneer settlement, and it would have looked like a country fair had the site been more florid and pleasant, and if the Athenians, like all southerners for that matter, had not had the funereal habit of always dressing in black. This, added to the color of their hair and beards, and to the abundant growth that thickened their eyebrows, emerged in tufts from their nostrils and ears, and sprouted in curls on their moles, transformed that human assembly into an assembly of black beetles.

The uproar grew, until all of a sudden an august silence fell on the crowd and froze it. The men uncovered their heads, the women bowed theirs, and a respectful path was cleared for the advance of a horseman. Informed of these singular happenings, the king in person, His Majesty George I, had come to see "the Achaeans." He rode a gentle white mare, which advanced at a walk through the human channel, turning her soft, melancholy eyes a little to right and left as though in apology. His Majesty as usual wore an admiral's undress uniform, and with his white-gloved right hand sometimes toyed with the ends of his long mandarin moustaches, sometimes touched the visor of the flat cap he wore tipped over his ear. A few shouts of *zito*[4] rose from the crowd, spontaneous but untimely, because the person most eagerly awaited on that day, when this most mysterious case of palingenesis or metempsychosis was about to be resolved, was not the king but Professor Mistriotis.

He was the holder of the chair of philology at the university, the one man in all Athens who knew ancient Greek not only *de jure* but *de facto*. Such at least was his reputation, since no one was able to provide any certainty based on experience.

Mistriotis was a classicist and carpophagous. He had roused the University against the irreverent attempt to present Sophocles in modern Greek, and every day, once his lectures comparing the Dorian, Ionian, and Attic dialects were over, he stopped at the fruit stalls on Patissia Street and slowly and shamelessly chose the fruit destined for his monkey diet. He stuck a finger into the bruises on peaches, squeezed the drop of milk from the necks of figs, held melons up to his ear, then loaded with his meal, went away to consume it, dragging his feet on the ground and raising a cloud of dust; for Mistriotis, like Michelangelo, suffered from

---

4. "Long live . . ." in Greek.

a strange deformity of the lower limbs, and walked without lifting his feet from the ground, in the manner of little boys who move their arms like pistons and go "chug-chug" with their mouths to imitate the action of a locomotive. "Goodbye, *kyrie katheghetè!*" the fruit seller called after him, whereup the offended philologist, turning around with the face of an ape whose backside has been scorched by a red-hot iron, shouted back: "*Katheghetá,* you jackass!" Mistriotis resembled his distant ancestor Socrates, but unlike the son of Sophroniscus, he wore a tall hat and frock coat, steel-rimmed glasses, and large flapping shoes.

While the procession was wending its way up Kopanos, a few farsighted individuals had gone to seek out the philologist in his bachelor quarters, he being the only man capable of entering into communication with the "Achaeans." And now the professor was ascending the hill in great pomp, his tall hat on crooked and his body lying among amphoras like a drunken Silenus. For knowing that with his usual pace of a toy locomotive he would have taken six months to arrive on foot, they had hoisted him onto a *susta* decked with festoons and bells, one of those two-wheeled carts with painted sides that are used to transport Amaroussi water, which for the Athenians is what Acetosa water is for the Romans—a thirst-quencher and a mild laxative.

At the sound of the harness bells, the crowd swayed and an excited hubbub broke out. The philologist was lifted down from the amphoras, deposited on the ground like a shapeless mass of rags and hair, and pushed forward on soft rubber feet to the edge of the crowd, beyond which the area of the mysterious colony began.

The Achaeans were going on with their lives, without even looking around. Having finished their supper, they spoke among themselves in low voices, while washing and drying the metal knives and forks, the collapsible drinking cups. The child had been put to sleep on a modern folding cot.

Mistriotis took off his hat, adjusted his steel spectacles, and with a voice that emerged from the pit of his stomach pronounced:

"O andres . . ."

But he stopped with his mouth open, and turning around with staring eyes, said: "But these ancient Greeks are talking English!"

And he added, sighing: "With an American accent!"

II

In this iron age in which we are living out our lives, we still retain a few glimmers of the ones that preceded it. Depending on a person's habits, his tastes, and especially his degree of nobility, there are some who more easily recall the age of gold, others that of silver, still others that of bronze. But does anyone still remember the basic reason for these metallic eponyms?

Men were once as full of gold as decayed teeth. The awful suspicion arises that the world began as a colossal cavity. Cities glittered with these noble creatures who, clapping each other confidentially on the shoulder to rejoice in their common incorruptibility, gave out a sweet and ringing sound, like castanets suspended on a wire and stirred by the breeze.

Even the most carefully contrived deluge leaves behind a few survivors. It is not unusual to encounter very rigid men, with harsh expressions, and some actually with bronze faces, who, should you bump into them, give off from under their clothes a subdued and mysterious "bong." They are men of metal, survivors from the age of gold, silver, or bronze. Then there are the survivors from the age of heroes, and in their presence one must get to one's feet and salute. Then there are those from the age of stone, hard and heavy people, and if by chance they tread on your foot, you will remember it for the rest of your days. Finally there are the survivors from the ornithic age, the light and flying bird people, who, not being sufficiently numerous to occupy a whole age by themselves, constituted a special hidden clan in the bosom of others, and lived there fluttering and twittering where the distance from other men was the greatest and the danger of meeting them least. Aristophanes spoke of the bird men with Attic elegance, and Cyrano de Bergerac with experience and erudition. When a bird man crosses the sky at nightfall, his body aslant and his arms swinging, or passes on foot through a city, so lightly that he scarcely touches the ground, and with his wings folded on his back like a pair of skis, other men say it is an angel and wait openmouthed for some astonishing news. For angel means "one who announces," and men still pay strict attention to the meaning of words, without stopping to think that it was they themselves who invented words.

Need one add that these extraordinary light creatures, subject like everything that lives to implacable Necessity, seek in the corps de ballet a condition suitable to their nature, and that those of the finest quality are called Zambelli or Aida Boni if female birds, Nijinsky or Serge Lifar if male? One can never sufficiently praise as a trainer of bird men the unforgettable Diaghilev, who transformed his Ballets Russes company into an enormous musical aviary.

Mr. Duncan, of Scottish origin and a citizen of San Francisco, having put his wife in the condition to give birth to the fruit of their love, departed for Los Angeles to found a new family. The pioneer spirit of the Americans did not limit itself in those days to exploring deserts and founding cities. The pregnancy of the forsaken lady ripened in a dark sadness, amid the splendor of that marine landscape known as the Golden Gate, or Porta d'Oro in Italian. Strange phenomena were taking place in her, as in mythical times in women impregnated by gods. Not the usual movements, the "kicks" of a little creature obscurely "tasting" life, but a *dance*. Loyal to an old and glorious tradition, the doctor understood nothing, but he ordered for Mrs. Duncan chilled oysters and champagne, or rather he unwittingly chose the food most suitable to the coming baby, for as everyone knows, oysters and champagne are the food of Aphrodite.

The dancing baby came into the world on 27 May 1878. May derives from *maius*, two and seven make nine. So why was so much misfortune to fall on the dancer's head?

Scattered elements of divinity stream through the air, and some people catch them on the wing to create ineffable apparel for themselves. Isadora Duncan was one of those who created for herself a dress of "divine elements," and this explains the extraordinary ease, so deplored by fainthearted souls, with which she showed herself in the nude.[5] Of the four elements that according to Empedocles go to make up nature, Isadora Duncan was on familiar terms with fire, water, and air. With the fourth element, earth, she maintained good but less than excellent relations. In any case, she tried to touch the earth as little as possible, which in a dancer can be a purely technical feat. Fire dominated her in all senses, and the first memory that glows in the darkness of her childhood is that of a blazing house. From an upper window Isadora at the age of three was thrown into the arms of a gigantic policeman. To tell the truth, fire is not the only protagonist in this memory. The three-year-old child felt so secure and happy on the breast of that colossal guardian of law and order that this childhood memory can be considered more than anything else as an anticipation of Isadora's extraordinarily amorous life, of her urge to fling herself into the robust arms of men.

Water, more imperious than fire, held sway over Isadora's destiny. "I was born by the sea," she wrote in *My Life*, "and . . . all the great events of my life have taken place by the sea." Her art was also inspired by the sea. "My first idea of movement, of the dance, certainly came from the

---

5. Shelley was another who clothed himself in "divine elements." Naked, he felt dressed. He had invited the English consul and his wife to lunch at his house in Viareggio. Returning at noon from his swim, he found his guests awaiting him in the drawing room. Naked as he was, the poet greeted them graciously, apologized for being late, and with a slight bow asked leave to retire and get dressed.

rhythm of the waves. . . .[6] I believe, too, that it must make
a great difference to a child's life whether it is born by the
sea or in the mountains. The sea had always drawn me to it,
whereas . . . the mountains . . . always give me an
impression of being a prisoner to the earth. Looking up at
their tops, I . . . feel . . . only a desire to leap over them and
escape." Water witnessed her birth, water killed her
children. River water, winding and treacherous. She adds: "I
was born under the star of Aphrodite . . . and when her star
is in the ascendant, events are always propitious to me."
Isadora trusted in celestial signs. She shared the error,
common to many, that the gods are our friends. She was
unaware that between gods and men the class struggle
continues. Friends of man so long as he is humble and
submissive, the gods become vindictive and ruthless once
they discover in him a possible competitor. For her part,
Isadora never missed an opportunity to irritate them. In
Vienna, aspiring to be loved by Hermann Bahr, Isadora
confided to him that she was built rather "on the lines of the
Venus de Milo." In making this remark she hoped to melt
the inhibitions of the overly timid music critic of the *Neue
Presse.* At the same moment in Paris, in one of the
ground-floor galleries of the Louvre, the Venus of Milo
experienced a tremor of rage followed by a furious cough,
and without delay descended from the pedestal that had
held her for so many years in order to go and give that
insolent woman a good slap in the face. But remembering as

---

6. Her dances were always inspired by some natural movement.
She herself wrote: "At that Villa in Abbazia there was a palm tree
before our windows . . . I used to notice its leaves trembling in the
early morning breeze, and from them I created in my dance that
light fluttering of the arms, hands and fingers, which has been so
much abused by my imitators." She also derived instruction from
painting. "[In Florence] it was Botticelli who attracted my youthful
imagination. I sat for days before the Primavera. . . . A nice old
guardian brought me a stool, and viewed my adoration with kindly
interest. I sat there until I actually saw the flowers growing, the
naked feet dancing, the bodies swaying."

she was about to cross the threshold that she had no arms, she went glumly back to her place and resumed her pose.

Isadora saw her father only once, amid cakes and ice cream. She was eight years old. The doorbell rang. Isadora went to answer it and found herself face to face with a handsome gentleman looking like a plainclothes Apollo. Into the two-room lodging that then constituted Isadora's maternal home, this man had dropped like a hawk into a chickenyard. "Tell him to go away, tell him to go away!" cried the deserted wife from the next room, and the little voices of Raymond, Augustin, and Elizabeth, Isadora's brothers and sister, took up the cry of their mother like chicks around a hen. So the Apollo in frock coat and top hat took the little girl by the hand and led her to the best ice-cream parlor in San Francisco. He stuffed her with ice cream and cakes, and watching her eat he called her his "Princess Pug." Isadora did not see her father again. She learned later that he was a poet, and among his poems she found the tragic prophecy of her own life. Currents circulated in that family that were sure to make the fallen but still extant gods of Olympus jealous. When little Princess Pug returned home, the silence was damp with tears.

Her idea of the dance took shape very early. Isadora opened her first school in San Francisco. But soon San Francisco was too small for her ambition. The Duncans moved to New York. In New York Isadora found more art and greater beauty. So? This is merely the sign that *est deus in nobis.* A subtle hint is enough to arouse the inner god, and unlimited horizons open out before the host of divinity. To paint his dragons, Böcklin posed those tiny fishes that lovers of fish fries eat head, tail, and all. The false Gothic of New York was enough to make Isadora Duncan understand that architecture can also be art and poetry. Later, looking at the Brandenburg Gate and the façade of the Neue Wache, she was to discover that Berlin is a *Greek city.* Happy nature! Like the man with a cast-iron stomach who is able to digest anything. Like the girl whose charms are so undisputed that, as the French say, *"un rien l'habille."*

In New York Isadora had her first encounters with the impresarios, actors, and directors of that immortal form of slavery that tries to subject the artist to the basest instincts of the crowd, and against which no Lincoln has ever issued an emancipation proclamation. She had an engagement at the Daly Theater. They dressed her as Columbine, and made her do whirling movements. "The dance must express freedom," Isadora kept repeating with a grim face that brooked no discussion, "it must express the feelings and emotions of humanity." Augustin Daly, his rabbit's eyes ringed in pink, looked at the preaching maiden, then clapped his pale little flutist's hands and ordered the pirouettes to begin again. Between rehearsals Isadora took refuge in the dressing room, and clutching her head in despair read Plato, Aeschylus, Marcus Aurelius. An area of suspicion formed around the bookworm. To change her ideas they gave her a small singing and dancing part in *The Geisha*. "In those days," Isadora remarks, "they considered artists as inferior—a sort of upper servant." And she adds, as one bites a piece of lemon peel after taking a purge, "This feeling has changed very much since, especially since Paderewski became the Premier of a republic." The mind comes up with some very acute observations behind their slipshod surface, observations that pass from Stendhal to Nietzsche, and from Nietzsche to Isadora Duncan.

This habit of offering partridges to those who asked for turnips was to accompany Isadora for the entire journey of her life. She dreamed of "setting the Ninth Symphony to dance," and people wanted her to do the saltarello. At the Karlstheater in Vienna, the public received the chorus of *The Suppliants* coldly, but went into ecstasies over the *Beautiful Blue Danube*. The dancer approached the footlights, hushed the storm of enthusiasm with her hands, and said it was necessary to revive the beauty of the ancient chorus. *"Nein! Nein!"* cried the Viennese from the darkness of the auditorium, like children who have been promised chocolate cream puffs and find themselves offered boiled potatoes: *"Noch nicht! Tanze! Tanze die schöne blaue Donau! Tanze noch einmal!"*

In New York the sea once again intervened in Isadora's destiny. The Pacific, which the girl had seen from her window in San Francisco, had reflected upside down the cloudy mirages of Asia, the spider webs of China, the sails of sampans resembling the wings of yellow bats. But in the Atlantic Isadora saw reflected the whole history of Europe by stages, and the closest image went back to the age of heroes. In the Pillars of Hercules, the predestined girl discovered the beautiful face, veiled with sadness, of Greece. Once again the sea revealed that its purpose was more to unite continents than to divide them.

We must reverse our position as Old World inhabitants to understand how, for those on the other shore, the march toward Europe can become the exploration of a new world. The Duncans did not travel as Americans usually do, in first class and to the sound of cocktail shakers, but on a freighter black as a water beetle, which was transporting a load of cattle to Hull. One of these was Jove, white, hoary, and down on his luck. The clan was complete, with Raymond, Isadora, Elizabeth, Augustin, and their mother—she who had unwittingly brought into the world four angels with mutilated wings but in whom the wish to fly was as irresistibly natural as the tides of the sea, or the rustling of leaves in the forest.

It was a stormy crossing. The good-hearted captain tried to keep up the morale of his passengers by offering them whisky and grog. Amid the roar of the sea and the whistling of the wind in the rigging, agonizing bellows arose from the hold. Tossed and pitched, rolled from side to side, crowded together in a fearful stench, that tragic cargo of horned animals, snatched from the green pastures of the Middle West and destined for the stomachs of the people of London, was suffering from seasickness. Isadora approached the hatch, she grew melancholy at the torments of that ox in whom she had recognized the father of gods and men, still capable of transformations but now incapable of abducting nymphs, swimming away with them across the blue sea, depositing them on some harmonious strand, and there impregnating them to give birth to the kindest, most cultivated, most human continent on earth, the only one where the life of man is divided like the last act of *Aida* into two levels: spirit and matter. When calm returned and the moon emerged from the clouds, Isadora and the first mate climbed to the crow's nest. He was Irish like the girl's mother, but these lunar encounters were justified more by elective affinities than by affinities of race. And up there, between sea and sky, the dancer and the sailor confabulated endlessly as Christopher Columbus and Pedro Gutierrez had done four centuries earlier, but on matters of another kind, while the cattle boat escorted by dolphins dragged its bottom over the phosphorescent ocean, and below, in the now subdued hell of the hold, Jove, foam at his nostrils and his flanks quivering, lay in his own vomit. Even in the most obtuse of men Isadora inspired pure and sublime feelings.

Some months later Isadora met Jove again in Paris. The same one who in the guise of a sick ox had lain in the hold of the cattle boat? Who can say? In any case, extraordinarily regenerated and restored to his most glowing taurine state. Like Sophroniscus, the father of Socrates, he practiced sculpture, and he called himself Auguste Rodin. Those plaster legs that walked away on their own, freed at last from the useless weight of a head and torso; those fists that clenched the air to the point of spasm; those human trunks that though deprived of limbs and head were magnificently alive and breathed from the depths of the heart—all these revealed true art to Isadora, and the way their great creator despised the superfluous and stuck to the essential. If entomologists do not deceive us, the magnified claw and the part for the whole are the ant's way of seeing, that little creature for whom our world is a synecdoche. What does it matter? By that time Rodin had brought his winged-bull nature to perfection, and the title of "new Michelangelo" resounded agreeably in his huge and hairy ear. Isadora, who had already met him socially, went to pay him a visit one day in his studio in the Hôtel Biron. Upon the dancer's entrance, Rodin with a nod dismissed Rainer Maria Rilke, who in the pose of Narcissus was taking down in a notebook the thoughts the Master dictated to him on art. Isadora slipped out of her street clothes like a banana out of its skin, and danced angelically nude among the statues. Women imagine that art justifies everything. And which art? The dance—this *Ersatz* of art. Rodin followed these circumvolutions of flesh with a bovine eye, and his forehead became tragically furrowed. He said nothing, but the silence was filled by his anxious breathing. When the circles narrowed, were reduced to a point, and the girl came to standstill, the bull detached himself from the mantelpiece on which he had rested his elbow during the chaste and awesome dance and moved slowly forward. Still he said nothing, but he was breathing more heavily than ever. He approached the panting and fragrant dancer, and touched her hair with his huge hand, accustomed to molding clay; he touched her neck, her arms, her legs. His chest swelled, fumes came from his nostrils. Then Isadora stirred as though coming to her senses, defended herself with her hands like Daphne against Apollo, and fled in a series of great arching leaps. "What a pity!" Isadora Duncan remarks many years later in her autobiography. "How often I have regretted this childish miscomprehension which lost to me the divine chance of giving my virginity to the Great God Pan himself, to the Mighty Rodin!" And Nivasio Dolcemare, from whose living voice we have culled this recital of Isadora Duncan's exploits, comments at this point: "It's easy to be wise after the event."

To get back to the cattle boat. In the horror of its hold, Isadora had recognized Jove transformed into a bull, and from a bull reduced to an ox. This is a sign of how living and present for the dancing maiden that world of human super-humanity was, which for most people is over and forgotten. As for Raymond Duncan, the spectacle of those ruminants tortured by the sea was responsible for his abjuration of meat-eating and conversion to vegetarianism. This is not only

nutrition, it is religion.[7] Raymond became one of the most
fervid apostles of the green faith. Anyway sarcophagy is
absurd in a Raymond Duncan! The Duncans, as we have said,
are bird people. True, Raymond has never been a flying bird,
but rather a flightless one, like the chickens and turkeys. He
has the hooked beak of a turkey, wattles like Dante's, and his
neck moves like a connecting rod when he walks. So not even
grass is appropriate for such a creature, but corn—and not to
be eaten but pecked. Of the four Duncan children, Raymond
for importance and the doctrine of the dance is second only to
Isadora herself—that Isadora whom he, still among the
living, now mourns in Paris with his round eyes of an old
turkey cock.

III

What does Nivasio Dolcemare think of the dance? "The
dance," he has told us, "is the language of deaf-mutes as
propagated by the hands to the rest of the body. Deaf-mutes
and dancers are equally distressing. Both would like to tell us
something, but what? The same could be said for a dog,
except we know the dog will never speak. So never say of a
dog: 'If he could only talk.' The expectation of what cannot
happen is the most painful form of unhappiness. What are
the dancer's gestures meant to express? Not ideas, leaving
aside those rudimentary ones expressed by semaphore, two
sailors speaking to each other by waving their arms from one
ship to another. Beyond that, one moves immediately to the
absurd, equivocal, opaque area of *states of mind.* Now do you
understand why we who have discovered a new poetic reality
have always been suspicious of the dance, even in the period

7. Vegetarianism is a kind of Reformation. It has its Counter-
Reformation in the vegetarian's return to meat-eating. Nietzsche
provides us with an example of this. In a passage in *Ecce Homo,* he
expresses his gratitude to Wagner, who showed him the error of
vegetarianism and its "softening" effects.

of its greatest triumphs? What we love in the word is its meaning and object: they love movement. Deaf-mutism rises to the eyes, the brain. The dance is a harmless form of madness, a silent and flickering illness. But the years go by and the mind grows calm. From the comfort of an ever broader perspective, even the most useless things acquire a desirable reality. We think back nostalgically on the words of our parents, on the now forgotten art, which they practiced so wisely, of speaking in order to say nothing. Dislike diminishes little by little, and now it is with sympathy, no longer with hostility or indifference, that we recall this woman who by the drama of her life satiated for a moment the voracity of fate, as the seven youths and seven maidens of Athens year after year satisfied the hunger of the Minotaur. Poor Isadora! Too simple to conceive the utility of the useless, she offered her absurd gestures to anyone, and her dancing concealed a religious purpose. Isadora was also an archaeologist, a Petrarch in skirts, a Winckelmann with breasts. She found the ballet and its practitioners reduced to gyrating dolls: she resuscitated the Greek dance, the gravity of its rhythms, the austerity of its movements. Unlike those who sought to imitate her, her dancing was neither frenetic nor hysterical, but always contained within a stately measure, a great dignity." Thus spoke Nivasio Dolcemare. Did the British understand the revolution in dance brought about by Isadora Duncan? We will never know. Their good manners prevent the British from expressing judgments.

The Duncans' debut in London society took place in Mrs. X's house in Grosvenor Square. Mrs. Duncan sat down at the piano and Isadora danced Nevin's "Narcissus" and Mendelssohn's "Spring Song." Elizabeth for her part recited some Theocritus idylls in English translation, and Raymond gave a brief lecture on the influence of the dance on the psyche of future humanity. A program to send the rustics of Colle Val d'Elsa into paroxysms of delight. Isadora danced barefoot, her adolescent body enveloped in a few yards of veiling. A youthful divinity, reawakened after two thousand years of slumber, had dropped from the ceiling in the middle of that

Operatic Lives

London salon. Ladies and gentlemen followed the unusual spectacle with their lorgnettes and monocles, their faces set in a common smile that allowed no expression of surprise. "Delightful!" they murmured. "Charming!" But did anyone notice that those light veils were more shocking than frank nudity? Good manners overcame puritanism itself. Meanwhile in other salons, all things being equal, Francesco Paolo Tosti was garnering the same sort of praise after singing, with goatee uplifted and eyes rolled back, "Vorrei morir" amid general indifference. Also present was the Prince of Wales, the future Edward VII, but not even he, endowed as he was with the political acumen destined to shine so brilliantly in the Entente Cordiale, penetrated the mystery or sounded the depths of Isadora's art. But he made up for it by his appraisal of the dancer's physical qualities: with the sureness of an expert, the future king exclaimed that she was "a Gainsborough beauty," and this praise, formulated by such authoritative lips, made Isadora the rage of the moment. Ephemeral glory! Her successes in London drawing rooms were purely honorific, and while Mrs. Duncan, the few dollars brought from New York having been spent, nourished her flying offspring on tea in which she dipped the stale crusts of leftover buns, Isadora, her limbs weakened, gave benefit performances that netted plenty of gold sovereigns for the lady sponsors. In England piety and ferocity wear the same face. When Jack London began playing at poverty as an experiment, and along with other tramps entered a Salvation Army soup kitchen in the Whitechapel quarter of London, General Booth's lieutenants, before handing over the bowl of stinking dishwater and the piece of grayish bread that constituted the goal of that sad pilgrimage, obliged the starving men to spend an hour singing psalms in praise of the Most High, when salami would have been rather more appropriate. From her stay in London, Isadora made certain observations on the life and character of the British that go far beyond anything George Bernard Shaw has had to say or write on this subject. Listen:

218

[In Mrs. Wyndham's house] I had my first experience of an English afternoon tea before an open fire.

There is something about an open fire, bread and butter sandwiches, very strong tea, a yellow fog without and the cultural drawl of English voices which makes London very attractive. . . . There was in this house a magic atmosphere of security and comfort, of culture and ease. . . .

It was in this house that I first noticed the extraordinary demeanor of good English servants, who move about with a sort of assured aristocratic manner of their own, and, far from objecting to being servants, or wishing to rise in the social scale as they do in America, they are proud of working for the best families. Their fathers did it before them, and their children will do it after them. This is the kind of thing that makes for the calm and security of existence.

And Nivasio Dolcemare adds: "Evil cannot be suppressed in the world. So why not conceal it under a uniformly angelic face? There is no reason to seek any meaning for the word hypocrisy other than the one contained in the word civilization."

In Paris the avian nature of the Duncans underwent a splendid development. The atavism of Ornix, their remote ancestor from the age of birds, manifested itself with renewed vigor. They got up before sunrise, and since according to the testimony of the philosopher Amelius birds are the happiest creatures in the world, they went to dance in the dewy Luxembourg Gardens, among the marble queens of France. Isadora made her debut in the salon of Madame de Saint-Marceau, before the Tout-Paris of art and finance. André Messager was at the piano. When the dance was over, a gentleman with the face of a mummy and a body of ectoplasm rose from the depths of an armchair where he had been coiled like an anaconda digesting a meal; little by little he began to extend himself, not stopping when he might reasonably have been expected to, but continuing to rise. He

219

was very tall indeed. Around his body shone an opaline halo, the manifest presence of what metapsychists calls "vital irradiation." The unlikely gentleman thrust out two octopus tentacles and seized the dancer as though to devour her.

"Quel est ton nom, petite fille?"

"Isadora."

"Mais ton petit nom?"

"When I was a little girl they called me Dorita."

"Dorita! Dorita!" exclaimed the immeasurable gentleman in a little thread of a voice entirely suited to his tubular body. Then availing himself of the privileges granted to a personage so different from other human creatures, he kissed the girl on her eyes, her cheeks, her mouth. When Isadora asked the hostess who this singular kissing gentleman was, Madame de Saint-Marceau replied that he was the "great" Sardou.[8] It was Isadora's fate to be kissed by all the great men of France.[9]

Besides the meeting with that famous and by now forgotten puppet master, two events mark this period of Isadora's life,

---

8. "Vital irradiation" and the appearance of ectoplasm are justified. Victorien Sardou was less important as a dramatist than as a cultivator of occult sciences, and ever since being reduced to the state of a wandering soul, he has responded most obligingly and as an old colleague to the questions put to him by mediums, both by automatic writing and table-rapping.

9. One of the few illustrious Frenchmen of the time who did not seek labial contact with Isadora's skin was Eugène Carrière. A painter of opacity and fog, Carrière was also a pure and beautiful soul. He lived a humble and saintly life in a top-floor studio among his books, his family, and his friends. "When coming into his presence," says Isadora, "I felt as I imagine I would have felt had I met the Christ." Meager and of an apostolic tastelessness, meals in the Carrière household were consumed in a silence occasionally broken by some beautiful thought uttered in a deep voice and with hieratic movements by the Master, in the small circle of light that streamed like a divine ray from the lampshade. In this pious penumbra Isadora met Mechnikov, Pasteur's successor and discoverer of the life-extending properties of yoghurt.

both of great importance to her: the tragic process of *anthoptosis*, and the discovery that the center of dance movements lies not at the base of the spinal column, as ballet teachers erroneously believe, but at the level of the solar plexus.

"I spent long days and nights in the studio seeking that dance which might be the divine expression of the human spirit through the medium of the body's movement. For hours I would stand quite still, my two hands folded between my breasts, covering the solar plexus. . . . I was seeking and finally discovered the central spring of all movement, the crater of motor power, the unity from which all diversities of movement are born, the mirror of vision for the creation of the dance—it was from this discovery that was born the theory on which I founded my school. The ballet school taught the pupils that this spring was found in the center of the back at the base of the spine. From this axis, says the ballet master, arms, legs and trunk must move freely. . . . This method produces an artificial mechanical movement not worthy of the soul. I on the contrary sought the source of the spiritual expression to flow into the channels of the body filling it with vibrating light—the centrifugal force reflecting the spirit's vision."

Lest the reader make any rash assumptions, we declare that the above quotation is taken directly from the writings of Isadora Duncan.

"After many months," Isadora continues, "when I learned to concentrate all my force to this one Centre I found that thereafter when I listened to music the rays and vibrations of the music streamed to this one fount of light within me—there they reflected themselves in spiritual vision—not the brain's mirror, but the soul's, and from this vision I could express them in Dance—I have often tried to explain to artists this first basic theory of my Art. Stanislavski mentions my telling him of this in his book: 'My Life in Art.'

"It would seem as if it were a very difficult thing to explain in words, but when I stood before my class of even the smallest and poorest children and said: 'Listen to the music with your soul. Now, while listening, do you not feel an inner self awakening deep within you—that it is by its strength that your head is lifted, that your arms are raised, that you are walking slowly toward the light?' they understood. This awakening is the first step in the dance, as I conceive it." And Nivasio Dolcemare adds: "Stanislavski was one of Isadora Duncan's most intense, albeit 'unrequited,' loves, which proves once again that the senses are still the best means of comprehension between a man and a woman." "When I had finished this colossal experiment," Isadora confesses in another part of her autobiography, "I realized that the only dance masters I could have were Jean-Jacques Rousseau ('Emile'), and Walt Whitman and Nietzsche." And Nivasio Dolcemare: "Too bad one couldn't see their expressions when they found themselves assigned such unexpected tasks!" As for what we have called *anthoptosis*, borrowing from the language of botany a term signifying "fall of the flower," and which stands for Dorita's passage from the state of maiden to that of woman, Isadora carried it out in Budapest, with the help of a Hungarian actor. Time and time again Isadora informs us that she is a *"cérébrale."* "My love affairs of the head," she says, "were as interesting to me as those of the heart." Of three young men who court her in Paris, she picks the ugliest, bespectacled one. "But what a mind!" she adds, as though having to justify her choice. She expresses her distaste for the four officers of the guard, magnificent specimens of flowering manhood, who come to her dressing room in the Opera House in Saint Petersburg bringing flowers from the czar. On another occasion, and still for reasons of the head, she prefers a fifty-year-old man in poor health to a muscular, broad-shouldered youth. Nevertheless, she tells us that the young Hungarian of the *anthoptosis* was "of god-like features and stature," and that "he might have posed for the David of Michael Angelo himself." A sign that there are some initiations for which intelligence alone is not enough.

But what do London or Paris, Budapest or Saint Petersburg matter beside the great, the true, the only goal that had brought the Duncans from America to Europe? One day

Raymond declared that the time had come to go to Greece. "No more shilly-shallying," declared the young man, who wore knickerbockers and a flowing tie, and above his highly developed Adam's apple had the face of an inspired simpleton. And he added peremptorily: "The Parthenon is waiting for us!" Since Raymond for the moment was the only male in the clan of featherless feathered folk, his decisions were final: the Duncans lifted their invisible wings and flew south. Even storks break their flight from time to time and descend to rest on church steeples. The Duncans stopped in Abbazia, but found it almost impossible to get a hotel room. When the court of Vienna went to Abbazia for seabathing, the town became tightly packed with brilliant personalities, like an untouched box of candied fruits. As Elizabeth and Isadora, worried about the next night's lodging, were searching the town by carriage, they were noticed by the Grand Duke Ferdinand. He saluted them with two fingers to the brim of his military cap, and having given his reassurances, with great courtesy invited them to stay at his pavilion in the gardens of the Hotel Stephanie. The news of the grand duke's hospitality circulated with the rapidity of a lighted fuse, and immediately set in motion all the female tongues, lips, and jaws assembled around the precious members of the imperial family in the pleasant little town on the Adriatic. The gardens of the Stephanie were surrounded, invaded, and patrolled by the ladies of the court, as rigid inside their corsets as warriors in armor, their necks encased in high starched collars and their hair obliquely covered by hats so loaded with fruit as to resemble baskets of spring produce, and bristling with feathers that included birds with outstretched wings preparing for flight and streaming ostrich plumes. Discovering the two American girls taking a carefree stroll among the flowerbeds, or reclining at ease on the lawns and S-shaped benches, countless eyes armed with lorgnettes scrutinized them with severity, indignation, and horror, but also with the flame that the force of fascination kindles in the eyes, as when visitors to a zoo stare into the crocodile pond. Simply to undress them was no effort for those eyes: the two girls wore so little. In the dining room of the Stephanie, the court ladies curtsied deeply as they approached the grand duke's table, but they were unable to compete with Isadora, who, favored by her lack of a corset and the greater nimbleness of her joints, performed curtsies that were absolutely fluid in depth. At the bathing hour, while Isadora and Elizabeth played at being mermaids among the wavelets, scantily clad in light blue bathing costumes that constituted a daring anticipation of the future and an astonishing contrast with the black outfits of the time, elongated by equally black stockings and shoes, the Grand Duke Ferdinand, standing on the footbridge and observing these unsual bathers through mother-of-pearl opera glasses, was heard to remark: *"Ach, wie schön ist diese Duncan! Ach, wunderschön! Diese Frühlingszeit ist nicht so schön wie sie!"* But how deceiving are appearances! The grand duke's interest in the girl who was "more beautiful than springtime" was purely aesthetic. In other respects, the illustrious personage preferred the company of the handsome young officers of his entourage. And when later Isadora learned that by decree of the Austrian court the exquisite grand duke had been incarcerated in the sad castle of Salzburg, but not so he could listen to the Mozart festivals nearby, she wept disconsolate tears, as Echo in her time had wept over the impossible love of Narcissus.

There are all kinds of ways to go to Greece: the tourist way, individual or collective; the hasty commercial way, to negotiate a shipment of olives or sweet grapes; the Odyssean way, which is the most illustrious of all. Few use it, but among those few one name stands out: Victor Bérard, the last of the Homeric scholars, who devoted his whole life to the *Odyssey*, and for his honeymoon retraced the voyage of Odysseus in the company of his young bride, Alice, to whom the first volume of his immortal work is sweetly dedicated: *"Dilectae coniugi Alice Bérard gratiam persolvens pro annorum XXV vitae ac laboris societate concordi."* The Duncans held a family conference and for their trip to Greece decided to adhere as strictly as possible to the itinerary of the son of Laertes. They started out by embarking at Brindisi, a port where the "far-ranging" hero never dreamed of landing. They disembarked at Leukas, discerned the rocky ghost of Ithaca and the cliff where Sappho, desperate with love, threw herself into the sea; they betook themselves to the little town of Karvasaras, where in the presence of the assembled inhabitants, whose eyes were popping out of their heads, they knelt and kissed the sacred soil of Greece; that night they made the acquaintance of the bedbugs of Hellas, Homeric too in their way, and which the Greeks call "English" because of a certain similarity of color to the old uniforms of the British marines; they passed through Agrinion; paid homage at Missolonghi to the memory of Lord Byron, who died there of malaria in April 1824; they passed through Patras but did not pay homage to Matilde Serao since they did not know her, and that same evening they came in sight of Athens. But they did not immediately enter the city sacred to so many who worship beauty, intelligence, and reason. Just as the Muslim takes off his slippers before setting foot in the mosque, the Duncans divested themselves of the sad garments that had hitherto covered their agile limbs so desirous of light and air, and sacrificed them on a bonfire to the deities of Olympus, while pouring libations of unwatered wine that smelled of varnish.[10] Finally, in tunics and sandals, their hands gripping staffs and gourds filled with water teetering on their shoulders, they made their entry into the city of Pallas Athena. But has the power of the latter really been reduced to naught? At the approach to the Theseion, a brisk shower of stones greeted these people who were coming to restore the cult of the wisest of goddesses. We trust that even the most inattentive reader has understood by now. The "ancient Greek" whom the astonished Gargaras had seen crossing Parliament Square that day in the noon sun was

---

10. Falernian was called "smoky" because the skins containing this famous Campanian wine were customarily hung under the chimney of the fireplace and smoked like hams. For their part, the Greeks, ever since Homeric times, have mixed resin with their wine the better to preserve it, which gives the drinker the impression of drinking fresh paint.

Raymond Duncan; and it was Raymond, along with Isadora, Elizabeth, and their mother, whom the Athenians followed around the city and out of the city to the high ground of Kopanos, where the king himself, His Majesty George I, came on horseback to see these odd individuals. And then it was that the farce began changing into tragedy. Invisible eyes opened and glittered threateningly, mysterious ears pricked up and listened; and an arcane hostility, whose precursory signs had appeared in the storm in the Ambracian Gulf that all but sank the little steamer with the four Duncans on board, in the current of the Aspropotamos or "white river"[11] that almost swept Isadora and Raymond away in their eagerness to bathe, in the savage dogs that attacked the little clan on the road from Karvasaras to Agrinion, began to close more and more tightly around these rash souls who were trying to subvert the order of time and bring back to life things that repose forever among the dead.

IV

The Duncans' arrival on the sacred soil of Greece aroused not only the curiosity of men, but another kind as well, ineffable and much more profound. While the pilgrimage of the Athenians to the Kopanos campsite continued, a slight undulation rippled across the surface of Hellas, and was dispersed over that body which so resembles a vine leaf set in the sea. Barely a tremor in comparison with the frightful earthquakes that violently shook Delphi when the fury of the serpent-slaying god was unleashed, but still it was precisely at Delphi that this telluric ripple found its epicenter—Delphi, which in metaphysical times was the navel of the world. When rosy-fingered Dawn began to lift the shadows from the Phaidriades—just as in autumn the housekeeper strips the armchairs, divan, and piano of the sheets that have protected them during the summer season, transforming Madame's

---

11. The ancient Achelous.

drawing room into a silent reception of ghostly presences—a faint rumble of shifting earth was heard in the middle of what was left of the foundations of the temple of Apollo. Crickets lying on their backs bathed themselves in dewdrops, and little birds lifted their wings to the breeze to cool themselves. But the sun tarried and there was an obscure connection between this delay and the little upheaval of turf in the middle of the temple.

All of a sudden the chorus of birds fell silent, and with eyes round with astonishment stared at the unexpected creature halfway between man and beast who came wriggling with difficulty out of the earth.

"Who are you?" demanded the leader of the birds with a lion's courage, "you coming out of the earth like a stalk of asparagus?"

The creature's trunk was already out: it seized a clod of earth and flung it at the insolent bird.

"People who live in glass houses. . . !" cried the birds in chorus, and simultaneously spreading their wings, they flew away in a noisy flock and plunged into the nearby woods. The unknown creature now drew forth its legs, stretched its limbs, gave a yawn like a famished panther, then with the stride of a man made of volcanic tufa and covered with mud, it descended the sacred plain of Delphi toward the green ice-cold waters of the Pleistos. Remaining inside the temple foundations was a deep hollow that looked like the shadow of a sleeping man. Then, at a sign from their leader, all the birds broke out again in song, and the sun, suddenly liberated, leaped above the horizon.

Great trust was established between the Duncans and the people of Athens—all the greater in being a sincere reaction against the mistrust that had preceded it. A comical intimacy came to unite these blond Americans in their colorful cloaks and that dark-skinned and dark-colored populace, so similar to crickets obliged to live like men. Neither group could understand the other: the Athenians spoke Romaic, or the bastardized Greek of today, the Duncans a few ancient Attic

227

words found in the dictionary and pronounced with a trans-atlantic accent. The impossibility of understanding each other increased the cordiality of their relations. Evolutionists deem mutual understanding between peoples to be an element of progress, and for this purpose fabricate common languages that are supposed to make peace reign on earth. Dreamers! It is ignorance that keeps people beautiful, the way ice preserves food.

The Duncans had chosen Kopanos as their headquarters, less in order to live at the foot of Mount Hymettus, famous for its honey, than to be on a level with the Acropolis. It was a steep and barren hill, unsuitable for any sort of cultivation or dwelling, and apparently free of property claims. But no sooner had the Duncans shown their intention to build a house on the top of Kopanos, when not one but five owners leaped forth, expressing first their astonishment, then their horror, and finally weeping at the idea of having to relinquish that heap of stones where nature, as they said amid sobs, had gathered so much splendor and abundance. But the Duncans had unfailing arguments at their disposal: from her tours of the principal theaters of Europe Isadora had brought back heaps of pounds sterling and *louis d'or*, and at the sound of this metal the hearts of the five landowners, though broken, gave in. The business was expeditiously negotiated through a horrendously hairy and sweating Athens lawyer named Panaghios Vlakas. The five families were invited to a banquet, and after copious libations of *raki*[12] and resinated wine, the head of each family traced his cross on the bill of sale.

Raymond lost no time in setting to work. The house was to be modeled on Agamemnon's palace. Its walls had been two feet thick and so the walls of the Duncan house must also be two feet thick. The only material permitted was that Pentelic marble from which the columns of the Parthenon had been hewn. The day came for laying the cornerstone. All the peasants from the surrounding countryside climbed Ko-panos, behind the black-robed priest, with his black hat

---

12. The cognac of the Greeks.

perched over his knot of hair, held in place by hairpins, and with a black gauze veil fluttering on his shoulders. The sun was about to set. Seven times the Duncans traced the outline of the foundations with dance steps. The priest seized a black cock by the legs, and as the sun was setting on the horizon, solemnly cut its throat and anointed the cornerstone with the blood. Then holding the still throbbing creature with his left hand and the bloody knife with his right, he walked three times around the invisible house. He intoned prayers and ritual spells. One by one he blessed the stones. He pronounced an invocation in which the names of Raymond, Elizabeth, and "young" Isadora constantly recurred, but before uttering the name of this last, he delicately cleaned his nose with two fingers. He prayed for their descendants, and at the end of the rite the *floghera* and *daouli* players struck up a Dionysian concert. Huge fires blazed in the night. *Ouzo* and *raki* flowed in streams. Roast lamb *à la palikara* was torn to pieces with the teeth right on the spit and devoured in a twinkling. The women danced the *sirtos,* which is danced in a chain, shuffling the feet[13] and holding to the ends of a handkerchief.

But someone was spying on them. He was still panting from the climb. Even had they discovered him and looked him in the face, no one would have recognized him, because except for ourselves no one had ever seen him before. Besides what was there to see on that face as devoid of human features as a melon? It was the man of stone and mud who had emerged "like a stalk of asparagus" from the turf in the temple of Apollo, and who with the gait of an enormous pair of walking compasses had set off down the holy plain of the Pleistos. Hidden in the darkness, and though without eyes, he watched with devouring curiosity the faces of the men and women dramatically illuminated by the flames from the braziers. The smoke rose like a ghost in the sky. No one noticed him, and the songs, dancing, and drinking lasted until the sun, which the evening before had witnessed the

---

13. Hence its name: *sirtos,* shuffled.

sacrifice of the black cock and in the meantime had given a day to people in the other hemisphere, returned above the summit of Hymettus.

At the same time that all this was going on, Nivasio Dolcemare was preparing for his piano examinations. The Athens conservatory is called the Odeon[14] and is situated on Piraeus Street. Why bother to repeat what has so often been said about music being a drug? Nivasio Dolcemare was living a musical dream. One hour of scales every morning and an hour of Pischna to "loosen" the fingers, before going on to the persistent repetition of the program to be executed at the end of June before the panel of teachers from the Odeon, presided over by the director, whose name was "Nose": Bach's *Italian Concerto,* Liszt's *Presence of God in Solitude,* Schumann's *Papillons,* and the Concerto in D flat major by Tchaikovsky. Intoxicated with sounds, Nivasio Dolcemare set out for the Odeon on Tuesday and Saturday, two days of weekly happiness. The sounds of the place were audible to him from afar, and as soon as he turned from Concord Square into Piraeus Street, his blood quickened. On those metaphysical afternoons the Odeon emitted torrents of diverse music from every window, which merged into a music of all and none, of everything and nothing, the music of music, the only kind that did not deceive, and the old people stopped in the street to listen, rejoicing to hear the sounds of childhood again.

Isadora, too, was immersed in the life of music. On moonlit nights the municipality of Athens did not light the city, deeming gaslight redundant in so much lunar splendor. The Duncans had been granted special permission to circulate at night on the Acropolis. Seated on the steps of the Theater of Dionysus, they heard a boy's voice rising in the night, "with that pathetic, unearthly quality which only boys' voices have." All of a sudden another voice joined the first, then another and still another. This nocturnal chorus gave Isadora the idea

---

14. I.e., Cantoria.

of reconstituting the choruses of *The Suppliants*. Ten little ragamuffins with limpid voices were chosen from the riffraff of the Theseion quarter, and having been washed, deloused, and dressed in light tunics, were handed over for their musical education to a seminarian from the college of Byzantine priests in Athens.

Nivasio Dolcemare was studying piano under Hermann Lafont, a Saxon of Huguenot origin and pupil of the great Reisenhauer. A formidable virtuoso and one of the high-speed performers of the international concert stage (he treasured the review in which Edmond Rurisch, critic for the *Musikalische Zeitung*, had dubbed him *"die Lokomotive des Klaviers"*), Hermann Lafont was also one of the purest specimens of *homo felis*, or cat man. Frau Lafont for her part was a violinist, extremely pretty in face and figure, and her name was Mariezybil, which means Mary Sybil. She also taught at the Athens conservatory, but Nose the director did not assign her any pupils over ten years of age, fearing that beyond that limit the respect a pupil owes his teacher would degenerate into culpable sentiment, or worse, sinful passion.

On 17 May, posters appeared on the walls of Athens announcing that on the evening of the 30th Isadora Duncan would dance at the Demotiko[15] Theater. The heart of the city stopped beating, then resumed anxiously and with the violence of a tolling alarm bell. It was not so much the novelty of the solo and "serious" dance that disturbed people's minds—though hitherto no other dances had been seen besides ballet on points and the high kicking in the "cafés concerts"—as the information, underscored on the poster, that Isadora Duncan would dance *with bare feet*. The word "gymnopodia" made its way into households and disturbed the peace of families. Sports and hydrotherapy were still in their early stages.

Feet! After nineteen hundred years of Christianity, feet were coming back into their own. For almost twenty centuries

---

15. Municipal.

they had remained forgotten in the darkness of people's socks. Fashionable society in Athens knew no other contact with its feet than the Sunday foot bath that preceded a change of stockings. Other than that, the feet of even the most elegant youths, the most ethereal ladies, stood there silent and reluctant at the bottom of their sheaths of calf or cowhide, alone with their bunions, corns, and hammertoes. Who was this "American," synonymous at that time with "unprincipled," who dared to unveil the mystery of her feet? Saint Paul had warned against the seductiveness of the female foot, and Athenian wives, though unaware of the saint's admonition, forbade their husbands to attend the spectacle of "that shameless woman." The last straw! A woman with bare feet.

Isadora's feet aroused equally strong feelings, though apparently softened by veils of "European" tone, among members of the diplomatic corps. The Baroness Güldenkrone, daughter of Comte de Gobineau and wife of the minister plenipotentiary of Norway, said that Isadora Duncan's feet must be longer than *pieds d'Anglaise* since they were American feet, and this witticism made the rounds of the legations. On Nivasio Dolcemare, too, these posters made a profound impression, but of another kind: they announced that Isadora Duncan's dances would be accompanied at the piano by Professor Hermann Lafont. Nivasio thought he must have misread it . . . But no: it really said Lafont. "His" Lafont.

In Germany, a country more advanced along the path of nature worship, Isadora's feet had produced a different effect. One day in Paris Isadora had had a call from a fat and ceremonious gentleman, wrapped in a sumptuous fur coat and with fingers sparkling with rings, who introduced himself as Herr Binenbaum, impresario.

"I am from Berlin," said Herr Binenbaum. "We have heard of your barefoot act. I have come from the largest music hall in Germany to make an engagement with you at once."

Isadora contracted her arm muscles to keep her hand from seizing the bronze dog with a clock in its mouth on the mantelpiece and hurling it at Herr Binenbaum's head. Affable and uncomprehending, the latter went on: "I have the contract ready. All I need is your signature."

"My art," Isadora replied, "is not for a music hall."

"*Sie verstehen nicht!*" exclaimed the impresario, his pasty cheeks flushing red. "You do not understand. The greatest artists appear in our hall, and there will be much money. I already offer you five hundred marks a night. There will be more later. You will be magnificently presented as the 'First Barefoot Dancer in the World.' "

"Certainly not!" repeated the inflexible Isadora, while the impresario ran his watery and astonished eyes over the wretched furnishings of the rented studio. "I will come to Berlin some day, and I hope to dance to your Philharmonic Orchestra, but in a Temple of Music, not in a music hall with acrobats and trained animals. *Quelle horreur!* I bid you good day and adieu."

"*Dummes Mädel!*" growled the impresario, striking his forehead in vexation, but three years later, when Isadora's prediction came true and she danced at the Berlin Opera accompanied by the Philharmonic Orchestra, Binenbaum came into her dressing room more ceremonious than ever, and presenting a magnificent bouquet of roses with a gem-studded hand, said: "*Sie hatten recht, gnädige Frau. Küss die Hand.*"

Despite the veto by the wives of Athens, a human avalanche pressed against the doors of the Demotiko Theater on the evening of 30 May. Due to this exceptional turnout, extra policemen had been assigned and the ushers clamorously enjoined the order to "have your tickets ready." Standing out in the crowd, like a bell tower over the houses of a village, was a broad-shouldered and extraordinarily "simplified" man. That the face was that of a man was not entirely obvious. The eyes, mouth, and nose could barely be seen, as on a stone that a sculptor is only beginning to rough out. A hat, ridiculously small in comparison with the enormous head, rested on top of the wild mass of hair, like Noah's ark on the summit of Mount Ararat. He advanced through the crowd like a buffalo through the reeds of a swamp. His pace was slow but relentless. He did not have to exert himself, but simply rolled his body slowly. He stepped ruthlessly on people's feet, and every contact with him must have been painful, since an empty space had formed around him, almost as though his visible body were contained in another larger but invisible one.

When the usher at the entrance asked him for his ticket, he paid no attention. "Ticket," repeated the usher in a peremptory voice, but as he raised his eyes at that moment to the other's face, his voice choked in his throat and his body shriveled as though a lethal current had passed through it.

"Why didn't you make him give you his ticket?" asked the second usher. And the first: "Didn't you see? It's the king of Portugal."

He was lying. No one knew who that shapeless man was, except for ourselves who have seen him emerge from the turf in the temple of Apollo and later scrutinize the faces of the Duncans by the light of the braziers.

A prodigious silence fell on that human marmalade, every movement stopped, and in the enchanted void the notes of Chopin's Nocturne in E flat major were ignited one by one.

Lean and triangular as a seated thunderbolt, Lafont offered up the sound of the grand piano, its lid raised, to Isadora's dance. His arms moved inside the sleeves of his tailcoat with the motions of a piston. His fingers came down on the keys like spider legs, and immediately shot back up as though scorched by the keyboard. And meanwhile the gymnopodist, free in her body, like seaweed afloat in the sea, filled by herself the blue space in front of the curtain. The charm of her swaying movements operated like an invisible caress on the eyelids, on the heart. After so much glitter, so great a press of men and things, the performance returned to the elementary process of growth. The spectators, most of them students, men who had not yet found their place in society and were still charged with obscure hopes, were enraptured to see how flowers are born, how man is born, how life is born; and at the end of each dance the silence gave forth the roar of a reawakened beast. Isadora, once again small as a top when it stops its iridescent spinning and falls lifeless to the ground, took repeated curtain calls, and gazing at that quivering mass of humanity, bristling with noses, dotted with eyes, pierced by howling mouths, thought, in imitation of Caligula, if only all those men had a single body by which to give life together to a creature of health and beauty: to a new Meleager.

What a joy it would have been for Nivasio Dolcemare to see the pistonlike movements of his idol, to hear the welcome sounds that emerged from his fingers like air bubbles from the mouth of a fish! But in the hour that Lafont was playing and Isadora treading the boards of the Demotiko with her naked feet, children were asleep, each watched over by his guardian angel. And indeed Nivasio's angel, wings folded behind its back, was seated at the sleeping boy's bedside, and by the glow of the night light placed in front of the three-color reproduction of the *Madonna of the Goldfinch* was reading with obvious delight *The Adventures of Pinocchio*, which it had found on the bookshelf of its little charge, illustrated with drawings by Chiostri. But Nivasio's sleep was not tranquil. It was troubled by sinister dreams in which the adored Lafont, taller and more skeletal than ever, was threatened by frightful dangers. Nivasio wanted to protect him, to save him. But what could he do, small and helpless as he was, and especially with his weak legs that folded up under him like sausages?

George I, on hearing of the spectacle, expressed the wish that the barefoot dance be repeated at the Royal Theater. The evening was a brilliant one, the best that Athens had to offer in the way of décolletages and starched shirtfronts, and the king applauded with white-gloved hands from the royal box, but the flaming enthusiasm of the popular evening was lacking. As Isadora remarks in her memoirs: "The Ballet will always be the dance *par excellence* for Royal personages."

It was spring, the season of impurities and perils. Man is deluded by the possibilities that crowd upon him, and wants more than he is able to have. Among the promises of that acclaimed and obscure season, Nivasio felt an anticipation of death. The day after the evening at the Royal Theater was Tuesday—a fateful day. Nivasio turned into Piraeus Street, and immediately noted that in the web of sound woven in the air around the conservatory a stitch had been dropped. This time his blood quickened not with joy but with fear. As though a tree had been uprooted from the heart of a forest. Infinitely small as it was, the void left by the missing stitch opened up before Nivasio like an abyss into which his life was about to plunge. Nivasio knew by now, and if he persisted in not recognizing it, it was only out of a desperate need for comfort. Papadaros, the old doorman at the Odeon, informed him the minute he saw him enter: "No point your going upstairs. Lafont hasn't come in." Then, though Nivasio hadn't opened his mouth to answer: "He won't be in." Now all those sounds were the empty sounds of Nothingness.

Nivasio left the conservatory and started walking. He came to the outskirts of the city. Scattered dwellings, skeletons of unfinished houses, rose in the middle of uncultivated fields. Instinct led him, as a dog leads a blind man, to the point where two roads, barely to be seen in the sparse and yellow grass, met. A one-story cottage stood at the point of intersection. Night had fallen. How many times he had been in that house, for advice on technique, for the interpretation of a difficult passage! The arm of a gas lamp projected from the corner of the house, the diffused light from the flickering little flame accentuating the dreariness of the four closed shutters, the façade four times blind. Deserted by her husband, Mariezybil Lafont had taken refuge in the house of Max Wassenhoven, he too a teacher at the Odeon, but of the flute. And it was in thinking back on the sadness of that abandoned house, on the loss of his idol, on his shattered dream, that Nivasio Dolcemare, many years later, wrote the little musical poem known to a few initiates scattered over the principal capitals of Europe, in which like a threnody (a song of lamentation, a dirge) occurs the refrain:

> *In this house*
> *My teacher died,*
> *Let go, my heart,*
> *Goodbye, goodbye . . .*

That same night, Isadora Duncan and Herman Lafont embarked at Patras on the *Bulgaria* of the Florio & Rubattino shipping lines. They had been preceded on board by the chorus of ten Greek boys, who, lined up on the deck by the seminarian, beating time with his monstrously long index finger that ended in a black and rounded nail, launched into the Greek anthem as soon as the steamer got underway:

> *From the sacred, resurrected*
> *bones of the Hellenes . . .*

The lights of the port traced moving diagrams on the water. Leaning against the rail, her gaze fixed on the receding city, Isadora said:

"We have revived the ancient dance. We have replaced the uncomfortable and funereal modern costume with light tunics, we have restored freedom to the body. But that's not enough. We must create a new race, of healthy and beautiful children, worthy of the life that we have restored."

In a third personage, also leaning against the rail a short distance away, we can recognize the man of volcanic stone who had emerged from the soil in the temple of Delphi. His features have become more pronounced: the eyes wide and devoid of pupils, the nose perpendicular, the lips curved in a bow. The body is still swollen, and in the gray checkered suit that gracelessly covers those athletic limbs it is easy to recognize the style of the large Universal Department Store on Hermes Street, direct importer of merchandise from Mainz. As for the straw boater purchased at the Little Lord shop, once on board he has put it back in the tissue-paper wrappings supplied by the store, and on his head with its crown of golden curls substituted a visor cap. His face is impassive and cruel, but at Isadora's words his ear begins to

237

vibrate, doubles in size, and the better to listen contracts to the shape of an agaric mushroom.

"Would you like to, Hermann?"

Hermann doesn't answer, but the pressure of those fingers, accustomed to pounding out Chopin polonaises and Hungarian rhapsodies by Liszt on the keyboards of Kaps and Blüthner pianos, is more eloquent than speech.

"O my 'Greek' love!"

Holding each other up like two invalids afflicted with flaccid paraplegia, Hermann and Isadora descend below deck.

Patras is now only a faint glimmer in the distance, over the shining, throbbing blackness of the sea. All on board are asleep: asleep are the ten young warblers with their mouths open and drooling and their fists closed, asleep is the seminarian and ominous braying noises issue from his nose, asleep are the first- and second-class passengers between sheets, and those in third on the benches of the forward deck, and the mice come to whisper in each one's ear the subject for a beautiful dream. Four bells. Then the stone man, putting his ear back in place with a hand still as shapeless as a potato, also goes below to sleep.

> *Let go, my heart,*
> *Goodbye, goodbye . . .*

V

Isadora's ideas were as deep as the dreams of statues as yet unearthed by the archaeologist's spade. This elementary woman did not stray; she went right to the source and, like Faust, entered the august presence of the Mothers. We have seen the dance of the Russians, touching but insensate, violent but sterile, dazzling but unnatural. The whirlwind of Nijinsky, that body transformed into a moving sign, a living arabesque, was nothing but vanity and desperation. Furthermore, the dance of the Russians eliminates anthropomorphism and reduces man to an abstract figure. Even when present, Nijinsky was already a memory. Not so Isadora, favorite daughter of nature, whose dance was hope. Her hands and feet obeyed the voice of destiny. Simple ideas flowered in her, primitive ideas, only transported to a higher register, repeated in a larger format. Nothing in her offended nature, aspired to overcome it, or tried to divert it from its course. On the contrary, she wanted to serve it, manifest it, celebrate it. There was in Isadora the naive symbolism that one finds in a statue of Justice on the pediment of a court-house. She stood above the things of life as Böcklin's *Night* wrapped in its veils stands over the houses of the sleeping city. Unaware and trusting, she had come from across the seas, from the golden Far West, just as Truth, Goodness, and Beauty, equally unaware and trusting, leave their mysterious centers to come into humanity's midst. Art was for her so much a "natural thing" that Isadora saw motherhood shining on its summit. Thus was born in her—or rather arose in her, since it had been dormant there from the start—the idea of becoming a mother, of bringing children "more beautiful than the ancients" into the world. And the gods heard this proud proposal and picked up the gauntlet. Unseen but present, Retribution set out on Isadora's trail.

In order to produce "divine specimens," Isadora thought of uniting herself, her beautiful body, with "exceptional" men. She considered herself as matter and asked others for the spirit. This thought has been subjected to irony and derided, but what simpler or more natural thing is there to say against it? It offends, and above all irritates, the "exceptional man." But it offends ordinary people, who, not wishing to look inferior, would like to cut others down to their own size. Scorn is often nothing but the mask of envy.

The eugenesis attempted that night on the Aegean, in the darkness below the deck of the *Bulgaria* and with the cooperation of Hermann Lafont, did not produce the desired result. One can see that on other keyboards the "locomotive of the piano" was a simple cart. Later Isadora made the same proposal to Stanislavski, but he, though he loved Isadora like the light of his own eyes, stared at her wildly as though all of a sudden she had been transformed into the image of Death, and exclaimed, "And Polia Trofimovna? What will Polia Trofimovna say?"[16] It is comforting to think that there are still people in the world for whom conjugal duty is not an empty word. Invited to participate in the conception of a creature who would combine his brain and her legs, George Bernard Shaw is known to have replied, "And if it should have her brain and my legs?" In which the pungent Irishman was once more mistaken, since Isadora not only surpassed George Bernard Shaw in physical qualities but in judgment as well. Strindberg too received Isadora's invitation, and in fact the dancer, to whom one trip more or less did not make much difference, went to Stockholm to deliver it to him personally, repeating the usual formula: "Come and see me dance." What a misfortune for women that even the purest invitation should take on an equivocal tone! Strindberg replied that he hated mankind and never went out of his house. "I'll give you a seat on the stage, behind the curtains, for you alone," Isadora promised, but Strindberg would not be persuaded. It was Isadora's view that there are two kinds of women in the world: inspirational ones and vampires. Strindberg's pessimism could be attributed to the fact that he had loved only vampire women. The same invitation went to Ernst Haeckel, last of the great Darwinians and author of *Monographie der Radiolarien* and *Anthropogenie oder Entwicklungsgeschichte des Menschen*. Haeckel accepted. The meeting took place at Bayreuth.

Life at the Villa Wahnfried at that time was like a symposium. No less than fifteen guests sat down daily to luncheon and dinner at the Wagner table, and when Isadora arrived in Bayreuth and checked into the Hotel Schwarz Adler, she soon received a luncheon invitation from the woman on

---

16. The name of Stanislavski's wife. Some years later, Polia Trofimovna, to whom Isadora recounted the incident, remarked, "I'm not surprised at my husband, he takes everything so seriously!"

whose breast the composer of *Tristan* had rested his head to sleep. Dressed in a flimsy white tunic, her curls dancing on her head, and for all the world like a big shining angel descended to earth to demonstrate the beauty of paradise, Isadora found herself in the midst of the most illustrious representatives of the republic of music—the athletic Hans Richter, Humperdinck, the fascinating Mottl. The dining room was arranged in such a way that from the table around which they sat, the guests could see the Master's tomb standing in the park. Cosima, whom Nietzsche in his madness had called Ariadne, sat at the head of the table.

When the meal was over, Cosima took Isadora's arm and they went for a walk in the park, which lay gilded with the colors of autumn. Cosima asked Isadora to compose dances for the "Venusberg" music, and in her choreographic outline Isadora wrote that "in this music [*Tannhäuser*] is concentrated the unsatisfied senses, the mad longing, the passionate languor; in short, the whole cry of desire in the world."

Haeckel arrived in Bayreuth on a rainy day. He alighted from the train carrying a carpet bag bearing the diagonal inscription "*Gute Reise.*" He was bearded, gigantic, and childish. Isadora took him by carriage to her Phillipsruhe villa, where she showed him his room decorated with flowers. A professed monist,[17] Haeckel found that even Isadora's dancing was an expression of monism, because "it came from one source and had one direction of evolution." In the state of mind in which the monist found himself, any praise, even the highest, would have appeared to him as lower than the truth. In the afternoon they took a walk in the countryside. Arriving at the top of a hill, Haeckel looked around with the gaze of a demiurge and contemplated the

---

17. From a recent definition of "Monism" supplied by Adriano Tilgher: "Affirmation of the unity of the cosmic principle, conceived as a vaguely personal force that draws the world, its expression and manifestation, upward along the path of infinite Progress, in which this principle actuates and realizes itself indefinitely."

works of nature below with a satisfied and approving eye. In the evening Isadora took her friend to the Festspielhaus. They were giving *Parsifal*. While onstage they sang of Amfortas's incurable wound and the knights of the Holy Grail invoked the Lord, the monist sat quiet as could be in his seat, without making a gesture or uttering a sigh. How could Frau Cosima say that Haeckel was a materialist, incapable of grasping the things of the spirit? When the act was over and the lights went on again in the hall, Haeckel was sleeping like a bearded baby, smacking his half-closed lips in that air still charged with musical harmony.

It was Isadora's fate to commit a host of errors at Bayreuth. One evening at Villa Wahnfried, King Ferdinand of Bulgaria was announced. Everyone jumped to his feet, except Isadora who continued to recline languidly on a couch, in the position of Madame Récamier in David's painting. To Frau Cosima's pointed looks, Isadora replied that she was "fiercely democratic." The king entered, and by an inexplicable attraction ignored the guests bowing at right angles and made a beeline for the reclining woman. Having learned who she was, he spoke with enthusiasm of the rebirth of the ancient world and offered his palace on the Black Sea for a school of classical dancing. In return, Isadora prepared a magnificent supper in Ferdinand's honor at Phillipsruhe, and since she had a butler who bore a striking resemblance to the king of Portugal, the guests had the illusion that there were two sovereigns present instead of one.

The idea of children "more beautiful than the ancient gods" had taken up steady abode in the dancer's mind. One evening in Saint Petersburg, at the home of Anna Pavlova, Leon Bakst read Isadora's palm and discovered two crosses on it. "You will have much glory," said the clairvoyant painter, "but you will lose the two creatures whom you love most on earth." "Who?" asked Isadora, looking around with a questioning eye. Like those of Cassandra, Bakst's prophecy was scorned.

242

What Hermann Lafont could not do for the same reason that Theseus decided to abandon Ariadne,[18] what Stanislavski could not do because of an overly rigid adherence to his marital vows, what Strindberg could not do because of the inhibitions produced in his psyche by the vampirism of women, and Haeckel for reasons that escape us non-monists, was done by Gordon Craig, the wizard of scenography, he who for the harmless old stage sets substituted flights of stairs at whose top a cypress sways under infinite skies where one's gaze is lost.

Isadora saw Gordon Craig for the first time in 1905, in Berlin, but since meetings prepared by destiny are always somehow foretold, Isadora had "'foreseen" Gordon in a woman she had met many years before in London.

"Who are you?" Isadora asked this being, who looked like a combination of Endymion and Hyacinthus and stood before her like a memory dressed as a man.

"I am the son of Ellen Terry," he replied.

"Ellen Terry!" Isadora repeated, her voice faint with astonishment. "The great actress? My ideal woman? Give me a child!"

Gordon Craig lived in a studio on the top floor of a very tall building. The floor was painted black and strewn with artificial rose petals. The studio was completely empty of furniture, and equally empty were the pockets of the host. Isadora and Endymion slept on the floor, and a nearby delicatessen from time to time sent up a little food on credit. The patriarchs, the wives of patriarchs, and all those who have some experience of procreation and progeny will say that these are not the most favorable conditions for begetting children. But for once the patriarchs and their wives will have been mistaken. Besides, and by Isadora's own admission, Gordon Craig was a mixture of fire and lightning. And so

---

18. Theseus abandoned Ariadne because she was seasick between Crete and Naxos.

who cares about furniture, regular meals, and money in the bank?

Isadora dreamed of making her Gordon the most celebrated "scenic technician" in the world, and for this purpose she introduced him to Eleanora Duse. Eleanora commissioned Craig to do the stage sets for *Rosmersholm,* and a few days later Duse, Isadora, and Craig took the train to Florence.

Gordon Craig and Eleanora Duse were not made for mutual understanding, but since Craig knew neither Italian nor French, and Duse for her part did not speak a word of English, a tacit accord was established between them.

In the stage directions for the first act of *Rosmersholm,* Ibsen calls for "a comfortable, old-fashioned living room with a window looking out on the courtyard of an old estate," but Craig converted the comfortable, old-fashioned living room into an Egyptian temple with tall columns and dizzying perspective, and the simple window into an enormous picture window opening on a fiery landscape of reds and yellows. The interpreter between Craig and Duse was Isadora Duncan. "I see this as a small window," said Eleanora, bringing her famous hands together as though in prayer and imploring him with her sorrow-laden eyes. "Tell him to give me my little window!" And Isadora translated: "Eleanora says that you are the greatest genius in the world and that your stage sets are masterpieces." A short while later, and as a consequence of Eleanora's repeated lamentations, Craig in his turn said: "Tell this damned woman to stay out of my way or I'll dump a can of paint on her head." And Isadora translated: "Gordon says he considers you the greatest tragedienne of all times, and that he will do everything possible to infuse his sets with the sorrowful beauty of your soul." Why not adopt the Duncan method for diplomatic conferences?

Nothing better confirms the truth of the myth of Antaeus, namely, the deterioration of certain organisms when removed from their place of origin, as the fate of the ten young choristers taken on tour through Europe by Isadora Duncan. Beautiful as angels, pure as the air of the mountain tops, these ten boys were considered by Isadora her spiritual children, but everyone knows how often parents—honorary ones no less than actual ones—are mistaken when it comes to their children. To the owners of the hotels where Isadora and her retinue stayed, and thus to the managers and staff as well, these ten little angels, flowers of purity and goodness, revealed a violent disposition and marked tendencies toward crime.

Every morning, dressed in fluttering tunics, sandals on their feet, and their heads wreathed in roses, the ten singing boys trooped through the Tiergarten in Berlin, flanked on three sides by Isadora, Elizabeth, and the Byzantine seminarian.

One morning as the neo-Hellenic procession was parading along an avenue in the park, a horse on the adjacent bridle path neighed, and rearing up threw its woman rider. Passersby rushed to lift up the fallen equestrienne and retrieved her bowler hat, which had rolled among the tangled reins: it was the Kaiserin Augusta. To what was the fright of the gentle old steed from the royal stables to be attributed, if not to the sight of those ten boys dressed so differently from the other visitors to the Tiergarten? Isadora Duncan's chorus was becoming a public menace. The Kaiserin Augusta was reputed to be so modest that before visiting a sculptor's studio she sent court lackeys ahead to cover the nude statues with sheets.

Not only did the spirits of the ten boys begin to deteriorate but their voices as well. Pure and piercing under the skies of Greece, crystalline as the water of the Castalian Spring, in the air of Berlin the voices of the little choristers had become as rasping as sandpaper. While Isadora on the stage of the *Opernhaus* was impersonating the fifty daughters of Danaus, multiplying herself accordingly and with a hundred hands imploring the altar of Zeus, the chorus of boys accompanied these entreaties with jarring notes that grated on the ears. Between scenes Isadora tried vainly to explain to the audience the nature of Byzantine music, and how what seems jarring to us is actually the sweetest of harmonies, but patient and well mannered as they were, the Berliners looked at each

245

other in bewilderment and disgruntled murmurs spread through the hall.

Then there was the problem of diet. Cold cuts, soups prepared with beer and cream, and the other specialties of German cuisine were not to the taste of these young Greeks, who at first with timid voices, then with growing self-confidence, and finally in voices of command, insisted on having the dishes of their native land: *skordalia*, a garlic sauce similar to the *aïoli* of Provence; *bamies*, pods in the shape of horseshoe nails, which is to say okra; *imam baildi*, or eggplant and tomatoes cooked in oil, a dish of Turkish origin, which derives its name from the fact that the *imam*, the prophet's vicar on earth, is said to have tasted it and *baildi*, swooned with delight.

The passage of the ten *paides* through the hotels unleashed the wrath of God. As in the wake of Attila's footsteps, the grass no longer grew in the wake of these innocents. No need to mention such harmless jokes as switching the shoes left at the doors of the rooms, sewing up the sheets, or hiding brushes and chunks of coal in the beds, but another favorite game of these boys was to shoot lead pellets with peashooters at the mirrors and crystal chandeliers; and one evening in Munich, taking advantage of a brief blackout, they disemboweled the divans and armchairs of the Hotel Vier Jahreszeiten with penknives, and when the lights came on again, the sight of that horribly lacerated furniture expelling its soul of cotton batting made the blood run cold. Unmistakable signs of unheard-of abominations were discovered in the boys' rooms.

As for the seminarian, the shepherd of these lambs, he squandered more time in the *Weinstuben* and *Französische Restaurants* than he spent teaching his pupils the forms of Byzantine music. In addition to teaching, he was also expected to supervise the ten boys. But one night when the cries of a fearful brawl woke the entire hotel and brought Isadora running more naked than usual into the bedrooms of the little choristers, the seminarian's bed was found to be occupied not by him, but by three pillows placed in such a way as to simulate a sleeping body.

While the simulacrum of the seminarian[19] lay in bed in the Vier Jahreszeiten, his real form was seated at a table in the Simplicissimus, in company with a man who to us is an old acquaintance. Three bottles of Johannisberger, tall, slender, and shaped like Indian clubs, stood empty on the table, and the fourth was already more than half consumed. Kathe Kubos, proprietress of the Weinstube, stood leaning against the bar and singing with the voice of a drowning man, every so often interrupting herself to spit or to hurl insults at the customers.

In the man sitting opposite Panaghiotos Perivolarakis (whose name might be translated as Allholy Littlegarden) we can recognize the mysterious creature who emerged that morning from the soil in the temple of Apollo, and has now arrived at complete perfection. The agile, jointed limbs swell under the tight-fitting suit, threatening to burst the coarse, fawn-colored fabric. The features have been incised with an engraver's tool on the beautiful face, and a highly expert hand has colored the pupils with dilute lapis lazuli. A derby hat sits rakishly on the golden curls, its band fastened on one side with a metal buckle. On the oxblood waistcoat gleam two rows of spherical buttons, dotted in red like the backs of cockchafers. The jacket is tight at the waist and the pants tight at the ankles, where patent-leather shoes, half covered by gray spats, protrude like pointed steam irons. From time to time, when he makes a sweeping movement with his arm, his shiny cuffs stick out of his jacket; he speaks quickly and in a

---

19. The Greek custom of substituting for oneself a numen or simulacrum is very ancient. Euripides says that the Helen loved and abducted by Paris was actually only her numen, and that she in the meantime was the guest of the king of Egypt, where Menelaus, once the Trojan War was over, went to fetch her. Did the Greeks and Trojans thus fight over nothing? One can believe all the more readily that this has not been the only time that men let themselves be killed for a shadow.

whisper, and empties his glass in one gulp, throwing back his head. But why this equivocal appearance, this look of a cardsharper, of a hotel burgler, of an international crook in one who—for now we know it—though disguised as a man, is none other than one of the most illustrious, if not actually the most illustrious of the Greek gods?

The West looks through the lens of its own idealism at the Greek world and its creatures, in which nothing else exists but a splendid and witty bestiality. Winckelmann, Goethe, Nietzsche—what could they have known of the Greeks? What little there is comes in handy, wrote Nivasio Dolcemare concerning the mass of ambiguities and falsehoods produced by aesthetes on the real quality of the Greek spirit, which consists less of spirituality than of animal subtlety, much more recognizable in the ass than in the ephebe, in the goat than in the canephora, in the ape than in the panther. And what is one to say of the cruelty of the man now seated at a table in the Simplicissimus in the company of the seminarian, the magnificent, gleaming cruelty, which he whets like a knife while listening to the disclosures about Isadora supplied to him by Allholy Littlegarden through the fumes of the Johannisberger?

The sad experiment of the ten *paides* taken on tour through the capitals of Europe, with their pimples, their vices, and their souls of precocious delinquents hidden beneath an angelic appearance, lasted six months.

One evening, at the end of the six months, Isadora danced in the auditorium of the Künstlerhaus in the presence of Karlsbach, of Lenbach, the portraitist of Bismarck and Marshal von Moltke, and of Franz von Stuck, who painted women as green as boiled zucchini in the coils of serpents. But her spirits were low. And next day, she accompanied the ten boys and the seminarian, no longer dressed as ancient Greeks but buttoned up in dark overcoats and with steaming breaths, to the Munich Bahnhof. Banks of steam and fog turned stagnant under its roof. As the train started, a chorus of insults broke from the ten boys leaning out the windows. Their angelic faces were twisted in horrible sneers, and their still tender little hands formed obscene symbols. Insults and jeers were hurled at the "spiritual mother," and finally the ten choristers all together raised their palms, fingers spread like a fan, in the sign of the *munza*.[20]

At first Isadora did not understand, and when she did she burst into tears. But at that same instant, a miracle occurred: something alive stirred within her.

"My child!" cried Isadora, but her cry was drowned out by the whistle of the locomotive. What did the departure and ingratitude of her "spiritual" children matter now?

"My child!" Isadora repeated more softly, and her look met that of a tall young man wearing an imitation beaver coat and with his derby hat pushed back on his head.

"What did you say?" asked the young man, lifting his hat with two fingers.

"My child," said Isadora once again, and a mysterious fear ran through her like a current of air.

From the receding train a hand was still waving: Allholy Littlegarden's last farewell to the god in the fake beaver coat and with his hat pushed back, who waved in return from the station platform.

Who is this man, Isadora, and why does he dog your now heavy maternal footsteps?

VI

Haste, promiscuity, and mechanical life have ruptured the aura of respect around the great operations of nature. When one is born or dies, one does not want to be looked at, and the

---

20. To show the palm of the hand with the fingers spread is a very serious insult for the Greeks. This insult has a "historical" origin: when Mohammed II entered Constantinople on 6 April 1453, he placed his open hand in sign of possession on the inside wall of Hagia Sophia, and henceforth the mark of the conquering and infidel hand has never been erased from the wall of the church then converted into a mosque.

animal withdraws into solitude. Death in the middle of a café, birth in a tram have been reduced to small newspaper items, when instead they ought to provoke cries of fear and horror. A dancing Gaea, Isadora felt the obscure grandeur of the event that was about to take place. There was in her an "awareness of beginnings," as in Pyrrha, but even more, since Isadora did not give birth near her Deucalion, in a solitude prepared for the arrival of the desired and awaited child, but left him behind, a useless creature now, with his buckets of paint, his coloristic frenzies, his hysterical fits as an eccentric artist with an unfounded reputation for genius. Heavy with her precious burden, Isadora set out first for The Hague, then proceeded to a village called Noordwijk on the North Sea coast, and there she stayed, in a little white house at the top of the dunes. The school she had founded at Grünewald, and which was not only a school but an asylum for children rescued from the slums of Berlin and destined for an airy and musical life, had been entrusted to her sister, Elizabeth. And there, facing the dark and boundless sea, the sea without hope, Isadora waited for her child like Tristan waiting for Isolde. She waited amid the ever more insistent demands of that life "inside." She waited in that solitary house, which could only be reached by one hundred steps hollowed out in the dune. She waited, thinking back every so often on her past life, the dance that now seemed so remote, those light and silent movements that had been her pride, the song of her soul. She waited, standing before a cheval glass to follow the deformation of her body, which had once been so beautiful and agile as the wind. She waited in company with the nurse Marie Kist and a lovely friend named Kathleen, who had come from Paris to stay with her and who later married the explorer Captain Scott. Every day the local Dutch doctor came puffing up the hundred steps of sand to examine the position of the unborn child. She waited while August, and then September, slipped slowly by. She waited while the sky and sea darkened and the light diminished more and more. She waited until something dreadful struck her in the middle of the loins, followed by other pains, agonizing and racking, and from which, like light from the clouds, emerged a wail, a little face enclosed in its night and its mystery, a tiny baby girl, complete and perfect, who, in order to integrate her with her remote ancestors and the land of her fathers, was given the name Deirdre, a name so beautiful as to be almost unpronounceable and which means "Beloved of Ireland." Isadora had asked that a cast of the *Wounded Amazon* be placed in the birth chamber. And while little Deirdre, her first cries spent, lay beneath the curtains of the cradle, unseeing and still immersed in her original sleep, Isadora turned to the statue, her eye still dazed but relieved now of the fixity of her spasms, and said, "You too, my sister, will never be so gloriously fit for the battle again." But with what joy Isadora took up her future battles for the happiness of the sleeping child!

Isadora returned to the Grünewald school with her baby in her arms. She presented her to Elizabeth and to the children, who stood on tiptoe to see her, and as they gazed at her with their smiling little faces, she said, "She is our youngest pupil." Life went on as before, but richer, more beautiful, and illuminated by Deirdre's smile.

Walt Whitman in one of his poems claims to "hear America singing," and the sculptor George Grey Barnard, in no sense paraphrasing the fabulist La Fontaine, had the idea, since stupidity is rarely simple and more often calculating, that if America is singing, there is nothing to keep it from dancing. Isadora Duncan, more nude than usual, posed for the statue of *America Dancing*, and if the work was not carried to completion it was due to Mrs. Barnard's unexpected illness and perhaps her unacknowledged jealousy. Small events sometimes divert great destinies, and Bartholdi's Statue of Liberty came to lack a sister.

The first part of the American tour was a disaster. A great impresario but incapable of understanding the dance as art, Charles Frohman put Isadora on the level of a variety act, and booked her in mid-August into a Broadway theater. The few spectators who, with the thermometer at 90° Fahrenheit, turned up in that uncomfortable auditorium in search of light entertainment were infuriated by Gluck's *Iphigenia* and Beethoven's Seventh Symphony as interpreted by Isadora, and convinced that they had been cheated, loudly demanded their money back. But the second part, during which Isadora toured the United States with the Philharmonic Orchestra of Philadelphia and danced under the direction of Walter Damrosch, was a series of triumphs. The first flutist had the face of a calf and played the solo in the Dance of the Blessed Spirits from *Orfeo* with such piercing emotion that Isadora stopped in the middle of the stage and dissolved in tears.

Such sights soften the hardest hearts, but not those of the Protestant ministers of Washington, who denounced Isadora's dancing. One evening in the theater an audience composed entirely of puritans and their wives rose in unison and covered the dancer with insults.

"What harm can these ministers find in Isadora's dances?" a voice demanded.

All eyes turned toward the speaker. There in a box stood the manly figure of Theodore Roosevelt, president of the United States.

"Hurray for Teddy!" cried the spectators in chorus, with the volubility of a crowd, which according to Shakespeare's reckoning can change its opinion three times in the space of ten minutes.

"My friends," continued the president, "Isadora is as innocent as a child dancing through the garden in the morning sunshine and picking the beautiful flowers of her fantasy."

"Hurrah for Teddy! Hurrah for Isadora!" cried the spectators more loudly, and a chorus of whistles, equivalent in those parts to our applause, greeted the president and the dancer.

Lugné-Poë presented Isadora to the Parisian public, Isadora danced on the stage of the Gaîté-Lyrique, and certain men of letters sang her praises. At this point an observation of Isadora's in the middle of the twenty-second chapter of *My Life* is apt: "All money brings a curse with it, and the people who possess it cannot be happy for twenty-four hours." When there came a knock at the door of her dressing room at the Gaîté-Lyrique and Isadora saw a tall, blond man enter as shy as a boy, she thought: "Here is my Lohengrin." But the shining thought was immediately smothered by another: "Here are wealth and its inseparable companion misfortune." We are not supposed to know this man's real name, because like those things that according to Plato are not *retà*, that is to say nameable, Isadora never calls him by his name, but always uses the Wagnerian antonomasia Lohengrin.

Who was he? That he was Isaac Laquedem* was denied by the color of his hair and the regularity of his features. The Flying Dutchman perhaps. Someone in any case who by constant travel sought to escape an oppressive mood of unhappiness. "Always my mother's face in her coffin; wherever I am I see her dead face." Such was Lohengrin's continual drama. "What use to live," he added, "since it all ends only in death?" And there was no bank in Europe or America unwilling to extend immediate credit to this man persecuted by the idea of death. They sailed on the *Isis*, a yacht white as the swan of Parsifal's son; they rowed on the blue Mediterranean escorted by dolphins and seagulls. Deirdre, wearing a little white tunic, danced on the deck of the ship. The table was set with crystal and silver, but beyond the crystal and silver Isadora saw the blackened faces of the stokers down in the bilge of the pleasure ship. She saw the crew, fifty men toiling for the happiness of only two people. The memory came back to her of the coffins she had seen being carried across Saint Petersburg on sleds in the cold light of dawn, in which lay the bodies of workers who had refused to toil for the happiness of others. The thought of the people and its sufferings inflamed her. She sprang to her feet:

---

* Name in Flanders of the Wandering Jew. (Tr.)

> *Afoot and light-hearted I take to the open road,*
> *Healthy, free, the world before me,*
> *The long brown path before me leading wherever I choose.*

And with all the breath she had in her lungs, she declaimed to the sea and wind Whitman's "Song of the Open Road."

"What rot!" cried Lohengrin, pale with rage. "That man could never have earned his living!"

"That may be," Isadora replied, "but he had the vision of free America."

"Vision be damned."

"For you America means thousands of factories working to give you wealth. For me it means mysticism and idealism."

As we can see, Isadora nourished some illusions about America and its democracy, illusions that Theodore Roosevelt's compliments had surely helped to bolster.

As a token of reconciliation, Isadora promised Lohengrin to dance for him in front of the temple of Poseidon at Paestum. Lohengrin hired an orchestra of thirty players, but so well did he feed them before the dance and so generously did he ply them with drink, that at the moment of striking up their instruments all thirty musicians were dead drunk. The attempt was repeated aboard the *Isis*, but a light southwest wind having sprung up in the meantime, the thirty musicians, green in the face and bending over the rail, restored to Poseidon what they had consumed in front of the temple.

September came, the month of separations. Lohengrin returned to Paris, and Isadora went to Venice. As she sat alone in the basilica of San Marco, contemplating the blue and gold of the cupola, the face of a little boy came to life on the wall and smiled at her. Lohengrin came running at Isadora's summons. He was more racked than ever by the idea of death. They consulted a doctor, who said: "You, a unique artist, once again to risk depriving the world forever of your art? It would be a crime against humanity." The idea of crime undergoes strange modulations. And the knight of the Grail: "What does it matter, since everything must sink into the tomb?" But the smile of the little boy appearing amid the blue

254

and gold of San Marco was irresistible. How could she remain deaf to his appeal? When the blond baby was born, little Deirdre looked at him and said: "Oh, the sweet little boy. Mother, you need not worry about him. I will always hold him in my arms and take care of him." And she kept her promise. When they dragged their two bodies from the river, Deirdre was holding her baby brother in her stiffened little arms. By what horrible feeling of pride was Lohengrin shaken in seeing his forecasts so speedily fulfilled? The boy was likewise given an ancestral name. Deirdre's little brother was named Patrick, after the apostle of Ireland, bishop of the church of Armagh, and author of the letter to Coroticus.

Life went on, more luxuriously than ever, between princely sojourns on the Riviera, in Paris, in the castle built by Lohengrin in Devonshire and modeled on the Petit Trianon, and cruises on all the seas. During a fête in the park of Versailles, the Colonne orchestra, under the direction of Pierné, played a selection of works by Wagner, and as the sun went down behind Bernini's statue of Louis XIV, overrun with ivy and banished behind the Swiss basin by the jealousy of French architects, the solemn strains of Siegfried's funeral march echoed in the air. Even musical programs were arranged in such a way as to justify Lohengrin's pessimism.

In the United States, seeing with what enthusiasm she and Lohengrin were welcomed by that same society that had hunted Gorky and his mistress "from pillar to post," making their lives "a torment to them," Isadora noted that Yankee prudery was a bluff and that "travelling with a millionaire does simplify things." And while we are in the mood for quotations, let us pause before going on to the catharsis of this most tragic of lives and transcribe the "English day" as Isadora saw it in Devonshire:

In an English summer it rains all day long. The English people do not seem to mind it at all. They rise and have an early breakfast of eggs and bacon, and ham and kidneys and porridge. Then they don mackintoshes and go forth into the humid country until lunch, when they eat many courses, ending with Devonshire cream.

From lunch to five o'clock they are supposed to be busy with their correspondence, though I believe they really go to sleep. At five they descend to their tea, consisting of many kinds of cakes and bread and butter and tea and jam. After that they make a pretence of playing bridge, until it is time to proceed to the really important business of the day—dressing for dinner, at which they appear in full evening dress, the ladies very décolleté and the gentlemen in starched shirts, to demolish a twenty-course dinner. When this is over they engage in some light political conversation, or touch upon philosophy until the time comes to retire.

And Nivasio Dolcemare: "To safeguard the security of such a way of life, white men and red men, black men and yellow men toil day and night in sun and snow, in wind and rain, under the stars of this or the other pole. How much unhappiness, O Lord, is needed to balance the happiness of only one?"

Omens came thick and fast. The Cadum soap factory asked Isadora's permission to use Patrick's picture in its advertising, and when she returned from a long tour of Russia, she found Paris filled with the eyes, the cheeks, the smile, the splendor of her baby boy, whom the Parisians, with their passion for nicknames, had dubbed "Bébé Cadum."

Isadora had gone to Russia with the musician Hener Skene. Arriving in Kiev at dawn and going by sleigh to the hotel, it seemed to Isadora that she saw two rows of children's coffins along the sides of the road.

"But there is nothing," the musician assured her.

"What? Can't you see? All the children are dead!"

"No, there is nothing but the snow . . ."

In Paris, Isadora got off the train and saw the colossal image of her Patrick up close. An individual standing next to her pointed an index finger loaded with rings.

"Beautiful kid, eh?"

Isadora recognized the character she had seen at the station in Munich, the morning the little choristers had gone back to Greece. He reeked of cheap perfume and was dressed like something between a parvenu and a pimp.

In 1908 Isadora bought the painter Gervex's studio in Neuilly, and Paul Poiret, entrusted with the decoration, did the walls in purple and painted twin black crosses on each. Why don't they offer practical courses against the evil eye, and why are not aesthetes banished to a desert island, as was done to the poor innocent dogs of Istanbul?

There was not only work in the studio but play as well, and one evening in a pantomime improvised by Isadora, Cécile Sorel, and Gabriele d'Annunzio, the poet of the *Laudi* revealed an unsuspected talent as an actor.

From the terrace Isadora watched Deirdre dancing in the garden. The little girl made up her own poems:

> *Now I am a bird and I fly*
> *so, so high among the clouds . . .*
> *Now I am a flower looking up to the bird*
> *and swaying so, so . . .*

Patrick, too, danced to strange music of his own invention, but refused all instruction. He said, "Patrick will dance Patrick's own dance alone."

Raoul Pugno came to play pieces by Mozart. Deirdre and Patrick listened motionless beside the piano. When the music was over, the two children passed their heads under the pianist's arms.

"Where do these little Mozart angels come from?" exclaimed Pugno.

After the old pianist, with his beard of a biblical prophet and his poodle's eyes, had left, the little boy began knocking over all the chairs in the studio. The strange effects of Mozart's delicate music! There was a ring at the gate: an unknown person, someone whose name Isadora was unable either then or later to find out, had sent as a gift two splendid volumes of the works of Barbey d'Aurevilly. Isadora opened the first volume, and her eyes fell on the name "Niobe." "Patrick, don't make so much noise," said the nurse. "Can't you see that Mama is reading?" And Isadora: "I'd like to be alone. Take the children for a drive." The children asked, "Where do you want us to go today, Mama?" Isadora made no reply. She didn't know what to reply. She didn't know why she couldn't reply. And when the children had departed for their last drive, she again picked up the book from the mysterious donor and began reading the story of Niobe.

A profound solidarity unites children all over the world, as profound as the very souls of children can be profound, but which gradually slackens until it is converted into the rancor, hostility, and war of grown-ups. When two children meet, they look at each other with no uncertainty, they recognize each other even if they have never seen each other before, and if they do not smell each other as dogs do, it is because the instincts to which the appeal of odors corresponds are still unawakened in them. If a child is happy, all children rejoice from one pole to the other. If a child is suffering, all children suffer a little and almost without being aware of it. When a child dies, a gentle sigh escapes the mouths of sleeping children, lingers like a shining bubble on their lips, and is then extinguished.

In a house in Sydney, Australia, Maggy and Puck are alone in the nursery. Their little brothers and sisters have gone to a party in Mrs. Egerton's garden, but Maggy and Puck have a touch of pharyngitis and have had to stay home. They have played a little without much caring to, but now they have stopped, and their toys lie on the floor, lifeless and sad. All of a sudden a black curtain comes down over the sky. Maggy and Puck look at each other, and trembling with fear take each other's hands. Then in the silence that covers the earth and sky come the tinkling little notes of a music box.

"Did you hear, Maggy?" asks Puck, the younger of the two.

"Yes," replies his sister. "Somewhere in the world a child is dead."

He was leaning with his back against the wall of the Tuileries. Yellowish and swollen, the Seine ran between its stone embankments and under the low arches of its bridges. On the other side, the big double window of the Gare d'Orsay looked like the mouth of the sea monster in whose belly Pinocchio was reunited with his father, Geppetto. Infinite is the patience of murderers. It would be impossible to recognize in this character the mysterious creature who had emerged that morning from the soil of the temple of Delphi, had we not followed him in his various transformations, in his steady rise to perfection. The straw hat tipped forward over his eyes rests on an extraordinarily thick and curly head of hair. The checkered suit, white spats, and bow tie accentuate the ambiguous character of the "avenger." When the automobile carrying Deirdre, Patrick, and the nurse toward the Jardin des Plantes appears from the Place de la Concorde, the avenger unbuttons his cuff, turns back his sleeve, follows with obvious satisfaction the growth of his hand, which soon reaches a diameter of over six feet, and when the automobile is near, the enormous hand drops on it, stalls it, and pushes it in the river. This and nothing more.

Yellowish and swollen, the Seine flows between its stone embankments. Apollo, lightly massaging his right hand with his left, brings it back to its normal size, then pulls down his sleeve, buttons his cuff, and walks away whistling toward the Louvre.

Isadora had gone on reading. The curtains surrounding her are the same ones she carries with her on her trips in Europe and America, to Africa and Asia, and they constitute her "scenery." Not the sound of footsteps but that of a rushing wind. And the face is no longer that of a man obsessed with Death, but of Death itself, as Lohengrin appears on the threshold and cries, "The children are no more!"

When Isadora emerged once again from her house as after a long illness, Paris was spangled with the image of her

Patrick. In vain did the new Niobe beg that the "Bébé Cadum" posters be removed from the walls. In vain did she offer her money, all her money: the soap manufacturers had no ears for her suffering. And from all the walls the tragic mother was pursued by the big rosy face, the smile, the splendor of her little boy who had been turned into a swollen bladder of water.

Once again Isadora began traveling about the world. She surrounded herself with other children. She bought the Hôtel Bellevue at Meudon and filled it with children. The war came. The children in Bellevue were replaced by wounded men, shattered men who screamed all night and themselves cried out for a mother. Then the war was over and Isadora was summoned to Greece by Venizelos to open a Temple of the Dance in the Zappeion. But a monkey bit the young king of Greece. Alexander died and Venizelos fell from power. Isadora again took up her travels, pursued by the memory of Deirdre with her little brother in her arms. She went to Russia. She married—she who had sworn never to submit to matrimony—the poet Sergei Esenin. She left him before he committed suicide. She continued her wanderings. Poor and weary, she landed in Nice.

Everyone remembers the theft of the *Mona Lisa*, but does anyone know of the two-day disappearance of the Artemis in the Louvre? The authorities have maintained a prudent silence on this mysterious absence, and if Diana's presence among the public did not catch the eye, it was because around 1927 all women went about in short skirts and walked with the rapid, springing step of Diana the Huntress.

In Nice it was raining. Apollo and Diana stood at the curb, covered by black raincoats. When the automobile went by, Diana grasped the scarf fluttering behind Isadora's neck with two fingers and held tight. This and nothing more. A moment later, the woman whom Anne de Noailles with amiable wit had nicknamed "Isadorable" was only a heap of blood-soaked rags on the wet pavement.

That evening on the Promenades des Anglais, Apollo and Diana exchanged their goodbyes before parting.

"Where are you going?" asked Diana.

"I'm catching a boat at Marseilles for Patras. And you?"

"I'll take the train and go back to the Louvre. *Chaire!*"

"*Chaire,*" Apollo replied, despite Giorgio Pasquali's commentary on the Third Letter of Plato, apocryphal anyway, and which states that *chaire* is unsuitable for the gods, since it has the meaning of "rejoice," and the divine nature is subject to neither joy nor grief.

On the old Rue de Seine in Paris there is a portal leading to a dark passageway, at the end of which stands a door with a sign reading: "Raymond Duncan School of Classical Dance." It is there, in the company of his wife Penelope and a goat, that the feathered but flightless old man still lives. From time to time he thinks of dead Isadorable and the dead children, and his eye, circled with red like a turkey cock's, glimmers and stares but sheds no tears. Too old now and tired.

Bombastus's First Love

The standing audience applauded with fervor, their hands in the air and extended toward the stage, excluding any doubt about the goal of such thundering homage. The singers and the Kapellmeister, the one black figure amid those multicolored ones, took repeated bows in the limelight, hand in hand in a human chain, like a band of disguised alpinists roped together for a difficult climb. Signora Poma heaved a sigh of relief, and now that she was no longer hearing it, began to come to terms with the music of Mozart. Mozart who? Along with her batskin purse and mother-of-pearl opera glasses, the beautiful Signora Poma was clutching in her hands, gloved in white moleskin, the program printed by the tourist office in Salzburg for the special benefit of Italian spectators. She consulted it and read that Mozart's name was Volfango Amadeo. Amadeo I can take, thought Signora Poma, though we say Amedeo not Amadeo. (Signora Poma had an instinctive aversion for anything that did not fall within the very narrow range of her knowledge.) But Volfango, what a funny name! Sounds like his name is mud.* Signora Poma tried to collect her thoughts, under the impression that there was another famous man, often mentioned by her friend Egle, whose name was also Volfango, but much as she searched her mind, shrouded in shadow and replete with vast blank areas, the personality of this other Volfango

* *Fango* = mud. (Tr.)

stubbornly refused to come forth. To put a stop to this pointless effort, Signora Poma adjusted her permanent with expert, delicate fingers. She too applauded the singers and conductor, but softly and merely in gratitude to see them detached at last from their working spaces. One doubt chilled her beautiful shoulders. What if the show wasn't over yet? Twice already the hope of much yearned-for liberation had comforted her, but no sooner had it appeared than it was submerged again by the disappointment of seeing the curtain inexorably open, and those characters, some dressed as Turks, who kept running after each other for no reason, or, which was worse, stopped to sing endlessly in a language of which you couldn't understand a word. But no: this time it was for good. In an overheated crush, in which the velvety throb of Elizabeth Arden face powder, the sinuous strains of Arpège, and whiffs of armpit perspiration mingled on an equal basis, the audience of music lovers pushed its way slowly and solidly toward the exit of the Festspielhaus. Their faces were aglow with mystical fire, their lips curving with the smile of the soul, their eyes moist with spiritual joy. Multilingual exclamations echoed around Signora Poma, who at that moment was only anxious lest her pink organdy mantle, a Gori original, be crushed by those exhilarated souls, while the last fanatics, grouped in front of the stage, leaning out of the boxes, and dangling from the peanut gallery, went on flaying their hands and drawing forth the roped and disguised mountain climbers from behind the curtain. "*Ach wunderschön!—Épatant, mon cher, épatant!—Deistvitelno precrasno!*" Then, among those obscure voices, Signora Poma, native of the town of Isola del Liri, heard a word that sounded friendly to her scroll-shaped ear, slightly pink at the lobe, and where a pearl in the shape of a tiny pear hung like an opalescent drop: "*Meraviglioso! Veramente meraviglioso!*" And after so much perplexity in these strange worlds, Signora Poma was happy to find herself back among her own. It was Egle's voice. Her friend Egle. The voice of the person who had made it her mission to initiate her, Pina Poma, into the mysteries of culture. She who in order to promote her

263

intellectual education had made her read, duly translated, *The Prisoner* by Proust and the *Notebooks of Malte Laurids Brigge* by Rainer Maria Rilke, had had the Modernissima send her books on Van Gogh and the Douanier Rousseau, had had her buy recordings of Stravinsky's *Piano Rag Music* and Hindemith's *Schwanendreher*, and as though that weren't enough, in this year 1937 had got her to come with her to Salzburg for the July and August festival. But obviously she still had a long way to go on this fascinating but bumpy road if what drew from Egle exclamations of wonder, on her had the effect of those passages from the *Iliad* that she had had to memorize many years ago in school. Besides there was still some doubt that this effort to create what Egle called a "mental life" for herself would be enough to fill the emptiness of her life. Emptiness . . . Her mother, who even when she went on the first of the month to claim her pension signed the receipt with an X, gave no sign of having ever known, not even now when she was old and alone, the "emptiness of life." The same for Clotilde, her elder sister, who had married a farmer and stayed at home, to have children and cultivate her kitchen garden. As for herself, Egle had nicknamed her "Nora" and drawn up a program for her of will power, independence, and "self-sufficiency." But how? For the moment she was groping in an incomprehensible and shapeless world, and as for creating what Egle called a "higher and richer life" for herself, it seemed to her like trying to fill a basket with water.

The Abduction from the Seraglio had started at 7 P.M., and at the exit of the Festspielhaus Signora Poma saw on her wrist, amid a minuscule firmament of diamonds, the delicate hands that indicated 10:30. "Let's eat," said Egle, adding, "It makes better sense to have supper after the theater. Are you hungry?" Next to her watch Signora Poma wore a tiny pink tulle handkerchief tied to her wrist: a wisp of cloud made rosy by the dawn. Perhaps a badge to distinguish her from an identical twin sister, the same starry eyes without a hint of expression, the same spotless brow without a shadow of thought, the same lips like coral fresh from the sea and without a suggestion of a smile, the same solemn gait of a futile goddess who finds herself among men by mistake—a sister who herself was wandering among black and white throngs, and on her wrist wore a tiny handkerchief of blue tulle. Signora Poma wasn't hungry. The moon showed Salzburg and its surroundings as in a cold negative photo. From the massive shrubbery of Hohensalzburg emerged the towers of the castle, white as milk bottles and cloaked in melodramatic shadows. Signora Poma wasn't hungry. She looked at the towers of the castle, and she, who in the words of her husband, Commendatore Poma, was "plump" and a "brunette," thought herself anemic and blond. The lute that had accompanied Pedrillo's aria still tinkled in her ear. She saw herself leaning out from one of those roof terraces up there, in the riding habit just now worn by Konstanze, Belmonte's sweetheart, under the falconer's plume that swept in a broad curve from her hat to her shoulder. She heard a voice rising in the night and softly offering love, but it was not Ildefonso's voice. At the thought of her husband a little cloud crossed Signora Poma's brow, so white, so pure, usually so devoid of thoughts. Then, just as one closes a door to shut out draughts, Signora Poma said resolutely, "Yes, I'm hungry, let's go back to the hotel." And escorted by Egle the intellectual like Tobias by the angel, the beautiful Signora Poma, wife of Commendatore Ildefonso Poma, managing director and principal shareholder of the Poma Footwear Company, set off through the streets of Salzburg, resonant as the sections of a huge sound box extending over both banks of the Salzach, in the direction of the Hirschhof, or "Residence of the Stag." There are some reputations that one would just as soon conceal. Signora Poma trembled every time she made a new acquaintance in the drawing rooms of her friends in the Parioli quarter in Rome, for fear of the terrible question: "Are you related to. . . ?" In Salzburg, at least, no one had ever heard of Poma Footwear. Equally unaware of it were the Kapuzinerberg and the Mirabell garden; the skeleton in the Fauststadt of a naked guard in front of the terrestrial globe was unaware of it, as was the young Mozart in marble seated at a likewise marble spinet, who with his buckled shoe presses a pedal that isn't there. In this musical city Pina Poma is simply *Frau* Poma, and on more distinguished occasions *gnädige* Frau Poma, while back in the Eternal City and for long stretches of the Via Aurelia, Via Flaminia, Via Cassia, and the other main approaches to it, huge billboards announce:

ALL OVER ROMA
SHOES BY POMA

If Salzburg is a sound box open to the sun and stars, to enter the Hirschhof hotel is like entering the bowels of a Stradivarius. The inlay of colored majolica and polished seasoned woods generates a steady warmth of comfort and security around the guest. But how is Signora Poma to identify a feeling so different from the one that infuses her cold and desolate house in Rome when she doesn't know the word *gemütlich?* Above the window through which glittered the dining room with its guests, flowers and crystal, an amiable stag's head spread the regal trophy of its horns. Signora Poma looked at it as she went by. And a strange thought, for one so unaccustomed to the passage of thoughts, a nebulous and troubling thought, crossed her mind. It was only for a moment, but in that moment the amiable ruminant's head was miraculously replaced by that of Ildefonso Poma, known as "Fonso." At the table, Pina was once more astonished that the spaghetti was served as a side dish, not to mention being undercooked and without grated cheese. Egle had often scolded her for being so attached to native dishes. She herself ate her roast veal with raspberry jam and praised the combination to the skies. What a liberated woman! When supper was over, the two friends went upstairs to their rooms.

They were supposed to depart for Italy next morning at eight. Signora Poma suddenly remembered it, as though awakening from the dream. She rang for the chambermaid and told her to tell them at the desk to awaken her at 6:30, but actually she used the word "bureau." She started packing her suitcases. She didn't know where to begin. She had been in

Salzburg for two weeks, and there was a great confusion of music in her head. At the Festspielhaus she had heard *Don Giovanni, Fidelio,* and *Die Meistersinger,* orchestral concerts at the Mozarteum, organ concerts in the cathedral, and some serenades at the Residenz palace. In addition, she had visited the house where Mozart was born and Hellbrunn castle, she had climbed up to the citadel of Hohenwerfen, and under the portico of a church she had seen a strange pyramidal tomb, in which Egle had told her a magician was buried. A magician whose name she couldn't remember . . . A magician who continued to keep a vigil in death . . . a magician . . . She realized that she was standing motionless before the open suitcase, holding the skirt of her brown suit in her arms as though it were the child that fate kept denying her, and she made haste to go on with her packing. The Gori mantle lay spread out on the bed like a tall, flat girl who had fainted. Signora Poma picked it up with infinite care, hung it on a hanger in her traveling trunk, and as she lightly smoothed the folds to arrange them harmoniously like organ pipes, she was surprised by a second unpleasant thought, after the one about her imminent departure: she remembered that except for sending a telegram on the day of her arrival, she had not yet written to her husband. It was something that had to be done right away, and mailed next morning before boarding the train.

Signora Poma sits down at the writing table, lays out a large blue sheet of paper bearing two intertwined P's in the upper left hand corner, places the stem of the fountain pen between her index and middle finger the way film producers do, omits as many women do the locality and date, and writes in the middle of the paper: "Dear Fonso . . ." But having traced these two words in a script full of tall strokes, Signora Poma's literary headway is arrested. Pina sucks the end of her pen, gazes blankly at the luggage stand that holds her suitcase, passes from the stand to the half-packed suitcase, and rises from the suitcase to a picture in a dark frame that hangs on the wall, which shows . . . Signora Poma is uncertain if this picture shows a man or a woman, and finally settles for a man

267

"dressed like a woman." Fat in face and neck (this is all the more obvious since he wears no collar) and with long hair curled at the sides, in the fashion now current for women, and crimped, one would say, by a steam permanent. Despite the fat, the features are delicate. The left hand rests on a listel inscribed with a few letters, the index finger of the right separates the pages of a book as though marking the place. Someone who writes, thought Signora Poma. "Wrote," she corrected herself, since the man's appearance was of another time. Wrote . . .

Signora Poma returned to her letter. "Dear Fonso . . ." What to say to Fonso? That man's nose is thin and slightly hooked, the nostrils broad and slanting—a nose to catch the unnoticeable odors of others, a nose to guide its owner to the most exquisite intimacies. What is this strange tremor that runs down the loins of the beautiful Signora Poma, under the angora dressing gown trimmed with swansdown like foam on a wave? The mouth is fleshy and resembles the mouth of a fish that knows how to kiss. The keen dark eyes express a mysterious understanding in their sidelong movement. At this point sudden inspiration reanimates Signora Poma's fountain pen, and she restores it to a combative position: "Dear Fonso, forgive me for not writing you sooner, but here with all this music, the time has simply flown . . ." Behind the back of that man in his scarlet robe (there could be no doubt that he was a scholar) stretches a landscape quite different—very "'strange," very "far away"—from the places familiar to Signora Poma. On one side flows a shining river that washes a narrow white city, passing under the arches of a humpbacked bridge and a tall exposed citadel, to merge finally with the sea, which, on the left, extends all the way to the horizon, and behind that fat "mammonish" neck rolls up in two cylindrical, crested waves. "Dear Fonso . . ." But how can it be that in the two weeks she has lived here, she has not been aware of this portrait? A light, spirited breeze comes through the open window, stirring the white curtain, a mountain breeze that brings with it the memory of pure and solitary peaks; the silvery light of the moon comes in and yields without a struggle to the golden light spread by the lampshade from the table; scattered, fleeting voices come in that language she doesn't understand and which nevertheless has become familiar to her . . . Strange! Purified by silence, even the music of *The Abduction from the Seraglio* now re-echoes more clearly in Signora Poma's ears, and the spectacle witnessed a few hours earlier at the theater reappears to her like a landscape on which the fog has lifted. Konstanze's pure song breaks out once again, now more loving, more comprehensible, more sympathetic, and from the gardens of Selim Pasha rises in the sky like a luminous thread; the ship sailing slowly away that carries Konstanze and Belmonte, Blonde and Pedrillo, home to their country now becomes clearer in its reasons to the wife of the large manufacturer of mass-produced shoes, communicates to her its melancholy, infuses her with its great nostalgia for love. "Dear Fonso . . ." But what is there to write to her husband? What can she find to say to him, so that by writing very large she can arrive at the bottom of the first side of that blue sheet of paper, destined to be folded and put in a long, narrow, American-type envelope, and perhaps even turn it over to the other side for love and kisses and her signature? What can Signora Poma write to her husband, they who in six years of sterile marriage have found nothing to say to each other? They who sit at the table, he with *Il Messaggero* folded to the article he hasn't had time to read in the car that brings him home from the office, she with the latest issue of *Donna* open to the photographs of models, and propped against the napkin ring like a little missal on a lectern? What can she find to say to him, they who in their big double bed sleep with their backs to each other? She who in the face of Ildefonso's tender overtures, becoming increasingly rarer, drives hard bargains, such as the promise next day of a hat from Silvestri's, or a few pairs of shoes to be ordered from Sima's at seven hundred lire a pair, or, as once happened, a custom-built "1500"? For needless to say, Signora Pina and Commendatore Ildefonso live in a princely manner on the profits of the large shoe factory of which the Commendatore is managing director and principal shareholder, but just as the hunting dog does not eat the prey, they refrain from putting their feet into shoes of their own manufacture—which does not save Commendatore Poma's feet from the calluses, corns, and bunions with which his toes are emblazoned.

This time it is because of the need to "get away from it all" that Signora Poma turns toward the portrait of the Unknown Man, toward those fascinating eyes. Behind his face the sky rises clear and innocent, but a dark cloud thickens behind the top of his head, almost the fumes of his thoughts. What thoughts? . . . And what a strange hat! Actually it's three hats, one inside another, the third one of fur and set askew. It looks like the hats they make nowadays, Signora Poma thinks, a Silvestri original. Suddenly the light of discovery shines in Signora Poma's mind, just as at the beginning of the century the minds of all cultured Europeans were illuminated by the discoveries of Minoan civilization made at Phaistos and Knossos; and through the discovery that fashion repeats itself over a distance of centuries, periods, and eras, even Signora Pina Poma, like Pythagoras of Samos and Friedrich Nietzsche, has the intoxicating revelation of eternal return.

"Dear Fonso . . ." But those eyes! Signora Poma stands up, goes to look at the letters on which he rests his delicate "midwife's" hand, and reads: "Famous Doctor Pareselsus." She had certainly guessed he must be a doctor! Under her light dressing gown she feels those skillful and delicate hands, those "doctor's" hands, skimming over her, touching her . . . "Pareselsus . . ." Signora Poma tries to collect her thoughts, just as a few hours before at the end of *The Abduction from the Seraglio*, when she was searching for the other famous man who, like Mozart, was named Volfango. But this time her lazy little mind, always anxious to go to sleep, gives proof of a certain capacity to come up with something. Pareselsus, or something like that, is the name of the magician buried in the pyramidal tomb, under the portico of that church. The magician who keeps a vigil in death . . . Who keeps a vigil in death as she now keeps a vigil in the

night . . . "Dear Fonso . . ." The trite salutation of the
unfinished letter still feebly torments her, but she no longer
has the strength to go back to the table, to detach herself from
that gaze, that life. What is the mystery in that life? How
would it have been different if she'd been married to that
man? Did that man ever love? Did he ever love? . . . Without
realizing it, Signora Poma has uttered this question aloud.
She is amazed, and cringes with fear at the unexpected sound
of her own voice. Then another voice, from behind a glass,
from behind a membrane, a faded voice from other times
replies: "No, never did I love. I was born in 1493, but I am still
a virgin." And since Signora Poma has jumped to take refuge
behind the bed, the voice, stiff as bone but with a remembrance vibrating inside it of great tenderness, a profound
sorrow, an infinite desire, says: "Pina, why dost thou flee
me?"

Signora Poma is cowering behind the bed. For greater, and
let us say total, protection, it would perhaps have been better
had she crawled right under the bed. But her position is
determined by the direction of the danger, which does not
come from above, i.e., from the ceiling, but from the side,
i.e., from the wall on which hangs the portrait. In her choice
of the bed as a means of protection, Signora Poma has
unconsciously followed numerous and ancient examples,
some of them illustrious. Gaius Caligula had a terrible fear of
thunder, and when it thundered he hid under the bed with a
crown of laurel on his head as protection against lightning. A
pleasant and very beautiful lady from Modena, whom we met
by chance some years ago at the Abano spa, told us that in
case of danger she didn't stop to think twice, but ran to get
into bed, and if the danger was a serious one, she pulled the
sheet up over her head. And which of us, as a child, has not
behaved in the face of danger like the beautiful lady from
Modena? Which of us, when in the grip of fear, has not
pulled the sheet up under his chin as though he were at the
barber's? And if the fear grew, didn't he also pull in his hand?
And if the fear kept on growing, didn't he also stick his head

271

under the covers? The analogy between the child and the frightened adult is exemplary. Fear paralyzes the adult's reason, which is to say it puts the adult back in the condition of a child. And those who wish to impose their will on other men are fully aware that the quickest and most effective means of doing so is to infantilize them through fear. But was it fear that Signora Poma felt, wrapped in her angora dressing gown and squatting on the bedside carpet, like a siren devoid of cunning and intent on laying a prodigious emerald egg? Fear is generated in us by the threat of evil, and in none of its moral forms, much less in those physical ones of beating or stabbing, burning or cutting, smothering or flaying was evil at that moment threatening Signora Poma's soft and precious flesh. Quite the contrary. The voice that had spoken to her from inside the frame was not threatening but imploring. "Pina," it had said, "why dost thou flee me?" Fear is produced primarily by the sudden appearance of the unexpected, in which case it is the extreme of astonishment, but not even in this form was fear operating at that moment on Signora Poma's psyche, because she had been prepared for the sound of that voice by over an hour of contemplation, or rather, of identification with the portrait, besides which what is now happening to Signora Poma she has been expecting, insistently and uninterruptedly, for some eighteen years, ever since she was a little girl in second grade at the Istituto Santa Elisabetta, and wore her name, Pina, sewn slantwise with red cotton thread on her little white smock. And how would the astonishment of the unexpected have operated on Signora Poma when that voice, albeit not an ordinary one but the voice of a portrait, sounded so mild and familiar, and called her with the very same name with which she was called by her mother, her husband, her friend Egle, and a few intimates? To be sure, it remained to be seen how the man in the portrait had come to know that her name was Pina, and if it hadn't been for the fact that she had to stay hidden behind the bed to save appearances, Signora Poma would have asked him without mincing words. Signora Poma deemed it undignified to look at the portrait above the bed, all the more since from behind the bed she could see the wardrobe mirror in which the portrait was reflected, and out of the corner of her bright little eye she was able to assure herself that Doctor Pareselsus's eyes had not lost the gleam of life. In other words, Signora Poma during her contemplation of the portrait has unwittingly crossed the line dividing the rational from the irrational, the physical from the metaphysical. If these transitions did not happen so naturally and inadvertently, even the dead would be astonished and frightened to find themselves dead, even the newly born would be astonished and frightened to find themselves born, while, as we know, the cry that newborn babies let out on finding themselves in the world is not one of fear or astonishment, but in order to take possession of this air that they will breathe until their death. So instead of being astonished, instead of being frightened because the portrait had spoken, Signora Poma would have been astonished if the portrait had remained silent. Like Alice, she has entered Wonderland, and wonders, when we cross the line and live them, are no longer such. And so why had Signora Poma let out that cry? Why had she flown across the room? Why was she hiding behind the bed? It had been simply a childish and unexpected act. One of those unconsidered reactions produced by an excess of joy. The excited surprise of seeing what had hitherto been only a long and sterile wish suddenly come to life. Let us say the exact word: a prank. Which she now repents. And Signora Poma would ask nothing better than to break the immobility and silence in which she has foolishly trapped herself, and come out of her hiding place. So it was not fear that was in Signora Poma, but ineffable emotion, the softest trepidation, and if there is indeed some form of fear in her, it is that the voice of the portrait will no longer make itself heard. But the voice did speak again, saying:

"Pina, thy name brings to mind the tree that stands near the sea because it is its friend. It brings to mind the tree that has the shape of an umbrella. It brings to mind the tree that is the green and cheerful brother of the sad dark fir. It brings to mind the tree that I learned to know when I went down into thy fair and smiling land. When I went to Venice in 1522, as an army surgeon for the Most Serene Republic, in the war between Charles V and François I, for the possession of Naples. The tree I saw when I went down to Naples and from there proceeded as far as Salerno, whose illustrious School honored me with a doctor's diploma. And I am moved all the more by the name of that tree, because its name, in thine, becomes feminine as in Latin. Thy name, Pina, brings to mind the wholesome fragrance of the pine tree, that fragrance that as I breathed it on my meditative walks along the shore of that most pleasant gulf, confirmed my idea that the only medicine is in nature: in trees, in the soil, in the air."

The Italian spoken by the portrait was not exactly what is here transcribed, and for the reader's convenience we have thought it advisable to purge it of such expressions as "forsooth" and "forasmuch."

Signora Poma, still crouching behind the bed, was thinking: Just look, all the nice things he has to say about my name. And the variations on the name Pina seemed all the more pleasing and new to her in that this name, short for Giuseppina, which her parents had reserved for her without her knowledge and saddled her with against her will, had always been odious to her. As a girl, Pina had dreamed of being called Oretta, Grazia, or Melisenda. And while not appreciating as she should have the reference to the war between Charles V and François I, not to mention the illustrious School of Salerno founded by Robert Guiscard, she nevertheless understood that a poet had spoken from inside that frame, which made her judge her husband, Ildefonso, all the worse. Not only did he never make her name the subject of poetic ramblings, but he in his turn had abbreviated and reduced it to Pi, which meant that Signora Poma would hear herself called from one room to another: "Hey, Pi, where'd you put the shoehorn?" Or: "Hey, Pi, don't forget to give me back the change for the thousand lire I gave you this morning." In addition, Signora Poma found the adjective "wholesome" referring to the pine tree especially correct, since she herself made much use of soap with essence of pine, and dissolved essence of pine in the bathtub every morning, in the water in which she immolated her lovely body, which the lack of true and heartfelt love had preserved one might say in a state of virginity.

"Pina," the voice continued, "why dost thou hide? I see thee and thou seest me, and I see that thou seest me."

At this point Signora Poma took her eyes away from the mirror and scornfully turned her head to the other side.

"Why continue this game unworthy of my age and especially of thy youth? The night is short, tomorrow thou leavest, and I have been awaiting thee for four hundred and forty-four years."

Signora Poma did not stop to figure out exactly which years the man in the portrait had spent waiting for her, but still the sum seemed considerable, and the very fact that he had been waiting for her in that hotel room, enclosed in a picture frame, flooded her with pride.

"First of all, who gave you permission to call me Pina, and how did you know it was my name?"

Though Signora Poma had been mulling over some sentence with which to respond to the portrait, she would probably have kept silent until some external event intervened to free her from her paralyzing position. But these mad words emerged from her mouth unpremeditated, and Signora Poma, surprised by their sound, got up and ran to the middle of the room to recapture them, like that individual who, suddenly overwhelmed by drunkenness, jumped up from the table where he had been drinking and started running, not because he had somewhere to go in a hurry, but to catch his head on the wing, because he had the idea it was running away from him.

"How could I not know thy name is Pina?" the portrait replied gently. "For two weeks we can be said to have lived together, and it is what I have heard Egle call thee."

"Egle is a friend of mine and I don't allow you . . ."

"How can I call thee otherwise, when I know no other name for thee?"

"I am Signora Poma."

"Poma!" the portrait repeated in a burst of admiration. "Poma! Autumn! The golden fruit guarded by the Hesperides at the borders of Death! The fruit from which I myself extracted so many wholesome juices! Thou, O Pina Poma, art a sylvan grove, thou art a garden!"

Signora Poma, like women in general and dull-minded women in particular, was mistrustful and unable to take a joke. Need it be stressed that Doctor Pareselsus had not the slightest intention of making a joke, but was expressing the purest admiration of a devout disciple of nature and fervent alchemist? Nevertheless his praises of Signora Poma's name and surname sounded like a pun, and they were taken as such by Signora Poma, whose mood, at the suspicion that the man in the portrait was making fun of her, contracted and became exasperated.

"You've spied on me! You've been in my room! You're not a gentleman! You have no manners!"

"Pina . . ."

"Stop calling me Pina!"

"Signora Poma, I appeal to your reasoning faculty."

Reasoning faculty? thought Signora Poma. What would that be?

"Consider," continued the portrait. "It is not I who have entered your room, but rather you who have entered mine. I have been in this room for ten years. Before that I was in an antique shop in Vienna. And before that in the house of an alchemist, who paid with twenty years in prison for his curiosity to discover the connections that unite man with nature, that is to say, the copy with the model. And it is a good four hundred and twenty years that I have been in this portrait, which was painted of me in 1517 in Paris by the painter Jan van Scorel, and the original of which is in the Louvre. As for my quality as a gentleman, it cannot be doubted, although I am enough of a philosopher not to boast about it. My family's coat of arms bears three keys on a blue field over bars of silver. The castle of my ancestors stood near Stuttgart. My paternal grandfather in 1468 accompanied Count Eberhard to the Holy Land and ended his life devoutly in the Order of the Knights of Saint John. I, whom you see enclosed in this frame, which is moreover very ugly and unworthy of me, am Theophrastus Philippus Bombastus von Hohenheim. The name Theophrastus, a foreordained name meaning 'he who can be called God,' was given to me by my father in homage to Theophrastus of Eresus, physicist, botanist, and naturalist, for whom my father nourished a profound veneration. In 1510, when I was seventeen and left my father's house for the Collegium in Basel, I latinized my name in accordance with the custom of the time, and in imitation of Duchêne who became Quercetanus and of Roccatagliata who became Rupescissa, I turned Hohenheim, which means 'high-placed dwelling,' into Paracelsus. Have you a love of philology, Signora Poma? If so, you will know that with Paracelsus I created a hybrid, combining a Greek root, *para*, with a Latin one, *cels;* but in those days people paid little attention to such details. Do you like my name? It is auspicious. It means 'Toward the highest summits.' Oh, to be able to reach them together with you, Pina! I was also called Aureolatus, because of a halo of light that surrounded my head like those of the saints. Does that not astound you? The halo around my head is clearly visible in the portrait of me that you people attribute to Tintoretto. But I tell you in confidence: the attribution is false. When that portrait was painted, I was twenty-eight years old and Tintoretto was scarcely ten. Even precocity has its limits. Some of my zealous admirers gave me the name Aureolatus, some of those fanatical and servile men of the kind you now call, if I am not mistaken, a 'pain in the neck.' I made use of that name only once: on a document, so as to impress the frontier guards. Among my other qualities, I can also list modesty."

During the enunciation of the various names of Theophrastus Philippus Bombastus von Hohenheim, known as Aureolatus Paracelsus, and of the explanations for them, Signora Poma had been immobilized by a sudden preoccupation that prevented her from listening to these names and much less their meanings, and the portrait had scarcely ceased speaking than she burst out with great vehemence, "But then if for the whole two weeks I've been in this room you've gone on looking at me from up there, it means you've seen me in every possible state . . ."

"Every one of them," Bombastus replied sweetly.

"Even naked?"

"Even naked," replied Bombastus with even greater sweetness.

"Oh, my God!" cried Signora Poma, beginning to shriek and stamp her feet. "You're a monster! A monster! A monster!"

She was silent for a moment and her face lit up with a sudden idea.

"But you can't see into the bathroom, can you?"

"No," replied Bombastus with the greatest sweetness. "I cannot see into the bathroom, but every morning, I have seen you, in the middle of this room, glowing with nudity and doing your Swedish gymnastic exercises, legs up, legs down, legs open . . ."

Bombastus was engrossed in a pause filled with memories, then more softly and with a sweetness that would be difficult to match, he added, "Beautiful . . . very beautiful . . ."

"My God!" sighed Signora Poma, pulling her angora dressing gown tightly around herself, but it would be hard to say whether it was to cancel with this gesture of modesty the spectacle of her nudity, which Bombastus from inside his frame had enjoyed for two weeks in a row, or so as not to allow the pleasure that these praises gave her to evaporate.

There followed an anxious silence, and in the silence someone knocked on the wall: a tardy response to Signora Poma's stamping and shrieking. *"Ruhe! Wir wollen Schlafen!"* said a sleepy voice from the next room.

"What does it matter, Signora Poma?" Bombastus resumed in a whisper. "No, let me call you Pina . . . what does it matter if I have seen you naked? Not only could I be your father twenty-two times over, but I am a doctor."

A doctor, thought Signora Poma. And her mind painfully re-evoked the visit her husband had forced her to make to Dr.

Rosci, in order to determine which of them was to blame for their sterile marriage.

"Pina," continued the portrait, "I have seen the supreme nudity: Death. How could eyes that have seen Death offend you?"

Signora Poma did not exactly understand what the portrait was talking about, but she had an inkling that it had to do with profound things. She was particularly struck by the words Death and Offend. The lazy mechanisms of her mind began slowly to move. The truth of that sentence was not long in becoming clear to her, that someone who has seen death could only look at her nakedness with innocence. In picturesque confusion the figures of death, her mother, her sister Clotilde, and of her friend Egle appeared to her merged into a single figure, which stood there watching her as she did her indoor gymnastic exercises, lying on the floor but reduced to the size of a two-year-old child. Whether the idea of the eyes looking at her nudity with innocence pleased or displeased her, we cannot say, and it may not have aroused in her either one feeling or the other. The thought of the eyes "that have seen Death" excluded any other thought. Signora Poma was unable to tear her eyes away from the eyes in the portrait, the eyes that had seen Death. And those eyes, loving and smiling, were looking back at her.

So far only the eyes in the portrait had been alive, and the mouth, which now smiled. But now the hand too comes to life: the hand holding its forefinger between the pages of the book. It draws forth the forefinger, spreads all its fingers, and emerges from the portrait.

"Pina," says the portrait, "Help me to descend. Help me to live the last act of my life, so that I can finally die." And since it was obvious that Signora Pina did not understand, the portrait added, "I will explain it to thee later. Now help me to descend."

The little hand sticking out of the canvas confirms the request. Signora Poma does not understand, does not stop to think: she is under the sway of the eyes that have seen Death. She approaches like an automaton, lifts her arm, and takes hold of that hand, so small that two fingers are enough to hold it. But on contact with life, contact with warmth, contact with Signora Poma's hand, the little hand grows suddenly and fills her whole hand. And behind the hand, the arm stretches itself forward, emerges from the canvas, and grows to the normal size of a man's arm. As do the head, the shoulders, the trunk, the legs. Finally the portrait is completely enlarged and outside the frame, on which only the heel of the right foot still rests.

"Leave me not," says the portrait turned man. And with his hand in Signora Poma's hand, like an acrobat descending from a trapeze, Theophrastus Bombastus von Hohenheim, otherwise known as Aureolatus Paracelsus, jumps to the floor with an elegant pirouette.

"Much thanks!"

Paracelsus stretches himself, yawns with the long meows of a panther, and realizes that Signora Poma is standing there looking at him stunned.

"Excuse me. I know it is not something that is done. But you will understand: I have been inside that frame for four hundred years . . ."

Having finished stretching himself and begging Signora Poma's pardon, Paracelsus shook himself from head to foot as though to throw off four centuries of dull, motionless life on a thin primed surface, after which he gave signs of a sudden ambulatory seizure, and launched himself on a mad walk around the room. First he circled several times about the table on which lay Signora Poma's unfinished letter to her husband, Ildefonso Poma; then he strode back and forth the entire length of the room from one wall to the other; then as though to alternate flat surfaces and obstacle races he again traversed the room, but this time by climbing over the chairs, armchair, and bed; then he added to these obstacles the table and dresser, which he climbed with truly surprising agility for a man carrying four hundred and forty-four springs on his back; finally he also made an attempt to walk up the wall, but failed at this boyish prank and caught himself just in time before falling on his rump to the floor.

Signora Poma stood glued to the wall, where she was imitating those figures in half relief that decorate the bar of the Teatro Eliseo in Rome, and was witnessing in terror the bedroom marathon of the man who had squeezed himself out of the portrait. But when Theophrastus started toward the window, open to the moonlit night, climbed on the sill with the same heedlessness with which he had just climbed on the dresser, and stuck his left foot out into the void to continue his bold walk beyond the window, Signora Poma tore herself away from the wall, ran to the window, seized the foolhardy man by the skirt of his doctoral robe, and managed to drag him back inside.

Theophrastus passed through Signora Poma's soft, fragrant, and encircling arms like a circus rider through the circle of fire, and found himself again standing upright on the carpet of the room. He continued to hold her beautiful hands in his, and closed his eyes as though it were the effect of that contact. A wrinkle creased his forehead, the kind that like a solitary wave sometimes cuts the broad and luminous sea of joy with its dark shadow. And indeed it was joy, an extraordinary joy, an unparalleled joy, that at that very moment was running through Paracelsus's reconstituted body and branching out in countless tributaries. If Paracelsus did not open his eyes, it was so as not to allow that joy an exit, not lose a particle of it.

"I've saved your life," said Signora Poma, red in the face and pleased with herself. "But you're crazy, that's for sure."

"Much thanks," replied Paracelsus. "I am not crazy. To be such I would have had to be formed in my embryonic life by arcae, or imperfect volcanoes, so to speak. If I were crazy I would wear amber rings on my fingers, which as I demonstrate in one of my seven magical books, in the chapter 'De origine dementiae,' curb the overwhelming effects of madness. Besides, O Pina, madmen manifest deeper intelligence than those who call themselves sane. Wisdom, to be sure, comes from the reasonable and immortal spirit, but it mani-

281

fests itself through the animal essence. The healthy man furnished with an animal body in good condition tends to let his body operate above all, whereupon his properly human faculties atrophy. We then see his true wisdom become attenuated and vanish, while he descends to living like a fox or a wolf. The madman is not the master of his animal body, but when the latter dozes the immortal intelligence gains strength to express itself and speaks through the mouth of the madman. For this reason, O Pina, it is better to listen to the madman rather than the sane man, and in imitation of the Muslims honor in the madman the prophet and saint. But it is not this that intoxicates me, not this. Anyone who swims is not afraid to get wet. To the extent that I am already dead, I cannot die any further. I do not know if I have the faculty of walking on air because I have not tried, and what is not tried by experience cannot be said to exist. But even were I to lack this faculty and to have fallen into the street, by that law that bodies heavier than air obey and which if I am not mistaken you call the law of gravity, the only trouble I would have had would have been to awaken the doorman of the hotel and have him bring me back up here in the lift."

"What? Dressed like that . . ."

"What would it matter? He would have taken me for one of those characters who performed *The Abduction from the Seraglio* this evening at the Festspielhaus, and who had not had time to change his costume and remove his makeup."

"But you know everything!" exclaimed Signora Poma in astonishment. "And the law of . . . what do you call it. . . ?"

"Of gravity," suggested Paracelsus.

"And the lifts! And that this evening they did *The Abduction from the Seraglio!* How could you, when you were such a little painting locked up inside that frame, how were you able to know all these things?"

"I know everything," replied Theophrastus, "but by hearsay. I am like those diplomats who attend international assemblies not as participants but as observers, like the delegate of the United States to the sessions of the League of Nations."

282

"League of Nations?" repeated Signora Poma angrily, with the indiscretion of people who have no understanding of political and cultural matters, and who burst out without restraint at the slightest mention of these problems. "My husband," she added vehemently, "says the League of Nations is a bunch of crooks."

"I have heard that myself," replied Paracelsus, slightly annoyed that Signora Poma had broken his train of thought. Then he went on: "I learned of *The Abduction from the Seraglio* from you, you had talked about it with your friend Egle. How I would have liked to accompany you! To immerse myself too in the sea of music . . ."

What a funny idea! thought Signora Poma. And I was so bored!

". . . immerse myself in the sea of music, next to you wearing that dress the color of dawn which left so much of your beautiful shape on view!"

"You mean my pink dress?"

"Yes."

"It's an original model."

"It could not be anything less," replied Paracelsus. "Everything about you is an original model. Everything about you is exemplary . . . O Pina! O my model! O my paradigm!"

"Paradigm. . . ?"

Signora Poma understood more or less a third of the words uttered by Paracelsus, and it was precisely for this reason that these words had such an effect on her. If you choose the films you go to see in a language you do not know, they will seem to you obscure but more beautiful. The fascination of many writers is in direct proportion to their obscurity. Understanding is less required than it is said to be. It is required by those few who are capable of reasoning, and therefore of receiving light from reason, as well as comfort and pleasure; but for the others reason is sterile and of no use. For women, and also for men who live by sensations and impressions, a language devoid of precise meanings would be more suitable, one that would merely be the modulated sound of their desires. To that little pink shell that was Signora Poma's ear, where the pear-shaped pearl hung like a drop of milk, Paracelsus's words sounded like the language of the horses in the land of the Houyhnhnms. But what did it matter? Signora Poma could hear that that forest of obscure words referred to her, bowed to her, surrounded her, and raised her up to the top of a monument, and for her that was enough.

Paradigm, thought Signora Poma. I'm his paradigm . . . That's cute!

So far Theophrastus had spoken with his eyes closed, like someone asleep on his feet and telling his dreams aloud, but at this point he opened them and irradiated Signora Poma with rays infinitely more living, incomparably more ardent as compared to those albeit very living, albeit very ardent ones that had irradiated her before. Nor did his hands leave hers, but rather squeezed them still harder.

"Thou didst not save my life," said Paracelsus, "thou hast given me life. Life I did not know except by hearsay. I lived by virtue of the Nefesh, which is the animal soul, and the Ruach, which is the cogitating soul, but I lacked the Neshamah, which is the spiritual soul. And what kind of life is it, tell me, O Pina, what kind of life is that which lacks the Neshamah? But thou hast appeared to me. Thou hast appeared as the Law appears to the elect. And like the Law thou hast appeared to me first through a curtain, revealing to me the Derashah, or interpretation by syllogisms, then through a transparent veil and revealing to me the Agada, that is to say, interpretation by symbols."

"You don't mean to insinuate that now you see me through a transparent veil?" Signora Poma asked in a rather worried tone.

"Hush," replied Paracelsus. "Hush. The Zohar, vainly studied for so many years, is finally about to reveal to me its terrible secrets. Through the Thirty-two marvelous Ways of Wisdom; through the Sefer, the Sefar, and the Sippur; through the Ten Sefiroth and the Twenty-two Fundamental Letters; through the Three Mothers, the Seven Doubles, and the Twelve Simples, I feel, O Pina, I feel that the Copy is about to achieve the perfection of the Model. Speak not. Our synergy is being accomplished. Our sefirotic relations are about to begin."

Paracelsus's jaws began to swell as in a fish when it breathes, his hands to tremble, while his pupils sank within his eyeballs and remained half submerged there, like two tiny black suns about to set in a sea of milk.

Despite the experience that had come to her from six years of marriage, Signora Poma, faced with such vivid manifestations of desire, felt the obscure terrors reawaken in her that her reluctant spirit had known as a girl, and she took fright. Violently twisting her wrists, she wrenched herself free from Paracelsus's burning hands.

"Don't you feel well, doctor?"

Paracelsus recovered himself, and his pupils returned to normal. "Do not take away your hands!" he implored. "I feel that through your hands the mysterious bond is about to occur that will unite my Microprosopon with your Macroposopon. Give me your hands again! In forty-eight years of living life, and in three hundred and ninety-six of pictorial life, this is the first time, O Pina, the first time I have touched a woman's hand."

"Liar!" exclaimed Signora Poma, still on her guard.

"The first," Paracelsus insisted.

To receive the homage of a man who for four hundred and forty years has kept his virginity is not something that happens to women every day, even when they are endowed like Signora Poma with exceptional attractions. Under the shell of her reawakened girlish terrors, the offer of this homage flattered and gently disturbed her.

Paracelsus's hands were supplicating and waiting. Signora Poma restored her hands to his, but for greater prudence she deemed it expedient to lead the conversation onto serious ground.

"Did you never touch your mother's hands?"

"Never even those," replied Paracelsus in a lower voice.

"Poor baby!" sighed Signora Poma, and for the first time in her life felt like a mother.

"I never saw my mother," continued Paracelsus. "She died

285

giving birth to me, but she left me her thought. At home they never spoke of her, whether so as not to stir up memories and thereby allow them little by little to go to sleep, or so as not to sadden my childish mind, but her faint sweet ghost never abandoned me. Alive, I never thought of woman except through the thought of my mother; and my mother, of whom neither at home nor elsewhere did I ever find portraits to show me what she looked like, I saw always in the image of the Madonna of the Abbey of Einsiedeln; in the little bronze Virgin with short wavy hair gathered around her childish face, by the gaze she directed to the Child seated on her short folded arm, by the body that never saw the sun enclosed in the long pleated habit and bending at the hip to balance the weight of the divine Son; the celestial Mother to whom the pilgrims came to ask for comfort and healing, and whom I was accustomed to seeing ever since I was a child, for the Abbey of Einsiedeln, founded in 829 by a Benedictine named Meinard, is situated in a deep valley near Zurich, not far from the little town of Etzel, where I was born on 10 November 1493. To return time and again to Einsiedeln was all the more dear to me, since they had told me that the hospital lodged in the abbey had been directed by my mother, and over the door of it I saw the sweet ghost disguised as the Madonna who still welcomed the sick pilgrims, and inside those vast vaulted rooms took care of them under the large black crucifix. All my life I thought of my mother, certain of finding her in death, and the thought of her kept far from me any other thought of woman. About my reputation for chastity, my enemies, and without boasting I think I can say there is no man who has had so many, spread rumors as wicked as they were false; some that I had been emasculated during my sojourn in Turkey, where by the way I had never even dreamed of going, others that as a child I had been bitten in my private parts by a pig. How can they be made to understand certain truths, those who of the three souls have only the Nefesh, the animal soul?"

Paracelsus's hands quivered again in those of Signora Poma, who felt as though she had hold of one of those large hot-air pistols called Föhn from the name of a hot dry wind that blows in certain valleys in Switzerland and the Tyrol, and which is the translation of our *favonio*, but since in these new vibrations she did not as before feel an impure emotion, she allowed the "synergy" between her and Paracelsus to be accomplished through this contact. Meanwhile she was thinking: What's synergy? And her ignorance of the meaning of the word increased its charm.

Paracelsus was silent for a few seconds, again concentrating his thoughts. Then he went on:

"If my life, as long as I was alive, had been entirely consummated, if my need for love had not been enclosed and dried up in that unattainable wish, if I had not left behind me any wish still in need of fulfillment, I, O Pina, would not be here with thee in this hour to accomplish the gentle synergy that to me will give death, or the completion of life, and to thee that flower of love that so far thou hast lacked and without which life is root, trunk, branch, leaf, but flower does not become; and I would be dead, completely dead, entirely dead, wholly dead in this city of Salzburg that now houses us, and in which so far as men and History are concerned, I died on 24 September 1541, while Uranus passed into Leo in opposition to Saturn, master of the Ascendant in these matters, and forming a correspondence with the Eighth House or House of Death in the sky of my birth; while Neptune passed into Aries and was in exact quadrature with radical Mars, indicator of trials and tribulations for its situation in the Capricorn of my birth; which demonstrates, O Pina, considering the correspondence of Aries with the head or more exactly with the neck, and of Capricorn with the legs or more exactly with the act of climbing; and considering at the same time the transition from Neptune to Mars in coincidence with the circumstances of death; which demonstrates, I repeat, clearly demonstrates that on that day I was supposed to die and on no other."

Let us be truthful. If Signora Poma at that moment had found a way to free herself, and ring the bell, and call for help; or better still if she had been able to leave her room, and pass into the adjoining room, and take refuge in the bed of her friend Egle, she would have done so without a moment's hesitation. But she could not. The synergy through the joining of hands had arrived at such intensity that to try to break it was not even thinkable. And so she yielded. She yielded as we yield to death, because we feel there is nothing else to do. She yielded to that shadow and to that dream, at the end of which a strange happiness nevertheless shone.

Although she was submerged up to the eyes in the darkness of the irrational, a glimmer of rationality still shone, or, it would be better to say, kept blinking in Signora Poma's mental night, similar to the last beacon on an immense ocean, over which all other beacons have been extinguished. A light fed by her still very lively curiosity to know by what miracle this man of many names had been able to live inside a portrait and descend from the frame to the floor just as he pleased, like the tenant of a ground floor apartment who instead of using the door enjoys leaving his home by the window. But how was she to ask Theophrastus Philippus Bombastus von Hohenheim, otherwise known as Paracelsus Aureolatus, about such intimate and personal things? By that singular phenomenon of adaptation that we have already noted, Signora Poma had familiarized herself from the very first moment with this strange situation, but it was perhaps for this very reason that she presented in this strange situation too the modesty, the reticence, and all those small but troublesome mental reservations that clog more normal situations, and if Signora Poma could not decide to ask Paracelsus the question that was on the tip of her tongue, it was for the same reasons that prevent us from asking someone who has been introduced to us a quarter of an hour before whether he has false teeth, wears long underwear with strings tied to his ankles, or suffers from hemorrhoids. But while the question that could not be formulated continued to weigh heavily on Signora Poma's mind, Theophrastus spoke and with his usual sweetness said:

"Be not troubled, O Pina, I will now explain to thee how I

have been able to live in this portrait of myself, and to climb out of the frame according to your picturesque image of the tenant on the ground floor who leaves his house by the window."

At the sound of these words, Signora Poma's astonishment knew no bounds, and in an abrupt movement of recoil she freed her hands from Paracelsus's albeit very strong grasp, like a ship moored in a port that at the surge of a sudden storm breaks its moorings and heads out to sea. "How . . . how did you know . . . what I was thinking?" she stammered, when she was again able to speak.

Paracelsus looked at Signora Poma the way a mother contemplates the amazement of her child, and with infinite tenderness replied:

"By the effect of synergy, my dear. After all, were we not, I and thou, in the middle of a synergetic operation? By the effect of synergy I had already been completely transferred into thee, and thou too—oh, deny it not!—thou too in thy turn wast about to transfer thyself into me; but thy untimely movement of recoil has broken the channel of sympathy that ran through our joined hands, and now we must begin again from the beginning."

Backed against the wall where her astonishment has driven her, and under the frame inside which the river, sea, rock, and coastal city still surround the white silhouette from which Paracelsus has shortly before detached himself and which deprived of his features looks like a portrait of Mr. Blank, Signora Poma is thinking that if a dressing gown is enough to protect our nakedness from the gaze of others, there is no dressing gown, whether angora or some even more solid fabric, that can protect us from the eye that can see through skin and bone to our naked brain, and the thoughts that arise from it like insubstantial fumes from the labyrinth.

Such an awful and endearing situation! An ineffable state of defenselessness and helplessness! In the end it is a great pleasure to feel weak.

Nevertheless, and by a new and equally rapid process of familiarization, Signora Poma adapts herself to this new condition of not being allowed to have secrets, and exposes herself to Paracelsus's scrutinizing gaze with the submission, not to say the pleasure, of a victim offering itself to sacrifice.

"Our lives are completely made up of desires," Paracelsus went on. "It is our desires that keep our lives alive. This strength of desires Schopenhauer rather inappropriately called will, and it is presumably by reason of this same strength of desires that Wolfgang Goethe . . ."

"Did you say Volfango!"

"Goethe. Why?"

"That's the one!" exclaimed Signora Poma with manifest satisfaction.

"Who?"

"Oh, nothing . . . I read this morning in the opera program that Mozart's name was Volfango, and remembered that there was another great man with that name, somebody Egle keeps talking about, but I couldn't remember his name. How nice to get educated!"

Taking advantage of the digression on the name of Mozart and Goethe, Paracelsus again took Signora Poma's hands in his.

"Thou sayest well, O Pina. Science too, that is to say, knowledge, is nothing but the way to unite ourselves with the universe, and to establish great synergy between ourselves and the whole."

Conscious of this truth, Signora Poma bowed her head and made no further efforts to withdraw her hands. As though to slake her thirst for knowledge, Paracelsus continued:

"It is presumably by reason of this strength of desires that Goethe asserted that man does not die from outside causes, but because he no longer has the will to live, meaning when he has fulfilled all the desires that support him in life. Indeed, O Pina, what else is death but the end of our desires?"

Signora Poma, though directly challenged, did not reply, but her serious and absorbed attitude left no doubt with what concentration she was forcing her weak mind to the thought of death as the end of our desires.

"Thus," Paracelsus continued, "some of the dead go on

living in a state of unfulfilled desire: conquistadors in their desire for conquest, scientists in their desire to bring to light a discovery barely glimpsed, philosophers in their desire finally to contemplate the longed-for Truth naked and entire. And it is perhaps because of the impossibility of fulfilling some desires that so many ambitious men continue to succeed each other in pursuit of the same desire: Napoleon resumes in his turn the desire that was formerly Alexander's, and Alexander resumes in his turn the desire of one of his predecessors, whose face has been dimmed and name erased by time.

"More fortunate than the others, artists too sometimes survive death, and not even in an absurd and incorporeal manner, but, as people say, in their works. And in the latter they survive not only in spirit but also a little in substance, through that feeling common to all true artists that the work is never finished and always desirous of perfection. And if thou shouldst try, O Pina, to wound the Madonna della Sedia with a knife, or to fire a revolver at the Hermes, or to tear the manuscript of the Ninth Symphony, thou wilt see no blood, but wilt hear the faint but agonizing cry of a great life that yet persists in that wood, that marble, that paper."

Signora Poma was on the point of tears. "No! No! I'd never do that!" And she shook her lovely head as though to drive away the specter of such an iconoclastic eventuality.

"As for me," continued Paracelsus, "when in September of 1541 I returned here to Salzburg tired from my long travels, and on the twenty-fourth of that month, in a wretched hospital ward and with a great cry of liberation abandoned my corporeal remains, I for all intents and purposes died, except for a desire that in my life I had not succeeded in fulfilling: the desire to love. And it is for this desire alone that I continue to live in a reduced way, the way of those disembodied entities that in my *Archidoxes Magicae* I call *Lemuri* or *Caballi*, and will continue to live until I fulfill it, making use of the corporality of certain objects that were familiar to me in life and in which I had reposed my affection, and particularly this portrait that so faithfully reproduces my

291

likeness, and which many years after my death had the honor to be copied by the great Rubens."

"But then," exclaimed Signora Poma in a burst of perspicacity, "if by giving up love you prolong your life, you could live forever, and go on spying from inside your portrait on the secrets of ladies who come and go, and starting amorous conversations, and once in a while coming down out of the frame . . ."

"I could," replied Paracelsus gravely, "but I do not wish to. I am tired, much more tired than that day when still alive but already prepared to renounce life, I knocked at the door of the Hospital of the Holy Spirit, and told the friar who opened the door and asked me my name, 'In the world of the flesh I had the name Theophrastus Paracelsus, but in the world of the spirit my name is already Nobody.' And besides it is well that the living are alive, and the dead dead; because just as the living desire to live, so the dead, if I may say so, desire with the same ardor to die. I, in my capacity as a dead man, cannot wait to fulfill this sole wish of mine, which for three hundred and ninety-six years has kept me anchored to life, like the last hawser that keeps a balloon from taking to the sky and immersing itself in the infinite vastness of the All. As for starting amorous conversations with passing ladies and descending once in a while from my frame like a Romeo from the balcony, believe me, O Pina, this is the first time . . ."

"Nonsense!" cried Signora Poma, twitching her shoulders and laughing a nervous flirtatious laugh. "You don't mean to tell me there's never been a woman to your liking . . ."

"Never!" Paracelsus insisted, maintaining the serious tone whereby he felt that, however inexpert he might be as a wooer, he would be led sooner and more surely to his goal. "Never! The women I have seen come and go in this room have been either too old or too ugly. Once one of them, having undressed to go to bed, sat for three quarters of an hour in the chair. I have seen couples go by who more often than not were accompanied by another couple, Vulgarity and Boredom. How fortunate, O Pina, that portraits are not subject to nausea! Much misery have I seen, much shame, much turpitude. I have seen single men go by. Once . . . but let me not think of it . . ."

"And never a woman you liked? Don't make me laugh!" And indeed, with a gargling sound in the back of her throat, Signora Poma went, "Ha-ha-ha!"

"Never," Paracelsus repeated once more. But all of a sudden, as though coming upon a needle in a haystack, he went on: "Yes, once. I do not remember the year, but it was during one of these music festivals. And that time, I confess, I was on the point of manifesting myself. I gathered my strength, concentrated my will, but push as I might this way and that, my pictorial life ran up against an invisible wall."

"Really?"

"It did not take me long to understand the reason. She, a Neapolitan, was wearing a little coral crescent on a chain between her breasts, and red coral, as I demonstrate in the chapter 'De Corallis' in my *Herbarius Theophrasti*, prevents ghosts from manifesting themselves."

A few wrinkles had altered Signora Poma's lovely features, giving her the look of a sulky child.

"So," she said in an angry voice, "if that woman hadn't been wearing that coral between her breasts . . ."

"Perhaps . . . I know not . . . I do not think," Paracelsus stammered hurriedly, aware too late that he had made a mistake. "And besides finding a few physical qualities is not everything . . . there are other necessary requisites . . . it is that state of purity, of virginity, that illuminates thee, O Pina, like the dawn."

From the rosiness of dawn, Signora Poma went red as a beet.

"I don't allow you to insult me, and especially to insult my husband. I have been married for six years, and my husband, Commendatore Poma, if you really want to know, is a man in the true sense of the word. As for you . . ."

Assailed by Signora Poma's anger, Paracelsus desperately ran for cover.

"I doubt it not . . . yes . . . a magnificent man . . . but that is something else . . ."

"What else, for God's sake!"

"I mean . . . when there is no interpenetration of sidereal principles, when the marriage of the two spiritual principles does not occur but only the contact of the physical bodies, virginal purity does not undergo alterations . . . And you, O Pina, are pure, you are intact, you are immaculate . . . You are the woman, the only woman, the sole woman for me, who like the unicorn cannot die without taking refuge on the breast of a virgin, you are the only woman who can fulfill my last desire, release me from life, and place me in the sweet lap of death . . . O Pina, I love thee! I love thee! I love thee!"

In the crescendo of these three I love thee's, Paracelsus broke the synergetic bond of their hands, stretched out his arms, and was about to put them around Signora Poma's waist, but she repulsed the amorous ghost by beating her fists on his chest, saying in a cold voice:

"Take your hands off me! You could have asked your Neapolitan woman to take off her coral and done it with her. By this time you'd be dead and satisfied, and you wouldn't be here propositioning me, who's got plenty of other things to do besides listening to your stupid talk!"

A grave silence fell after these words. Signora Poma adjusted the curls on her forehead, rubbed her wrists, which were slightly reddened from the synergetic grasp, then, looking very serious, went and sat down at the writing table, took up her pen, and made as though to resume the letter she had begun.

The moon, setting behind the Kapuzinerberg, prolonged its last light on the carpet, and advanced it under the table to pay homage to Signora Poma's naked, silvery feet, whose toes were barely ensconced under the tiny strap of her swansdown-trimmed mules.

Paracelsus had not moved. Finally, breaking the silence, which at the sound of his voice laboriously opened its lips to swallow it, Bombastus whispered:

"Pardon me. I did not want to offend you. And even had I wanted to, how could I? I know not how you could have thought of such an eventuality. Perhaps because you do not know me, do not know who I am."

Paracelsus continued to stand still in the same place. Then while Signora Poma held the point of her pen suspended over the paper like a threat, and looked straight in front of her, pretending not to hear him, Paracelsus, in a slow whisper, drawing forth his memories like a long ribbon, began to tell the story of his life.

In keeping with his nature as a propounder of riddles, Paracelsus began the story of his life with a question. "Have you ever happened to awaken in the middle of the night and had trouble understanding who you were, where you were, and what had happened to you?" he asked.

Paracelsus's question prolonged itself for its entire length in the silence, and after a brief existence died. And since Signora Poma continued to stare fixedly straight ahead and to pretend not to listen, refusing to honor the question received with a reply, which to a question is a hand grasping a hand, the second portion of Paracelsus's discourse emerged, with the difficulty of a surgical childbirth and after a very extended pause that threatened to compromise all possibility of renewal, from the same void from which the first one came. First with a gurgle of water that gushes with difficulty from the mud:

"Eh . . . ah . . . uh . . ."

Then with the fluidity of water liberated from the mud.

"It is like arriving at night in an unknown city. Like removing the blindfold in a place where we have been led with closed eyes. Like emerging at night from a station in the underground, in a neighborhood where we have never been before."

Was there a birdcatcher's cunning in the third example offered by Paracelsus, and did he really consider Signora Poma as a hunting bitch to be lured by letting her glimpse a couple of hare's ears from behind a lump of plowed earth?

No way of saying, but in any case the effect was striking. Signora Poma pricked up her shell-like ear, looked suddenly at Paracelsus with the eye in profile, shook her well-groomed head that shone like a fine dumbbell, and with the staccato little voice of a mechanical pullet exclaimed:

"It's true! . . . It's happened to me . . . when my husband took me to Paris . . . one evening when we were coming out of the Metro . . . I remember the name of the station . . . it was called *Barbès-Rochechouart*."

The six parts of this utterance were delivered very fast and in the manner of a wheel with six spokes that makes one complete rotation, blank in tone for all the perfect spontaneity that had generated them, like a little lesson learned by heart that has rhythm but not intelligence, motion but not comprehension, life but not thought.

Paracelsus's face was that of a chemist for whom a difficult experiment has turned out well. The ice was broken but it was necessary to profit by the heat of the result. Paracelsus made a jump and landed next to Signora Poma. He seized her hands and drew her to her feet. In the collision the pen fell at the feet of the reconstituted couple, and at the sharp little sound Signora Poma awoke as from a brief slumber, and looked at Paracelsus as though seeing him for the first time, almost as though his appearance were that of her prison.

"You again! . . . But what do you want? . . . Leave me alone!"

But by now the hands of the Motherless One were two soft, warm tongs, his arms a noose ready to be tightened.

"I will not leave thee! . . . I will not leave thee again! . . . Thou alone doth understand me! . . . Thou alone!"

To tell a woman that she alone understands us is like firing at a barrel with a precision rifle at a distance of four paces. And not for the supposed play of vanity, but because woman's profound function here finds its natural outlet, which is to understand the man in the literal sense of the word, and give him the refuge of herself in this desert called life.

"To leave thee would be to lose once again the mother I did not find on my entry into the world, and who now, having been found in thee, sweetly and piously will help me in my entry into death."

These repeated references by Paracelsus to his mother and at the same time to her, Pina Poma, as to an integral part of the former, disturbed Signora Poma, not because she didn't understand them, but because she understood that at the end of her not understanding there was a mysterious truth to be understood.

"Woman is attracted to profundity," added Paracelsus, as though to illuminate this thought with sound. "She is attacted by profundity more than by anything else in the world. Because woman is profound, much more profound than man, this practical and superficial speculator, and more than he may think. It is only that woman's profundity is natural, and therefore not conspicuous. And not only profound, woman is the very profundity of the world. Everything profound in the world is woman, and feminine: birth, life, death, eternity. And if rumor has it that woman is attracted by frivolity, it is to deceive the grave and motionless profundity of woman, and at the same time to save the kingdom of man. Now tell me, O Pina, dost thou not feel thyself to be birth, life, death, eternity? Art thou not the woman as large as the universe revealed by the Cabala, which does not mean magic as the ignorant think, and trafficking with demons and intrigue, but the tradition of truth?"

Signora Poma nodded her head twice and murmured something that might even have been: "Yes, I am."

Satisfied, Paracelsus went on: "I was sleeping. I was sleeping the prenatal sleep and all of a sudden I awakened. I awakened in the middle of this unknown life—the middle of this unknown life, which continues for me to be such even now when I am dead.

"This is what it means to come into the world and not find the woman who has generated us. This is what it means to come into the world and not find the woman who will take us by the hand and lead us through the unknown city, through the quarter where we have never come by day, and teach us the streets, the squares, the intersections, the inhabitable and salubrious places, the inhospitable and dangerous ones, the secrets of the houses and what is hidden in the shadows; she who when the blindfold is removed from our eyes points in a circle with her finger and says: 'That is north, that is south, that is east, that is west. If you go straight ahead, you will find a city. If you take this direction instead, you will find the sea and a port filled with traffic, where the great steamers weigh anchor that will carry you to the Fortunate Isles. But beware of going in this other direction, because you will find nothing but dangers and hostile people, and then the desert and death.' This is what it means to come into the world and not find the mother.

"Now imagine an entire life, then a life prolonged beyond life, and both diffused, lost in this perpetual perplexity, in this inability to find light in the surrounding darkness; in this inability ever to know who you are, where you are, what has happened to you. Because only through the mother can we understand who we are; only through the mother can we understand where we are; only through the mother can we understand what has happened to us, what is happening to us, what will happen to us.

"True, I found my father. He was sitting in the solitary house, the house without light, the house without sound. His eyes were glassy and empty, like two ship's lanterns in which they have put out the light to clean them. And he was waiting. He was waiting for the woman who had gone away. Because when the woman leaves the home, the men, sons, husbands, and brothers, do not know when to expect her to return.

"I found my father. But what can a father do? What can a man do? A man, who lives detached from the universe, and thinks himself to be the universe? At most he can suggest to us some way proved by experience, by the experience of this chain of men who go by repeatedly in life holding each other by the hand; he can light some small flame in our minds; he can teach us to imitate, to repeat, what other men have done; he can transmit to us some so-called secrets—when they are not to be called tricks. But the weight, the volume, the substance of life, the wishes of our hearts and the need for sympathy of our blood, our mental home, the radius of air that surrounds our bodies, the milieu of life in which we can confidently and easily turn over and over like the fish in water and the bird in the air—all these are things that only the mother can give us. And when the mother is missing, we spend our whole life wandering, without a body, lights lost in the night, hearts that beat aimlessly, blood that goes on circulating without rhyme or reason, finding no answer to our 'hows' and 'whys,' and all of life is nothing but one long, desperate, vain interrogation.

"Had I not found my father, perhaps I would not have hated the idea that I was to form of him. But why him and not her? Why this iniquity? A . . . how can one say it? . . . a dirty trick. Like saying to a starving man, 'Go to such and such a place and you will find a piece of bread,' and the starving man goes and in that place finds a stone. My father: a stone. What did his suffering matter to me, his gloom, that wretched look he had like a dog thrown out of the house? Furthermore he was hiding his pain from me, while for my part, and although I had never seen her, I had one much heavier, and perhaps it would have been good for me to share it with him, and there he sat chewing on it all day in silence. His pain . . . his pain as a murderer . . . his remorse. Yes. Because she had not gone away. She had not gone away like someone who goes away because she wants to go. No. He had killed her. He, the physician who had not known how to save her; he whose science had been insufficient to seize that precious, inestimable existence, hold it back on the brink of the black hole, and prevent it from falling to the other side. He, the murderer . . ."

Paracelsus waited for the tempest of sighs to subside a little in his breast—those sighs that out of sympathy were raising a tempest under the angora dressing gown in the bosom of Signora Poma—then went on:

"Although the attempt to save my mother failed, my father did not hesitate to exercise his profession of healer, and continued to receive the sick who came to him in hopes of a cure. Once he had finished deceiving those unfortunates, my father would take me with him on endless walks through the countryside and up the mountains—walks at a military pace and which he placed like a lid over his boiling remorse—and teach me the virtues of salutary plants, the dangers of poisonous ones and their antidotes. But how was I to believe him, or believe in his science? I waited.

"When I was eight years old, my father took me with him to Villach, where he had been transferred to teach chemistry in the mining school attached to the Fugger mines. We lived at number 18 on the Ledererstrasse, and if you go to visit our house, you will find in the room my father had set aside as a laboratory a bannister knob that I gilded with my own hands. If I too, as men customarily do for the beloved woman, wanted to make you a gift of something precious and metallic, that bannister knob is the only thing I could give you, but I doubt that they would let you take it away.

"The Fuggers, owners of the Bleiberg mines, by whom my father was employed, were reckless speculators and their name is written in letters of blood among the founders of capitalism. Their business organization, restricted to their relatives and in-laws and handed down from father to son along with the blood inheritance, anticipates that of the Rothschilds. Charles V made them counts of the Empire, because someone can always be found to reward those who starve the people, and it is from their example that I derived my hatred for the rich."

"What!" murmured Signora Poma, and a slight cloud veiled her brow, "you hate the rich?"

"I hate them," Paracelsus repeated more darkly. "Although the hatred I nourish for wealth has nothing in common with the hatred that goes to feed the so-called class struggle, both because my poverty was not the poverty of the poor man, and because the wealth at which I aimed was not comparable to the kind measured in ducats, pistoles, or banknotes. Can one who yearns to possess the supreme truth be called proletarian? Like other capitalists, the Fuggers concealed their 'execrable operations,' as the Church rightly calls them, under the splendor of art patronage, and their munificence gave as much luster to Augsburg as that of the Medici to Florence. And since in that time, unlike yours today, the enlightened humanists constituted an ornament of man, one Fugger, Ulrich by name, published some Greek authors at his own expense, among them Xenophon—yes, Xenophon, stupid Xenophon!—and this alone shows thee, O Pina, the criterion of this Ulrich—and gave a splendid library to the University of Heidelberg. Nevertheless, it was in the Fugger mines that I began to penetrate the secrets of nature; it was in the mines of Bleiberg that the similarity was revealed to me between the formation of the mineral in the womb of the earth and the gestation of the child in the womb of the mother; it was in those lead mines that I discovered the affinity and equilibrium between one thing and another whence the harmony of nature is composed; it was in those mines in Carinthia that my mind was opened to the light of alchemy, that is, to the search for the sympathies between one part and another of the universal whole.

"It was a terrible period and at the same time pregnant with hopes. Terrible because the world was torn by wars and violence: only recently had the Turks been driven back from the gates of Villach, Louis XII was waging war over the kingdom of Naples, the sky was reddened by the flames of the Inquisition, and the executioners knew no rest. But pregnant with hopes too, because Christopher Columbus had already made his fourth voyage to the West Indies; because Copernicus was discovering the true shape of the earth and the mechanism of the universe; because the printing press was beginning to disseminate thought; because Lascaris had printed the first grammar in the Greek language and the humanists were discovering the life of the ancient world; because the Cabala was disclosing secret truths to scholars; and finally because social customs and the organization of life were starting to develop toward more civilized forms, and the mail—that mail that tomorrow will bring to thy husband by the swiftest means the letter that lies unfinished on this table—at that time began regular services."

301

"Oh, God!" exclaimed Signora Poma. "The things you remind me of!"

"Worry not, O Pina," Paracelsus replied. "Another moment, and I will help thee to finish thy letter."

Such an educated man, thought Signora Poma, reassured. Who knows what a beautiful letter he'll write for me . . .

Paracelsus continued:

"The will to know spurred me on without letup. Today I would rather say the will to search, but then I did not yet know that the purpose of knowing is consumed in the pleasure of the search, and that we arrive at the end loaded with knowledge, yes, but without that knowledge for which we started out in the first place. Anyone who lives a vegetative life can say of living: the speculative life is a mad whirl, an hysterical fit as long as life itself, and a senseless effort."

"So which is better?" asked Signora Poma.

"The speculative," replied Paracelsus, "except that it passes in a flash and wrecks one's nerves. Besides, in my case, artificially raised and cachectic, a stutterer, locked in my inferiority complex . . ."

"No one seeing you would say that," said Signora Poma.

"The years bring strength and health. In four hundred and forty-four years I have had time to toughen myself. If men lived the life of the patriarchs, even the poorest and weakest of them would end by becoming bulls."

Signora Poma thoughtfully lowered her eyes.

"I could not continue to stay in Bleiberg," Paracelsus went on. "I was never able to become accustomed to places, or prefer one place to another. I know the possessive pronoun in theory but in practice I am unaware of it, and thou, O Pina, wilt perhaps be the first to teach me the profound meaning of the pronoun 'my' . . ."

Signora Poma thought the moment had come to yield herself, but some men, unable to stop talking, let slip the best opportunities. Paracelsus continued:

"If even the slightest sympathy began to form between myself and a place, myself and a house, myself and a person, an alarm bell immediately rang inside me to warn me not to stay . . ."

"An alarm?" interrupted Signora Poma. "The things you remind me of! One day, in the train from Rome to Frosinone, I had to pull the alarm cord to put an awful man who was with me in the compartment in his place."

What purity! thought Paracelsus, whose power of credulity had not been weakened by four centuries of life.

He continued:

"Movement was my natural state. But I was an innocent. I had not understood that when one is condemned to walk, one need only walk with the head and not move the legs besides, and this is the reason why the list of my journeys fills a whole page in my biographies, without counting those that fame has attributed to me to Tartary, Persia, and China, and which I never even thought of making.

"Why had I come into the world? Others, even though it is not a question of happiness, find a little corner of greater well-being or anyway of less discomfort on this earth, and there they stop as the swallow stops under the eaves to build its nest. And each of these places is determined by something that binds with the chains of sympathy or necessity, of interest or love: a father's house, the work by which one makes a living, a woman's love, a man's friendship, or some combination of these things. I alone did not find stations of love or necessity on this earth, and continued to wander. If other men too had been as I was, the earth would be bare of cities and villages, a bald sphere on which all humanity would circulate like a thick dark swirling sea from dawn to dusk and from birth to death; and had not Copernicus in the meantime given us the true shape of the earth, I would have deduced it myself, from my continual walking and from always finding myself retracing my footsteps. Let me add, however, that I would not have divulged my discovery. What would have been the use? After Copernicus, men still live and think as in the time of Ptolemy.

"So I left the Fuggers and betook myself to Würzburg, where the learned Benedictine Johannes Trithemius, former teacher of Cornelius Agrippa, instructed me in the doctrines of Plato, Plotinus, Iamblichus, and Porphyry; he guided me through the *Pimander* of Hermes Trismegistus; he opened to me the book of *Disputationes adversus Astrologiam divinatricem* by the omniscient Pico della Mirandola; he initiated me into the science of Nicola Flamello, Arnaldus de Villanova, and Bernardo Trevisano; he unveiled to me the mysteries of the Cabala in the interpretations of Ibn Gebirol and Maimonides. In Cologne I bowed my forehead over the *Azoto*, the *Car of Antimony*, and other manuscripts in which Basil Valentine investigates the properties of metals. In Paris, which already shone with the humanistic enlightenment spread by Guillaume Budé, I studied the local diseases, which at that time were not yet the pro-Communism of the salons and the painting of Cézanne, I saluted in reverence the spot on which Jacques de Molay, grand master of the Order of the Templars, had been burned alive, and laid a floral wreath on the pulpit where Abelard, the castrated friar, had taught that faith is not imposed by force but transmitted by means of reason. At the University of Montpellier I drew cabalistic knowledge from the tradition left by the Arabs, and was enraptured by the memory of Albigensian civilization. Italy at that moment was burning with humanistic fever, and in the splendor of that revival I visited the erudite universities of Bologna, Padua, and Ferrara. I went to Spain, where the memory of Ramón Lull was still alive, and from Lisbon went on to England, where Thomas More's *Utopia* was beginning to shine. I visited the mines of Cumberland, and at Oxford inhaled the agreeable odor of science left behind by Roger Bacon. From the island I returned to the Low Countries, which at that time were aflame with war; I was named surgeon in the Dutch army and took part in a few battles, the way Fabrice del Dongo took part in the battle of Waterloo, Wolfgang Goethe in the battle of Valmy, and Friedrich Nietzsche in that of Sedan, after which the stadtholder of Amsterdam presented me with that big sword which from then on, and with much difficulty because of my weak strength, I always wore at my side. From Holland I went to Stockholm, where a learned

Swedish woman, a follower of the faith healer Volupsa, taught me the composition of that decoction against hemorrhage that I mention in my *Grosse Wundartznei*. In Sweden I met the daring Olaus Petri, who propounded the laws of nature against the asceticism of the Middle Ages, and who can rightly be considered the precursor of nudism and Swedish gymnastics. From Sweden I went to Brandenburg, and from there to Bohemia and Moravia, where among those tribes of gypsies I collected some secrets of the Egyptian Thoth. I visited Lithuania, Poland, Walachia, and Dalmatia. At Fiume I took ship for Venice, and from Venice made my return to Villach.

"My father was sixty years old and sunk more than ever in the darkness of the Middle Ages, while I for my part was advancing ever more boldly into the light of the new times. We found nothing to say to each other. After a few months I said goodbye to him and once again set out on the road, nor did I ever see him again.

"I started a medical practice in Strasbourg. I was called to the bedside of the margrave of Baden, whom dysentary was carrying rapidly to the grave, and instantly cured him by administering some of my *labdanum*, which has relieved so much suffering, performed so many cures. In Basel I cured the printer Frobenius of a fracture in the right foot, and became friends with Erasmus, the praiser of folly and enemy of iotacism. Also in Basel, on 20 June 1527, to mark the end of the old theoretical medicine and the beginning of a medicine that studies diseases in patients and drugs in the great laboratory of nature, I threw Avicenna's *Canon of Medicine* into the bonfire that the students had lighted in honor of Saint John in front of the University, in imitation of what my friend Luther had done nine years earlier in the public square of Wittemberg, when he threw Leo X's bull into the fire. Fire, which in its principle of lightness we cabalists call *schinn*, was at that time the fashionable element for burning both heretics and papal bulls; just as today, when man flies in the sky, and from the sky drops bombs full of liquid air on the earth, I would say that the fashionable element is air, which in its principle we cabalists call *aleph*.

"But things began to go badly for me in Basel. My protector Frobenius, whom a year before I had cured of a serious and complex fracture of the foot, died of apoplexy while on his way to the Frankfort Book Fair, because the Book Fair, O Pina, is not an invention of your time. Certain wicked persons blamed the death of the great printer on the drugs I had administered to him, and a hue and cry was unleashed against me. I was accused of drunkenness and debauchery, because in a letter I had written to the students of Zurich I had called them *combibones optimi*, which means 'my dear bottle companions.' My name Theophrastus was turned into Cacophrastus, and the English derived from Bombastus the adjective 'bombastic,' which to them means 'puffed up and lacking in sense.' In a very few days I cured Canon Lichtenfels of the violent pains and persistent insomnia that were torturing him, but the canon, deeming that so rapid a cure did not deserve the fee I asked, sent me six miserable florins with the assurance that no one knew the value of life better than he. Not even the custom of paying the doctor poorly or not paying him at all is an invention of your time, O Pina, but this custom is likewise an iniquity. I asked for justice from the judges of Basel, hoping that they would decide in my favor, just as their colleagues in Berlin later upheld the miller of Sans Souci against Frederick the Great; but the judges of Basel decided instead to banish me and confine me on an island in the Lake of Lucerne, so that same night I fled toward Alsace, with no belongings and with only the sword given to me by the stadtholder of Amsterdam at my side.

"According to legend, this sword of mine is called 'Azoth,' and one version says that the hilt has an evil genie inside, another that it contains a sample of the philosopher's stone. I should like to show it to thee, O Pina, and convince thee that it is a good, simple, honest sword with neither devils nor deviltry, and moreover has never so much as sliced a turnip.

"I continued to roam. I took my *Treatise on the French Disease* to Nuremberg, but the Faculty of Leipzig did not appear to appreciate it, and indeed was able to have the Council of Nuremberg sequester it and other books of mine as well. I went on wandering between Saint Gallen, Ulm, Merano, Linz, and Graz. Finally I arrived one evening here in Salzburg and knocked at the door of the Hospital of the Holy Spirit, and a few days later passed from the hospital into this portrait whence a few hours ago I dropped into your arms, through that operation that you the living call death, and which for us initiates to the truths of the *Mysterium Magnum* is the reabsorption of being into the Universal All. But for me the reabsorption was accomplished in an imperfect manner, at the end of a kind of ineffable slide I bumped as though against a wall, and like a castaway on a rock I stopped. Hast thou seen *Modern Times?* Charlot dives into a canal and finds himself sitting in an inch of water. That is what happened to me.

"What was my life? Why did I ask questions of nature? Why did I scrutinize the mysteries of the *Ens seminis* and the *Ens proprietatis*? Why did I sharpen my eye in the *Evestrum*, which is clairvoyance, and my ear in the *Traramo*, which is clairaudition? Why did I consume my years in pursuit of a mystery? And what is this mystery? What is this principle of life and death?"

There followed a silence. Dawn began to break. And all of a sudden this word burst forth:

"Love!"

"Love, O Pina! Write that! Write that to thy husband! Write!"

With a strength that quite justified the four hundred and forty-four years of toughening of which Paracelsus had earlier spoken, he grasped Signora Poma's waist with his left hand, turned her around, pushed her in front of the table, picked her pen up from the floor and placed it in her hand, closed her right hand around it and guided it over the paper, and under the opening sentences written by Signora Poma, he wrote in angular Gothic characters in the middle of the sheet:

307

"Love sole principle of life and death."

"Now sign," said Paracelsus. And he signed: "Pina."

"This is the mystery that I have marked with a capital M," Paracelsus concluded. "This is the mystery that in its principle of materialization the Zohar ascribes to the heavy letter *Mem*."

And he added: "Thou, O Pina, art my capital M, thou my *Mem . . .*"

His voice broke in a rattle.

Then, as had happened to Paracelsus three hundred and ninety-six years before at the moment of his imperfect death, so now it seemed to Signora Poma that she was making a great slide; but before arriving at the wall she extended a soft hand, and turned the letter over to the blank side.

They were knocking at the door and a voice said:

"Bitte aufwachen! Es ist halb sieben!"

The room was full of light. They knocked again, but now it was Egle's voice:

"Pina, open the door. If you don't hurry up, we'll miss the train."

The door was locked, yet Signora Poma went to lean against it with all her might to keep Egle from coming in. And from the door she saw Paracelsus climbing up the wall, shrinking in size, and re-entering the frame.

"Open the door!" Egle kept insisting.

Once again Signora Poma saw Paracelsus in the portrait, but his eyes were still alive and shining with happiness.

"Open the door!" repeated Egle.

Signora Poma turned to look at the portrait: the eyes were spent.

They departed in a whirlwind. Egle threw Pina's clothes and other things into the suitcases. She helped her get dressed, since she seemed to be in a daze. She noticed the sheet of paper on the writing table, read "Dear Fonso" on the other side, stuck the letter in an envelope, wrote the address, and gave it to the desk clerk to be stamped and mailed. They caught the train just as it was leaving.

After repeated and fruitless attempts to learn the cause of her friend's persistent stupor, Egle left her "to stew in her own juice." At the station in Venice, she bought the afternoon edition of the *Corriere* and among the "late dispatches" found this news item from Paris:

"A guard at the Louvre museum, while making his rounds of the galleries last night, noticed that the portrait of Paracelsus painted by Scorel had 'whitened' in the middle of the landscape, as though the figure had been detached from the canvas. He called another guard, who also confirmed the whitening of the figure. But in the morning, the official to whom the two guards had taken their report went to see the portrait and found it intact, except that the eyes had lost the lively expression that had been their most outstanding quality, and now looked dead."

The newspaper added that the director of the museum was making an investigation, and the title of the article was "Wizard's Last Deviltry."

Egle read this news item aloud to Pina, who showed neither curiosity nor astonishment and continued to stare blankly in front of her, from which Egle concluded that Pina was really a nincompoop, and that it wasn't worthwhile going to all the trouble of trying to make an intellectual out of her.

Commendatore Poma was also unable to explain his wife's transformation. At first he attributed it to the ordeal of listening to all that music in Salzburg, and said that once he himself, having been to a concert at the Teatro Adriano, had come home as though drunk and with a terrible headache. Commendatore Poma's thesis seemed to be confirmed by the letter that arrived in Rome almost simultaneously with the two friends, in which a normal salutation was suddenly followed by the statement "Love sole principle of life and death," written in the middle of the sheet of paper in a madwoman's scrawl.

Upon Egle's advice, Commendatore Poma took his wife to an endocrinologist, who palpated her all over with solemn gestures in an office as bare and shining as the inside of an

309

icebox, diagnosed a serious glandular dysfunction, prescribed very expensive treatments, and charged a thousand lire for the visit.

A week went by, two weeks, a month, and since there was still no sign of improvement, Commendatore Poma, who had the reputation of being a "no nonsense" type, arrived one morning in his office smelling of more cologne than usual and with a gardenia in his buttonhole, told his secretary, Signorina Rita Pistacalli, to put a sheet of paper without the Poma Footwear letterhead in her typewriter, and began to dictate: "Dear Signorina Rita: It is now a considerable time that the sentiments I have nourished toward you. . . ."

He returned home like the flagship of a victorious fleet, only to be told that his wife had fainted. Urgently summoned, the doctor found that the lady was pregnant. Commendatore Poma fainted in his turn, but from joy. Returning to his senses and his office, the managing director of the Poma Footwear Company wrote a generous check to Signorina Rita Pistacalli, as compensation for the amorous relations that had been broken off before they had hardly begun.

At the end of the prescribed term, Signora Poma gave birth to a fine baby boy, on whom Commendatore Poma bestowed the name Geronzio, which had been the name of his sainted papa.

Commendatore Poma was an excellent managing director, but he was not an astrologer. Otherwise he would have seen that on the day of his son's birth the sun was in Scorpio, Jupiter in Virgo, and Mars in Capricorn, and he would have recalled that in November 1493 this same sky had witnessed the birth in the little town of Einsiedeln of a child whom his mother immediately abandoned to re-enter the Universal All. But Commendatore Poma was not an astrologer and was aware of nothing, though he was superior to many other husbands who are aware of nothing while having available much more specific signs.

One evening Signora Poma entered little Geronzio's room, but did not put on the light so as not to awaken the sleeping infant. The cradle stood out, white in one corner, and an aroma of talcum powder mixed with that slight stink of baby chicks that is the smell of newborn babies hung in the air of the room.

Signora Poma tiptoed forward, stopped at the cradle, and leaned over to look.

The tiny head rested on the pillow, and it was surrounded by a pale but precise halo.

No voice, no sound. Astonishment burst silently in Signora Poma's breast, spread through the room, and aroused general confusion; but not the slightest tremor stirred the veiling draped over the cradle.

Little by little the tumult subsided. Then, in the silence, in the shadow, in the faint smell of the nursery, Signora Poma, slowly and with difficulty, as though she were speaking for the first time, in a deep voice that moved the torpor of the centuries, said:

"Not Geronzio . . ."

And after a pause:

"Au . . . re . . . o . . . la . . . to . . ."

And after another pause:

"But I won't abandon you."